1912
FACTS ABOUT
TITANIC

SECOND EDITION

Lee William Merideth

Rocklin Press
7501 Palm Ave. #169
Yucca Valley, California 92284

1912 Facts About Titanic (Titanic Centennial Edition)
Lee William Merideth

©1999, 2003, 2012 by Lee W. Merideth

Includes bibliographic references and index

Titanic Centennial Edition: First Printing

10 9 8 7 6 5 4 3 2 1

ISBN 978-0-9836103-2-8 (cloth)
ISBN 978-0-9836103-3-5 (paper)

Rocklin Press
An imprint of Historical Indexes Publishing Co.
7501 Palm Ave #169
Yucca Valley, CA 92284
(408) 393-1606 (editorial and distribution)
email: rocklinpress@earthlink.net

Cover Design: James Zach
Cover Photography: Ross Mehan

This book is printed on 50# acid free paper. It meets or exceeds the guidelines for permanence and durability of the Committee on Production Guidelines for Book Longevity of the Council on Library Resources.

For Eleanore, my mother, who will read this,
for Edward, my late father, who never had the opportunity,
and for my family and friends who have had to put up with it.

I have not yet written the great American novel,
so this will have to suffice until I do.

Also by Lee W. Merideth

Titanic Names: A Complete List of the Passengers and Crew
Grey Ghost: The Story of the Aircraft Carrier Hornet
Guide to Civil War Periodicals, Volume II, 1995
Guide to Civil War Periodicals, Volume I, 1991
Civil War Times and Civil War Times, Illustrated 30 Year Comprehensive Index, 1959-1989

All books can be found at better bookstores or ordered from the author through Rocklin Press, 7501 Palm Ave., #169, Yucca Valley, CA 92284, email: rocklinpress@earthlink.net

CONTENTS

CHAPTER 1: BIRTH OF A DREAM   3

CHAPTER 2: THE WONDER SHIP   9

CHAPTER 3: FITTING OUT   29

CHAPTER 4: SEA TRIALS   41

CHAPTER 5: FINISHING TOUCHES   45

CHAPTER 6: THE CREW   55

CHAPTER 7: SOUTHAMPTON, ENGLAND   63

CHAPTER 8: CHERBOURG, FRANCE   87

CHAPTER 9: QUEENSTOWN, IRELAND   99

CHAPTER 10: DESTINY   111

CHAPTER 11: ENCOUNTER   129

CHAPTER 12: NOT ENOUGH LIFEBOATS   145

CHAPTER 13: RESCUE   181

CHAPTER 14: A SAD AWAKENING   195

CHAPTER 15: RECOVERY OPERATIONS   201

CHAPTER 16: LORD OF THE CALIFORNIAN   205

CHAPTER 17: AFTERMATH   213

CHAPTER 18: RESURRECTION   223

CHAPTER 19: A FEW MORE FACTS...   229

GLOSSARY   241

BIBLIOGRAPHY   244

INDEX   246

PHOTOGRAPHS

Titanic Fitting Out I	8
Olympic and Titanic Under Construction	28
Titanic Launched, May 31, 1911	30
Titanic Fitting Out II	32
Titanic Starting Her Sea Trials	40
Captain Edward J. Smith	48
Olympic and Titanic together	54
Stewardess Violet Jessop	60
Thomas Andrews	64
The Navratil Children	74
Father Thomas Byles	74
Reverend John Harper and daughter Nina	76
Isador and Ida Straus	78
Jacques Futrelle	80
The Countess of Rothes	80
James Bruce Ismay	82
Titanic Departing Southampton, April 10, 1912	86
John and Madeleine Astor	90
Molly Brown	90
Benjamin Guggenheim	90
James Clinch Smith	90
Sir Cosmo and Lady Lucille Duff Gordon	94
Lifeboat 1 Survivors	94
Douglas Spedden Spinning His Top	96
Titanic At Southampton, Easter Sunday, 1912	98
First Class Suite	100
Café Parisien	100
First Class Grand Staircase	102
Lawrence Beesley and T. W. McCauley in the Gymnasium	104
Captain Edward J. Smith Looks Over the Starboard Side	108
First Officer Murdoch and Second Officer Lightoller	110
Bandmaster Wallace Hartley	116
Archibald Gracie	116
John (Jack) Phillips	118
Harold Bride	118
Captain Arthur H. Rostron	182
Harold T. Cottam	182
Carpathia	182
Lifeboat Collapsible D	190
Lifeboat 6	190
The Iceberg	200
Captain Stanley Lord	208
Californian	208

PREFACE

On April 11, 1912, many of the more than 2,200 people aboard RMS *Titanic* watched the green hills of Ireland slowly disappear from view as the magnificent liner steamed west into a beautiful Atlantic sunset—and into history.

Early on the morning of April 15 she was gone. All that remained were bits and pieces of floating debris, a handful of lifeboats, and a long smudge of red paint smeared across the base of a floating mountain of ice. Of the thousands who boarded the great ship, only seven hundred and five survived to relate the extraordinary tale of her passing.

The passengers who rode *Titanic* into the unforgiving Atlantic Ocean were as diverse a group of individuals as you will find anywhere. Some of the richest and most prominent people on two continents, whether traveling for business or pleasure, shared the same ship with some of the poorest European emigrants to ever travel to America in search of a new life. Class distinction kept them apart during the first leg of their voyage. When disaster loomed out of a calm sea in the form of floating ice, that irrelevant distinction vanished. A short time later, after *Titanic* had slipped beneath the sea, those fortunate enough to secure a place in a lifeboat discovered (though did not voice) that class, gender, age, and religion meant nothing at all. And so they waited, together, for rescue, for death, for whatever fate had in store for them. And during the early minutes of their journey in the boats they watched and listened while more than 1,500 of their brothers, sisters, wives, husbands, children, and crew men and women screamed and died in the freezing water, praying aloud for help that never arrived.

Titanic's unthinkable demise has fascinated the world since word of her sinking first reached those ashore. Who could have predicted that the world's largest and most luxurious passenger liner—the jewel of the world's premier steamship company—would proudly set out on her maiden voyage only to strike an iceberg in the middle of the night and sink? As is so often the case, truth is more interesting (and stranger) than fiction. What author could have dreamed up a more fascinating cast of characters in a more dramatic setting with so many unusual intersecting circumstances?

Indeed, *Titanic's* entire short life brims with so many "what ifs" an entire book could be written about them: What if *Titanic's* officers had heeded ice warnings and slowed down? What if she had rammed the iceberg head-on? What if the lookouts had used their binoculars? What if the water had not been so calm? What if *Titanic* had not been delayed before beginning her journey? What if there had been more lifeboats? What . . . if?

Titanic's sinking has been the subject of hundreds of articles, books, movies, and videos. By many accounts it is the third most written about subject in history. It is perhaps little surprise, then, that James Cameron's *Titanic* was the highest grossing movie of the last century and is still being shown in theatres years after its original release. The movie sparked a renewed interest in the great ship and her loss, much of which has translated into the millions of visitors who flock to the *Titanic* Artifact Exhibition sites traveling around the world.

Many aspects of this tragedy linger with us, but one continues to haunt our thoughts: the demeanor of the condemned. Endless stories of strength in adversity, courage, and honor (with remarkably few examples of cowardice) grace what for most was nothing more than a prolonged and agonizing ride into their mass grave. While their wives, sweethearts, and children boarded lifeboats and rowed away into the night, many men stood back, most fully aware they soon would die in the freezing water. Most of the crew, too, sacrificed their lives so that others could live, guiding passengers above deck and loading them into the boats with a calm dignity befitting British honor. Far below in the bowels of the ship, meanwhile, the black gang—engineers, firemen, stokers, and trimmers, each of whom must have known they were voluntarily entombing themselves inside *Titanic*—worked to maintain the ship's generators to keep the lights on and the telegraph operating for as long as possible. Theirs was a truly horrific end.

In the early twentieth century, the dignified actions witnessed aboard *Titanic* were expected. One cannot help but wonder how passengers today would react if thrown into a similar nightmare. And therein rests one of the dilemmas inherent in writing history: we judge or condemn others who have gone before us at our peril, for someday others yet to be born will judge us.

Lee Merideth's *1912 Facts About Titanic* presents a collection of little-known facts and stories about this great liner, the people who experienced her, and the tragic events comprising her maiden voyage that ended so dramatically early that morning so long ago. It is not a definitive history of the ship and her brief life, nor is it intended to be. Instead, Lee's book is a collection of some of the most interesting information about the doomed liner, presented in a readable and chronological order. The "1912" in the title is a clever way of symbolizing the year in which the disaster occurred while communicating to the reader that the book is full of facts—indeed, far more "facts" than the title suggests.

The first edition of this book appeared in 1999. Since then, more than 35,000 copies have sold in seven printings. Lee, who once swore he would never make a public address to anyone, now speaks routinely to audiences around the country. His ongoing dialogue with fascinated students of the disaster, coupled with the new "facts" that have been learned since the book's first appearance, convinced him to produce a revised edition.

Titanic enthusiasts and historians everywhere will thank him for his efforts.

Theodore P. Savas
El Dorado Hills, CA

*   *   *

ACKNOWLEDGMENTS

I have been interested in the *Titanic* tragedy for over 40 years, ever since I read Walter Lord's excellent book *A Night To Remember* as a 5th grade reading assignment. Sometime thereafter I decided someday I would write my own *Titanic* book. The original version of my dream was in various states of repair and disarray long before the 1997 movie made *Titanic* a household topic of discussion. When friends and associates asked me about the *Titanic* story, they made it clear they were seeking only the "facts," and not an entire narrative history of the great ship and disaster. Their interests convinced me to rework the original material into chronologically arranged "fact-bites," the result of which you now hold in your hands.

As the years passed and numerous printings of the first edition continued to sell out, it became obvious that in addition to adding a few things, the book desperately needed an index. Including the index I have added a total of 24 pages of new and updated "facts," which included information on the discovery and recovery of the artifacts. I have also tried to answer some of the more commonly asked questions that arise from visitors to the Titanic Artifact Exhibits, which move from city to city around the United States and Europe.

For those of you (and there have been many) who have asked me if I am a survivor of the *Titanic*. Maybe I should feel insulted? The obvious answer (in addition to the next obvious one) is that if you can speak to someone who had been on *Titanic*, that person would, naturally enough, have been a survivor. But let me set the record straight once and for all. If you do the math (only simple arithmetic is required), you will discover that the great ship sank more than 90 years ago. Yes, at times I do look old enough to be a survivor, but I can assure you neither I, nor my parents, were alive in 1912.

I would like to thank Jerry Russell of Little Rock, Arkansas, for developing the concept for this series; my good friend Theodore P. Savas of El Dorado Hills, California, for giving me the impetus to get it done and helping all along the way; David Lang of Santa Clara, California, and Bill Haley of Huntington Beach, California, who both helped proofread this book; Ross Mehan of San Jose, California, for the cover photography; and Jim Zach of Mason City, Iowa, for the wonderful cover design. (Ross photographed a 1:350 scale plastic model I built and Jim turned the photo into the stunning cover of this book.)

Finally, and most importantly, I want to thank my mother Eleanore Merideth, who gently reminded me on a regular basis, as only a *mother* can, that if I didn't stop procrastinating I would never finish this effort, either the first time or this time. I heard the same arguments all through high school and college.

Mothers never change.

Lee W. Merideth
Rocklin Press
Sunnyvale, California
September, 2003

ti·tan·ic: a. Having great stature or enormous strength, huge; colossal. b. Of enormous scope, power or influence. (*Webster's Illustrated Encyclopedic Dictionary*, 1990.)

RMS TITANIC

When she steamed out of the harbor at Southampton, England, on her maiden voyage at noon on April 10, 1912, RMS Titanic was the largest movable object ever constructed by man. She was the engineering marvel of her time.

Titanic *represented state-of-the-art manufacturing, the crowning achievement of the industrial revolution, and the pride of a nation. The mammoth liner was the final word in Victorian luxury and opulence. Her construction was truly one of the monumental engineering feats of the century, and her sheer size bespoke safety and strength. Indeed few could conceive of anything that would cause her to sink.* "Titanic," *proclaimed a leading engineering journal,* "is practically unsinkable."

At 2:20 a.m. on April 15, 1912, slightly more than hundred and eight hours after leaving the dock at Southampton, Titanic's stern plunged into the icy waters of the North Atlantic Ocean and began its two-mile descent to the dark bottom of the sea. She took with her more than 1,500 souls in what is still the worst peacetime sea disaster in history. Her loss stands as a grim reminder that man, despite his abilities to produce grand engineering accomplishments, cannot overcome nature.

The story of the Royal Mail Steamer Titanic begins nearly one-half century before her launch . . .

CHAPTER 1

BIRTH OF A DREAM

Transatlantic passenger travel burgeoned in the mid-1860s. Much of this was the result of the westward expansion to the Great Plains and beyond, which in turn prompted the United States government to offer almost unlimited freedom to immigrate to America. In order to escape war, poverty and religious persecution, well over one million immigrants were entering the United States every year from European countries.

The only practical way to cross the North Atlantic in the late 19th and early 20th Centuries, before the invention of the airplane, was to travel by steamship. There were few considerations a passenger had to make in deciding which ship to take: cost, speed or luxury, (or a combination of all three).

- In 1867 British shipping line owner Thomas H. Ismay purchased the White Star Line, a fleet of sailing vessels providing service to the Australian emigrant trade. Ismay believed there were more profits to be made servicing the business and emigrant trade from Europe to North America after the American Civil War than there was serving Australia.

Financing for Ismay's plans was guaranteed by financier Gustav Schwabe, whose nephew, Gustav Wolff, was part owner of a shipbuilding company. Ismay could have the financing he needed as long as his ships continued to be built at a shipyard owned by Wolff.

- Thomas Ismay reorganized the White Star Line into a new company called the Oceanic Steam Navigation Company but he retained the White Star Line name.

There were dozens of steamship lines providing transatlantic passenger service and each steamship company had its own marketing angle. White Star Line advertised that their ships would be both fast and far more luxurious than any other ship in service. However, when balancing the two demands, White Star Line always built its ships for luxury over speed.

- The average transatlantic voyage took about six- and one-half days to complete at 22 knots (or just over 25 miles per hour.) A ship steaming at 25 knots reduced the trip by almost a full day, which theoretically allowed for a faster turnaround and ultimately more trips. However, because passenger ships always left a given port on the same day of the week, steaming faster didn't allow for more trips, only more time in port and a greater consumption of fuel. But six- and one-half days was a lot of time to spend crossing the ocean on a liner. As Ismay saw it, if he was planning to attract wealthy travelers, he needed something better than your competition: unsurpassed luxury and service.

- Steamship companies carried First Class passengers and catered to them to make their voyage worth the cost. Although some First Class passengers paid extraordinary amounts to travel on the best steamships, the fare paid by most First Class passengers covered the costs and provided the profits. It was the Third Class passengers who actually generated the revenue to keep most of the liners running. In theory, steamship companies wanted to carry a good mix of First and Second Class passengers for the prestige they generated, but plenty of Third Class passengers were needed to make a profit. Fares paid by Second and Third Class passengers covered the overhead while fares paid by First Class passengers generated the profit.

- In 1870 Thomas Ismay asked his friend William Imrie to join the White Star Line, and Ismay created a new management company. Ismay, Imrie and Company was formed to manage the White Star Line.

- Earlier, in 1840, Hickson and Company, Ltd. was organized as a shipbuilding company on the River Lagan in Belfast, Ireland. Fourteen years later in 1854 Edward J. Harland became general manager, and in 1859 Harland bought the company.
  Harland was an engineer who made several significant contributions to the art of shipbuilding, primarily the replacement of wooden decks and frames with iron and steel. This method of construction made a ship structurally much stronger and allowed for the building of larger ships with more than three or four decks.
  In 1861 Gustav Wolff joined up with Edward J. Harland and in 1862 Hickson and Company was renamed Harland and Wolff. That same year fifteen-year-old William Pirrie joined the company as a draftsman; thirty years later, in 1902, Pirrie was named the managing director of Harland and Wolff.
  With the purchase of the White Star Line by Thomas H. Ismay in 1867, and Ismay's agreement to have ships built at Gustav Wolff's company, Harland and Wolff became the sole provider of ships for the White Star Line. As the company grew, Harland and Wolff agreed not to build any ships for White Star Line competitors.

- In August 1870, the steamship *Oceanic*, the first ship built by Harland and Wolff for the White Star Line, was launched in Belfast, Ireland. Later, additional ships joined *Oceanic*, including *Atlantic, Baltic, Republic, Celtic* and *Adriatic* (White Star Line ships had names ending with "*ic*", including *Olympic, Titanic* and *Britannic*.)

  Harland and Wolff was considered to be the best and highest priced shipbuilding company in Europe. All work performed for White Star Line was done on a cost-plus basis, and no expenses were spared. The two companies worked so closely that Harland and Wolfe invoices were paid without question. No compromise on the quality of material was allowed—only the best material was used on White Star Line ships built by Harland and Wolff.

- In 1882 Joseph Bruce Ismay, eldest son of Thomas H. Ismay, joined the White Star Line and ten years later, in 1892, Thomas Ismay retired. When Thomas Ismay died in 1898, Joseph, (known by his middle name Bruce), became the managing director of White Star Line, a position he still held in 1912. Under the direction of Bruce Ismay and utilizing the talents of the extremely capable staff at Harland and Wolff, by 1910 White Star Line and Harland and Wolff were building the most modern and luxurious fleet of all the North Atlantic liners.

  The first large and modern steamship built for the White Star Line was *Oceanic II*, completed in 1899. This ship was the first attempt by White Star Line to provide quality service, luxury and comfort instead of trying to compete with its competitors for speed.

- American millionaire and financier J. Pierpont (J.P.) Morgan created the International Navigation Company of New Jersey in 1893 with the purchase of several smaller shipping lines. In 1902, Morgan changed the name of the company to the International Mercantile Marine Company (IMM).

  In late 1902 the stockholders approved the sale of the White Star Line to the IMM. The sale was opposed by Bruce Ismay. The stockholders, however, with some influence from William Pirrie of Harland and Wolff, approved the sale and the ownership of the White Star Line passed to the International Mercantile Marine on the last day of 1902.

  Bruce Ismay was still president of the White Star Line, and in 1904 J. P. Morgan offered him the job of president and managing director of the International Mercantile Marine. Ismay's acceptance gave him unlimited control of both the IMM and White Star Line.

  Although the IMM was an American owned company, any ship owned or managed by the White Star Line would continue to have its home port in Britain, carry the British flag, be served by British crewmembers, follow the shipbuilding guidelines, and be governed by the regulations of the British Board of Trade.

By 1912 the International Mercantile Marine owned 120 ships with a total gross tonnage of over 1.1 million tons, which made it one of the three largest ship owners in the world. White Star Line produced a significant portion of IMM's income and profits.

- The 1902 sale of the White Star Line to the IMM forced the British government to subsidize rival Cunard Line to insure that Cunard would not also be sold to a foreign company. This decision was seen as a potential military necessity because companies supported by the British government would have to allow their ships to revert to government service in the event of war. With the subsidization, any Cunard-owned ships would be part of the Reserve Fleet of the Royal Navy.

- New passenger ships kept getting larger and in 1906 the two largest, fastest and most luxurious ships that had ever been built were launched: Cunard's 30,000 ton ships *Lusitania* and *Mauretania*. These ships culminated Cunard's attempt to retain superiority in both size and speed. British government subsidies helped design new engines for these colossal ships, which meant the technology could not be passed on to any other shipbuilder. If a competitor was going to try to build a faster ship, it would have to foot the development costs of new engines itself.

- In 1906 William Pirrie, now Lord Pirrie, began a major two-year modernization program at the Harland and Wolff Belfast shipyard. Three existing building slips were demolished and two huge building slips were created in their place. Over this, a huge 240 foot by 840 foot steel gantry was built towering 214 feet over the building slips. The world's largest floating crane was built to assist in the construction and fitting out of ships after they were moved out of the slips and floated to a dock.

- The White Star Line's passenger safety record was about average for most steamship companies of the time. In the forty years prior to 1912, however, the White Star Line had survived several significant disasters.
    In 1873 the liner *Atlantic*, sister ship to *Oceanic I*, ran aground off Halifax, Nova Scotia, only fifteen miles from its destination. Some 546 people, including every woman and child on board, drowned in the worst non-military related maritime disaster in history up to that time. (The worst disaster involving an American-owned vessel was the 1865 sinking of the steamboat *Sultana* on the Mississippi River just north of Memphis, Tennessee. Over 1,800 former U.S. Army soldiers, mostly prisoners recently released from southern prisons after the end of the Civil War, were killed when the *Sultana* blew up and sank due to faulty steam boilers.)
    More disasters followed. In 1883, the largest livestock carrier in the world, White Star's *Noronic*, was lost without a trace. Then in 1893 the *Germanic* capsized in New York harbor because of an accumulation of ice on

its upper decks. There was no loss of life and the ship was eventually salvaged and put back into service.

In 1907 *Suevic* ran aground and lost 200 feet of her bow. Two years later *Republic* sank after a collision with the Italian liner *Florida*. Everyone on board *Republic* was saved except the two passengers killed in the initial collision. Survivors were transported by lifeboats to *Florida* and other nearby ships. This was the first time that a distress call sent out via the wireless was used to summon help for a vessel in danger. Only three years later *Titanic* would have to summon help with her wireless system.

Over the thirty-nine years from the time *Atlantic* sank in 1873 until 1912, millions of passengers made the transatlantic voyage on one of hundreds of passenger steamships; only four passengers were lost. Passenger travel on the modern steamships could justifiably boast an excellent safety record. In fact, from 1902 until 1912, more than two million passengers crossed the Atlantic Ocean on White Star Line ships alone; only two fatalities, both on *Republic*, occurred.

▪ The quest to build larger, faster and more luxurious ships continued. Each new class of ships was built faster or more luxurious then the previous class. By 1914, two years after the loss of *Titanic* and just in time to be influenced by the outbreak of World War I, the German-owned Hamburg America and North German Lloyd companies owned the world's largest passenger ships, which weighed in at 50,000 tons. The Hamburg America was the world's largest owner of passenger ships. Most of these would be sunk or commandeered by England and her allies during or after the war.

In order to maintain its superiority in shipbuilding, the British government contracted with Cunard to build *Lusitania* and *Mauretania* which weighed in at 30,000 tons each. The *Mauretania* set a speed record in 1909, crossing the Atlantic at an average of 26.6 knots, a record not broken until twenty years later in 1929.

Not wanting to be outdone, White Star Line had to improve on the design of the Cunard ships. White Star didn't have the resources to develop an engine to compete with them. If they couldn't beat Cunard with speed, then White Star would overwhelm them with size, luxury and service.

▪ In early 1907, Bruce Ismay and his wife were the dinner guests of Lord Pirrie. After dinner, Ismay and Pirrie retired to the study for drinks. During that time, while sketching ideas on a napkin, they developed the concept to build three mammoth ships to compete with all of their rivals. These ships would be so large they could carry more people than any other, ships so luxurious that even the Third Class passengers would be treated better than First Class passengers on many other ships, and so well built that they would be the last word in safety. The first of these ships would be called *Olympic*, and the three ships would be called the *Olympic*-class.

The second of these huge ships would be named *Titanic*.

TITANIC FITTING OUT. THE A DECK PROMENADE (THE LONG DARK LINE BELOW THE BOAT DECK) HAS NOT BEEN ENCLOSED. (*National Archives*).

"Everything about the ship was on a nightmarish scale."

CHAPTER 2

THE WONDER SHIP

The concept behind the design and construction of *Titanic* and her two sister ships that night in Lord Pirrie's study was the latest step in the evolution of steamship construction. In the forty or so years ending in the early 1900s, ship construction had made the complete transformation from the age of sail and wooden ships to the enormous steamships being turned out in several large shipyards around the world.

■ The reciprocating steam engine, turning one or more propellers and fueled by coal, had replaced the sail, the paddle wheel and the early wood-fired steam pressure cylinders of earlier ships. Shipbuilding technology had advanced in the previous forty years pretty much like aircraft technology would advance in the next forty. Bruce Ismay and Lord Pirrie had sketched out the design for their new ships in 1907, only four years after the Wright brothers flew their airplane in North Carolina. Ismay and Pirrie planned planned major advancements in construction, knowing full well that whatever they did would be superseded in the future. Ship construction was, and still is, one of evolving technology, huge costs and commercial one-upmanship.

■ The Cunard Lines' two huge ships *Lusitania* and *Mauretania* had been in service over a year the night Ismay and Pirrie had their meeting. Both ships had broken the transatlantic speed records, were the largest ships afloat and were by far the most luxurious. The rich and famous traveled by these two ships whenever possible. Ismay and Pirrie knew exactly what they had to produce in order to regain the prestige lost to Cunard. White Star Line had made it a business practice to place luxury over speed. Ismay and Pirrie went into the planning phase for their new ships knowing that they could not, and would not, attempt to match the speed of the Cunard liners.

To keep it from being sold to foreign investors, the British government heavily subsidized Cunard. Cunard and the Royal Navy worked together to develop a new type of reciprocating engine and they jointly held the patent on the design. White Star Line and Harland and

Wolff didn't have the development funds to design their own engines to match them, and so they didn't even try. They knew that the few extra hours that a passenger would spend on a transatlantic crossing on their ships would be offset by the luxury and innovations they would incorporate into them.

- There was never any doubt that White Star Line and Harland and Wolff would collaborate on the design and construction of the three ships on the usual cost-plus basis. No expense would be spared in their construction, and the latest technology would be used. The steel would be the best steel available at the beginning of the 20th century. If the technology required to do something did not exist, then it would be developed. Harland and Wolff agreed to build to White Star Line specifications and would be responsible for every part of the ships; very little work would be subcontracted out.

Three liners of the *Olympic*-class would be built. With the turnaround time of three weeks to New York City and back, plus port time to load and unload, (six days out, four days in New York City, six days back and four days in Southampton) the idea was that once all three ships were completed, there would be a departure from Southampton every Wednesday at noon and from New York City every Saturday at noon.

- Two of the three ships would be built almost simultaneously at the two newly enlarged slipways at the Harland and Wolff Queen's Island shipyard on the River Lagan in Belfast, Ireland. Approval to build the ships was given by White Star Line in April 1907 and preliminary design work was begun immediately. On December 16, 1908 the keel for the first ship, hull number 400, was laid down. On March 31, 1909 the keel for hull number 401 was laid down next to her sister ship. The keel for the third ship was laid down in 1911 after completion of the first ship. In keeping with White Star Line tradition, the names of the ships would end in "*ic*." To convey their size, White Star would name them, in the order they were built, *Olympic*, *Titanic* and *Gigantic*. (*Gigantic* would be renamed *Britannic* before she was completed). Hull number 400 would become *RMS Olympic*, and 401 would become *RMS Titanic*. They would be truly magnificent ships.

CONSTRUCTION SPECIFICATIONS

The *Olympic* and *Titanic* were built from the same plans. However, the addition of several First Class staterooms and two Promenade Suites before it entered service would make *Titanic* larger and heavier than her sister ship *Olympic*. The specifications for *Titanic* were as follows:

APPROVAL FOR CONSTRUCTION:	APRIL 1907
KEEL LAID DOWN:	MARCH 31, 1908
LAUNCHED:	MAY 31, 1911
MAIDEN VOYAGE:	APRIL 10, 1912
LENGTH:	882 FEET, 9 INCHES
BEAM (WIDTH):	92 FEET, 6 INCHES
HEIGHT, KEEL TO BRIDGE:	104 FEET
HEIGHT, KEEL TO TOP OF FUNNELS:	175 FEET
DECKS:	10
WEIGHT:	46,328 TONS
DISPLACEMENT:	66,000 TONS
SERVICE SPEED:	21 KNOTS
MAXIMUM SPEED:	24 KNOTS
PRIMARY DESIGNER:	ALEXANDER CARLISLE, BROTHER-IN-LAW OF LORD PIRRIE.
SUPERVISOR OF CONSTRUCTION:	THOMAS ANDREWS, NEPHEW OF LORD PIRRIE.
COST, 1912 DOLLARS:	$7.5 MILLION
COST, 2003 DOLLARS:	$135.8 MILLION

(IN 2003, THE VALUE OF A 1912 DOLLAR IS WORTH ABOUT $18.10)

EQUIPMENT

Anchors: Two at 7.5 tons each (port and starboard) and one at 15.5 tons (center), stored on the Forecastle Deck and lowered with a crane. The center anchor required a team of 20 horses to move it to the construction site.

Anchor chains: Two at 96 tons each and one for the center anchor at 101 tons. The anchor chain for the center anchor was 1050 feet long.

Engines: Two four-cylinder, triple expansion reciprocating engines. The pistons in each cylinder were eight feet in diameter and the engines weighed 1,000 tons each and were four stories tall—to this day the largest ever built. There was also one 420-ton steam turbine engine.

Horsepower: Each reciprocating engine produced 15,000 horsepower and the turbine engine generated 16,000 horsepower. The port and starboard reciprocating engines were powered by steam directly from the boilers. The excess steam, instead of being vented into the air as was normally done, was used to power the turbine engine.

Boilers: There were 24 double-ended boilers (they could be fed from both ends), 20 feet long and 15 feet 9 inches in diameter. Each boiler had six furnaces, and weighed 100 tons. There were also five single ended boilers, 11 feet 9 inches long, 15 feet 9 inches in diameter, and each with three furnaces.

Furnaces: There were a total of 159 coal-fired furnaces, the coal being shoveled into the furnaces by hand. The coal bunkers were located above and on each side of the boilers.

Coal capacity: Titanic could carry 8,000 tons of coal, enough for one round trip. When steaming, the furnaces would consume 650 tons of coal per day. Over four tons of coal had to be shoveled into each furnace every day by the stokers whose job it was to feed the furnaces.

Propellers: There were two three-bladed propellers, each 23.5 feet in diameter. These were counter-rotating (turned toward each other), which was a new design concept that allowed for a much smoother ride for the passengers. These propellers could also be reversed to allow the ship to back up or stop in an emergency. There was also one four-bladed propeller in the center, 16.5 feet in diameter. This propeller was powered by the steam turbine engine and could not be reversed.

Rudder: 78 feet high, weighing 101 tons. Tests and standard design ratios have shown that the rudder was slightly smaller (less than 2%) than it should have been. This, however, was not enough to have affected the outcome of the collision with the iceberg.

Funnels: There were four funnels, each 60 feet high, 22 feet wide and large enough to drive 2 locomotives through side-by-side.
Number 1: (closest to the bow), vented boiler rooms 5 and 6
Number 2: vented boiler rooms 3 and 4
Number 3: vented boiler rooms 1 and 2
Number 4: (closest to the stern) was a dummy funnel added to help with the aesthetic design of the ship. The public associated the number and size of the funnels with the size of the ship. However, although the fourth funnel wasn't used to vent the boiler rooms, it was used to provide fresh air to the engine rooms and vent the ship's galleys (kitchens).

Mast, forward: The forward mast was 101 feet high and made of steel except the top 15 feet, which was made of teak wood. Inside the mast was a 50-foot tall ladder used by the lookouts to climb into the crow's nest. The mast was raked (tilted) toward the stern 2 inches per foot.

Mast, aft: 97 feet high, with a teak top and also raked 2 inches per foot. This mast did not have an inside ladder nor a crow's nest.

Marconi antenna: What we would now call the radio antenna consisted of four wires that were stretched between the two masts.

Whistle: Triple valve, steam, so large that when blown it would rattle windows for miles around.

Structure, frame: Steel frames in the hull were three feet apart except for the bow, where they were two feet apart, and the stern where they were two feet five inches apart. The bow was built stronger to reduce damage in case the ship ran into something, such as another ship—or maybe even an iceberg.

Structure, bottom: Titanic was built with a double bottom, which was a series of sealed compartments seven feet high across the entire bottom of the ship. There were 44 of these sealed compartments which were in reality watertight compartments. The double bottom was another relatively new concept designed to prevent serious flooding if the ship grounded or collided with something. Most serious ship accidents, like the sinking of *Atlantic* in 1873, occurred when the bottom of the ship was ripped open. The tanks in the double bottom were (and still are today) used to prevent flooding. Also, the compartments were filled with water ballast. There was, however, no double hull on the sides of the ship.

Structure, plates: The ship was built with three-quarter inch or one-inch thick steel plates that overlapped by as much as three feet. They were double or triple- riveted with hydraulic rams. The areas where the plates were lapped were sealed with oil-soaked rope to prevent leakage.

Rivets: There were over three million of them, weighing a total of 1,200 tons. Once again, the material the rivets were made from was the finest steel available at the time.

Electrical supply: There were four 400-kilowatt steam powered generators with an output of 16,000 amperes providing electricity to power the following:

> 150 MOTORS (76 USED TO RUN THE VENTILATION FANS IN THE BOILER ROOMS);
> 10,000 LIGHT BULBS;
> A 50-LINE INTERNAL TELEPHONE SYSTEM;
> 48 CLOCKS;
> 1,500 PUSH BUTTONS AND LIGHTS TO CALL FOR ATTENDANTS;
> DOZENS OF ELECTRIC SIGNS;
> 520 PORTABLE HEATERS AND FANS;
> MARCONI WIRELESS SYSTEM;
> EIGHT 2-1/2 TON CARGO CRANES;
> THE HUGE WHISTLE;
> FOUR PASSENGER ELEVATORS;
> 15 WATERTIGHT DOORS;
>
> AND HUNDREDS OF LESSER ELECTRICAL ITEMS, INCLUDING KITCHEN MACHINERY (MIXERS, POTATO-PEELERS, ROASTERS, OVENS, STOVES AND HOT PLATES); PASSENGER SERVICES (FANS, LAMPS, ELECTRICAL REQUIREMENTS) AND SHIP OPERATIONS (WINCHES, WORKSHOP TOOLS, WATER HEATERS AND REFRIGERATION).

THE SAFEST SHIP AFLOAT

Titanic was designed to be watertight and to some extent the builders actually achieved that goal. *Olympic* and *Titanic* were the first ships that contained watertight compartments along the lower decks. In addition to the sealed tanks in the double bottom, the lower hull was divided into 16 watertight compartments by 15 transverse (across the hull from port to starboard) watertight bulkheads, or walls.

▪ The purpose of the watertight bulkheads in conjunction with the double bottom was to prevent the ship from sinking in case of a collision. The design allowed the ship to float if any two large amidships compartments (engine or boiler rooms) or the first four compartments flooded. *Titanic* would also float long enough to rescue the passengers and crew if any three amidships compartments or the first five compartments flooded, assuming that help would be available within a few hours. There were so many ships traveling the North Atlantic that there was usually at least one in sight at all times, so this was not as odd as it initially sounds.

▪ From the bow, the first two bulkheads extended up to D Deck, the next eight up to E Deck, and the last five up to D Deck. Generally speaking, the lowest deck closest to the keel has the highest letter assignment. Thus, A Deck is usually the highest deck on a ship. This was not the case on *Titanic*, where A Deck was the second highest (the Boat Deck was the highest.) Unfortunately, some of these bulkheads only went up to E Deck and extended just a few feet above the waterline. Due to the slant of the decks, rising higher toward the bow and stern, even D Deck amidships was only fifteen feet above the normal waterline.

▪ There were three major design flaws in the construction of the watertight compartments. Hindsight helps expose these flaws, but we must keep in mind that the entire concept was new, and these design flaws would only manifest themselves through trial-and-error.

First, the decks themselves weren't watertight due to the many openings for stairs, ladders, elevators, and so forth. The bulkheads did not extend above D Deck (or E Deck in some instances.) If the bow of the ship flooded, the weight of the water would pull down the bow of the ship. Eventually, the water would flow up through the deck openings, overflow the top of the bulkheads, and spill into the adjacent compartment down mores openings—even if the compartment hadn't been breached.

Second, the watertight bulkheads were transverse, but there weren't any longitudinal bulkheads running the *length* of the compartments. Thus if water entered through a hole in the side of the ship, it would fill the entire compartment the width of the ship. This could cause the ship to list (or tilt) to one side or the other as the water filled some compartments but not others, causing it to slosh back and forth, side to side. Without the longitudinal bulkheads, the ship couldn't be counter-flooded to correct the list. This improper weight distribution could, theoretically, cause the ship to capsize.

Third, a serious flaw was a 12-foot wide corridor that ran almost the entire length of E Deck. Used by the crew to move around the ship, it was also the only way Third Class passengers could move from the bow to the stern. There were no doors along this corridor, and thus it became an open channel for water to travel almost the full length of the ship.

- In the bulkheads between the sixteen watertight compartments were huge watertight doors. Only the doors on the lowest deck (Tank Top) could be closed from the bridge. There were, however, three ways to close them:

> 1) Electrically. An officer could close any door or all doors on the lowest deck from the bridge of the ship by pressing a button;
> 2) Manually. A member of the crew could also close any door;
> 3) Automatically. A unique float device located next to each door would close the door if there were more than six inches of water in either adjacent compartment.

The watertight doors on all other decks had to be closed by a crewman with a special key, and only upon receiving orders from a ship's officer.

- An innovation hailed as an important safety feature, tall enough for a man to stand in, was the double bottom. The ceiling (or actual floor of the Tank Top) plates were steel (3/4 inch thick) and the compartments inside were sealed. The double bottom was designed to provide an extra method of protection. If the hull plates below the Tank Top were pierced or sprung, the inner plates would prevent water from flooding the ship.

Unfortunately, the double bottom did not extend up the sides of the ship to create a double hull. It also did not extend past the water line and it was only effective if something pierced the bottom of the ship and not the sides.

- In spite of all of these flaws, *Titanic* was designed and built to be the safest ship afloat, combining all of the advances in modern shipbuilding then available. Because of its sheer size, there was absolutely nothing the designers or builders could envision that could happen to the ship to cause it to sink, or to sink so rapidly that the people on board would not have ample time to be safely evacuated.

If *Titanic* rammed another ship, which was a fairly common occurrence in the days before radar, the damage would be absorbed by the bow, the three watertight bow bulkheads, and four watertight bow compartments.

If *Titanic* was herself rammed by another ship, it was possible that two of the watertight compartments would be ruptured, but there wasn't a ship large enough, including her sister ship *Olympic,* to rupture three amidships compartments.

If the ship ripped open its keel by grounding, the double bottom would help prevent generalized flooding.

Finally, *Titanic* and her sister ships were equipped with the most powerful wireless station of any ship afloat. Ships for hundreds of miles around could be summoned immediately if there was a need for help. Ship traffic in the North Atlantic in the early 1900s was intense, and few ships traveling the normal traffic lanes ever went more than a few miles without coming into visual contact with another vessel.

■ Contrary to popular belief, no White Star Line officer or any other official ever called *Titanic* "unsinkable" because no ship is unsinkable. However, newspapers in the United States and Britain were always trying to come up with catchy things to say in order to sell their papers. Newspapers called *Titanic* "*the Wonder Ship,*" or the "*Last Word in Luxury,*" and even Wall Street called it "*the Millionaires' Special.*"

Ironically, it was the very prestigious journal *Shipbuilder Magazine* that called *Olympic* and *Titanic* "*practically unsinkable,*" and it was the word "*unsinkable*" that captured the imagination of the public.

A WALKING TOUR OF TITANIC

There were ten decks on *Titanic* and her sister ships. If you were to take a tour of the ship, starting on the bottom deck, and walking from the bow to the stern (front to back), this is what you would see: (Note: walking aft from the bow, the starboard side of the ship is on the left and the port side of the ship is on the right.)

TANK TOP

This was not considered a deck, but was in reality the top of the double bottom. It served as the foundation for all the engines, generators, boilers, coalbunkers, and some cargo storage. Fresh water storage was located under the deck in the double bottom. Passengers were not allowed in this area. This is the only deck that contained the electrically operated watertight doors that were located in the watertight bulkheads.

ORLOP DECK

The first (and considered the lowest) deck was the Orlop Deck, which did not extend the entire length of the ship. It was completely below the waterline, and no passengers were allowed on the deck. A crewman closed the watertight doors by hand. If you were walking from the bow to the stern, the significant areas you would find based upon the compartments created by the watertight bulkheads (compartments are numbered from bow-to-stern, numbers 1 through 16 on this deck, 1 through 15 on the remaining decks) were as follows:

Compartment 1: Forepeak (or the chain locker for stowage of the anchor chains);

Compartment 2: cargo stowage;

Compartment 3: cargo stowage, motor vehicle stowage;

Compartment 4: Post Office mail sorting room, First and Second Class baggage room. This was the end of the forward Orlop Deck.

Compartment 5: boiler room #6 and coalbunkers;

Compartment 6: boiler room #5 and coalbunkers;

Compartment 7: boiler room #4 and coalbunkers;

Compartment 8: boiler room #3 and coalbunkers;

Compartment 9: boiler room #2 and coalbunkers;

Compartment 10: boiler room #1 and coalbunkers;

Compartment 11: two reciprocating engines;

Compartment 12: one turbine engine;

Compartment 13: contains electrical switchboard; beer, wine, spirits, mineral water storage, tobacco and cigar storage; general groceries, beef storage and thawing room, bulk storage. This was the beginning of the aft Orlop Deck.

Compartment 14: refrigerated cargo stowage;

Compartment 15: general cargo;

Compartment 16: peak tank (this deck only);

G DECK (OR LOWER DECK)

G Deck was the lowest deck that contained passenger and crew accommodations. Because of the slope of the deck, the bow and the stern portion of this level were above the waterline, so there were portholes to allow air and light in. The amidships portion was below the water line. There were no doors in the watertight bulkheads between Second and Third Class accommodations, so the two classes were totally isolated on this deck. The only access passengers had to their cabins was from the deck above. From bow to stern again, the compartments were defined as follows:

Compartment 1: chain locker and stowage;

Compartment 2: There were crew accommodations for 45 firemen and greasers; foundation for the two-four deck tall spiral staircases used for crew access between the decks (these were open staircases without any means to close them to make them watertight. They may have played a significant role in the rapid flooding of the bow of the ship);

Compartment 3: Third Class open berthing. This compartment had bunks for 26 unaccompanied male passengers. The only access to this compartment was via the deck above;

Compartment 4: First Class baggage, Post Office with access to the sorting room below and to the deck above, registered mail room, 10 Third Class cabins and the Squash Racquet Court for First Class passengers, accessible from the deck above;

Compartments 5-10: continuation of boiler rooms and coalbunkers;

Compartment 11: continuation of reciprocating engine room, paint storage, engineer storage and workshop;

Compartment 12: continuation of turbine engine room;

Compartment 13: bulk storage for groceries, store rooms for flour, ice cream, ice, butter, fruit, fish, bacon, vegetables, mutton, milk, ice making machine, plus ready storage of all of the above for the restaurants;

Compartment 14: 40 Third Class or, if needed, Second Class cabins;

Compartment 15: 20 Third Class cabins and blanket/linen storage;

F DECK (OR MIDDLE DECK)

The first deck completely above water line. It contained mixed passenger and crew accommodations along with equipment to operate the ship. Arranged along the hull on both sides of the ship were the coal chutes, where colliers (coal barges) could load coal into the coalbunkers located above the boilers.

Compartment 1: chain locker;

Compartment 2: crew accommodations for 57 firemen and greasers with access via the spiral staircase;

Compartment 3: 26 Third Class cabins;

Compartment 4: Squash Racquet Court with access from the deck above, mail clerks cabins, linen storage, and 22 Third Class cabins;

Compartment 5: boiler casing, fan shaft, 33 Third Class cabins;

Compartment 6: boiler casing and fan shaft, swimming bath for First Class passengers with two showers and 13 dressing rooms, linen storage, washing and drying;

Compartment 7: boiler casing and fan shaft, Turkish Bath, three dressing rooms and two shampoo rooms for First Class passengers, Turkish Bath attendant's cabins, steam rooms and hot air tanks for hot water, dormitory for 11 cooks and 42 Third Class stewards;

Compartment 8: boiler casing and fan shaft, one half of the Third Class Dining Saloon;

Compartment 9: boiler casing and fan shaft, one half of the Third Class Dining Saloon and a pantry;

Compartment 10: boiler casing and fan shaft, dormitories for six butchers, six bakers and Third Class stewards, bakery, Third Class galley (kitchen), pots and pans storage and washing, dog kennels;

Compartment 11: reciprocating engine room casing, accommodations for all of the ships' engineers;

Compartment 12: turbine engine room casing, 13 Second Class cabins;

Compartment 13: 33 Second Class cabins, base of Second Class elevator;

Compartment 14: 18 Second Class cabins and one steward's cabin;

Compartment 15: 34 Third Class cabins;

E DECK (OR UPPER DECK)

All of the decks from the Tank Top up to E Deck were divided into watertight compartments. Most of the bulkheads had watertight doors in them. As on all the lower decks except for the Tank Top, these doors could only be closed manually by a crewmember. Crew and passengers were prevented from entering engineering spaces and the three classes of passengers with cabins on the deck were prevented from making contact by the closed and locked doors.

- E Deck was the first deck that lacked many watertight bulkheads—eight of them were missing in the middle portion of the ship. There were still watertight bulkheads in the first two compartments and the last five, but the majority of the ship on E Deck was wide open to an inrush of water.

All three passenger classes and the crew had accommodations on E Deck. Over two thirds of the starboard side was occupied by First Class passenger cabins, while most of the port side contained crew dormitories, cabins and accommodations for Second and Third Class passengers.

- One of the most noticeable features of E Deck was the 12 foot wide corridor on the port side that ran along the side of the boiler casings almost the entire length of the ship. This was the primary crew corridor and the only access that Third Class passengers had from the bow to the stern of the ship. This corridor was called "Scotland Road" by the crew in reference to the busy working class road in Liverpool. "Scotland Road" was always a hive of activity as the crewmembers traveled about their duties and the Third Class passengers visited friends and family that had accommodations at opposite ends of the ship. A narrower corridor connecting all of the First Class cabins on the starboard side was called "Park Lane" after a more fashionable street in London.

■   First Class cabins were virtually isolated from the rest of the deck and access was from the deck above. There were only three doors that would allow Second and Third Class passengers into the First Class areas. The doors were always closed and locked because they also opened onto "Scotland Road."

The deck plan for E Deck is a case study in throwing things together. It probably made sense to the designers and maybe the crew, but with its maze of corridors and hundreds of compartments, one can understand how the Third Class passengers would have had a hard time finding their way out of that portion of the ship.

Compartment 1: storage and chain locker;

Compartment 2: dormitories for 72 trimmers;

Continuing aft from compartment 2 to about where compartment 3 would end if the watertight bulkhead extended up this high was a dormitory for 44 seamen and numerous washrooms and toilets for the crew. Following this was a wide corridor extending to both sides of the ship. At each end of this corridor was the Third Class gangway where passengers entered the ship while in port. Facing this passageway, in the middle of the ship, was the Master-at-Arms office.

Next came the First Class accommodations on the starboard side. These ran all the way from about where the Compartment 4 bulkhead would have been if the watertight bulkhead had extended this high, to where the Compartment 12-13 bulkhead was. "Park Lane" ran the entire length of this section, broken only by two watertight bulkheads with watertight doors at compartments 10-11 and 11-12. These doors were always kept open and could only be closed by a crewman.

There were 91 First Class cabins in this area, about one-third of which did not have an outside view. These cabins did not have toilet facilities so there were also a large number of toilets and washrooms in this area. Also located among all of these First Class cabins was the base of the three First Class elevators and the five-story First Class Grand Staircase.

On the opposite side of Scotland Road, moving aft from the Third Class gangway were eight Third Class cabins; crew dormitories for quartermasters; carpenters; plate washers (20); Second Class stewards (62); library, smoking lounge and pantry stewards; saloon waiters (106); First and Second Class bedroom stewards; First Class cooks; barkeepers and storekeepers; engineers' mess; the restaurant staff; plus numerous storerooms, including some to store potatoes and even a room in which to wash them.

Compartment 13: Seven Second Class and three Third Class cabins and various storerooms separated by Scotland Road were located here. There was also a wide corridor that ran the width of the ship with a gangway door on each side that served as the main Second Class entrance to the ship.

Compartment 14: Next came 11 Second Class and 23 Third Class cabins, again separated by Scotland Road, plus the Second Class Purser's Office and cabin and a dormitory for the musicians in the orchestra and a separate room for their instruments.

Compartment 15: 30 Third Class cabins and various storerooms.

D DECK (OR SALOON DECK)

This deck contained accommodations for all classes and crew, and is where most people ate their meals. It was the first deck that did not contain watertight bulkheads or doors.

- In the bow were dormitories for 108 firemen and the top of the two spiral staircases for crew use. There was a solid wall running across the width of the ship to prevent the crew from entering into the passenger sections. Following this was a large open room, also extending across the width of the ship. This was the Third Class open space, which was just a huge room for social gatherings. Access to this room was from E Deck below and C Deck above. There was a solid wall between it and the next (First Class) space aft.

- Next came 49 First Class cabins and several cabins for stewards and stewardesses and a large number of toilets and washrooms, followed by the opulent First Class Reception Room extending across the width of the ship.

Beyond the Reception Room through several huge double glass doors was the magnificent First Class Dining Saloon, which also extended across the width of the ship. Large windows provided light for the room. The First Class Pantry came next, followed by the First and Second Class Galley, the Second Class Pantry and all the attendant storerooms and food preparation areas, including the bakery and butcher shops.

- Located on the starboard side, next to the Second Class Pantry, were the seven rooms of the ship's hospital, including two rooms reserved for infants.

The next room was the Second Class Dining Saloon, again stretching across the width of the ship, followed by 39 Second Class cabins. Another bulkhead followed with a single door through which another 11 Third Class cabins, including large cabins for families with several members, were located.

C DECK (OR SHELTER DECK)

This (C Deck) was the lowest deck to have open access to the outside. Only crew and First Class accommodations were located on this level, but this deck contained the common areas for both Second and Third Class passengers.

In the forward section were the seaman's and firemen's mess and galley, crew hospital, various shops and storerooms and the windlass gear, which was used to raise and lower the anchors. There were no access doors to the next section of the ship.

Next was the forward Well Deck, an open-air deck that served as an area for the Third Class passengers to congregate, also referred to as the Third Class Promenade. Also located here were two electrically powered cargo cranes and the hatch cover for the forward cargo hold.

- From the solid wall at the end of the well deck down to the First Class Entrance were 54 First Class, Purser's and stewardess's cabins. On either side of the First Class Entrance, with her Grand Staircase and three elevators, were 12 more First Class cabins, the Purser's Office and the Enquiry Office. Passengers used the Enquiry Office to arrange the sending and receiving of wireless messages or to pay for access to the Turkish Baths.

Next on the port side was the large suite containing cabins C62, C64 and C66, while on the starboard side was another three-cabin suite C55, C57 and C59. Each of these large suites was equipped with its own bathroom and servants quarters.

- The next section, almost one-half the length of the ship, contained 72 First Class suites, some with doors that made them into adjoining suites. About half of the suites contained their own toilet and bathroom.

Also in this area were the pantry and saloon for maids, valets, Marconi operators and postal workers. Cabins for the medical staff and surgery were also located here, along with the First Class stewardesses cabins, the First Class barber shop and the aft Grand Staircase that went up to the Boat Deck.

- Behind the First Class area, and accessible through locked doors, was the Second Class enclosed promenade with large floor-to-ceiling windows surrounding the Second Class Entrance and Second Class Library.

Through another bulkhead with locked doors, came the aft Well Deck which was another Third Class Promenade which was also open to the air. Two more of the electrically operated cargo cranes were located here. Following this was the Third Class Smoking Room on the port side and the Third Class General Room on the starboard side. The General Room was a large enclosed area similar to a lounge, where passengers could mingle, listen to music or conduct a dance.

Finally, the last section of C Deck contained the steering engines, capstan gear and the top of the rudder.

B Deck (containing the Forecastle, Bridge and Poop Decks)

The only accommodations on B Deck were for First Class passengers. However, common areas for both First Class and Second Class passengers were located on this deck.

- **Forecastle Deck:** This is the top deck at the very front of ths ship. From the bow to the opening for the Well Deck were located the anchor capstans, anchor chains, center anchor and a crane to lower it, and various mechanical equipment. This area was open to the weather, and is where Rose Dewitt Bukater (Kate Winslet) and Jack Dawson (Leonardo DeCaprio) did their "flying" scene in James Cameron's film *Titanic*.
  There was a gap between the Forecastle Deck and the main part of the superstructure on B Deck (also called the Bridge Deck). This gap was left for the opening created by the Well Deck, one level below.

- **Bridge Deck:** After the Well Deck gap was the First Class open corridor that ran the width of the ship and looked down into the Well Deck. The front of this corridor was open to the weather.
  Between the open corridor and the First Class Entrance were another 49 First Class cabins plus several toilets and restrooms. Next in line was the huge First Class Entrance. On either side of the ship were two gangways that First Class passengers used to enter the ship, and in the center was the Grand Staircase and elevators.
  Next on the port side was one of the two Grand Promenade Suites, made up of cabins B52, B54 and B56, with there own bathroom, servant's quarters and a private thirty-foot enclosed promenade. On the starboard side was the other suite, B51, B53 and B55. The two Grand Promenade Suites were late editions to the construction of *Titanic* that helped make the ship larger than her sister *Olympic*. The suites were added at the request of Bruce Ismay, and cost a passenger up to $4,000 (or $74,000 in 2003 dollars) for one trip.
  Following these, on the port side, were another 24 First Class suites, each with its own bathroom and 22 other First Class cabins without bathrooms, then the aft Grand Staircase, the à la carte restaurant, galley and pantry. Located on the starboard side was the Café Parisian.

- The next section of C Deck contained the Second Class Promenade, Second Class Entrance, gangway, bar, and the Smoking Room, which overlooked the aft Well Deck. Next came another gap here for the aft Well Deck, one level down on C Deck.

- **Poop Deck:** Still on the B Deck level, beyond the aft Well Deck was the Poop Deck, the raised open area at the stern of the ship. This deck was open to Third Class passengers and contained equipment required to operate and dock the ship. Above the Poop Deck, running across the width of the ship, was the Docking Bridge, which was used by the ship's officers when docking the ship.

A DECK

A Deck was reserved for First Class passengers and contained the First Class Promenade along each side that was covered and enclosed on the forward half of the deck. This enclosure was unique to *Titanic* and it is the only visible difference between her and her sister ship *Olympic*. The enclosure was added shortly before *Titanic* was completed because passengers on *Olympic* had complained about water spray from the bow blowing across this part of the deck.

■   Facing the bow and overlooking the Well Deck was the open portion of the Promenade Deck, with a corridor on either side of the superstructure that entered the enclosed portion of the Promenade. Behind the bulkhead were 34 First Class cabins and the First Class Entrance and Grand Staircase.

From the First Class Entrance, a glass-enclosed corridor with a revolving door extended to the First Class Lounge. This corridor was originally designed to allow passengers to have an enclosed passage between the entrance and the lounge because when designed and built, the Promenade Deck wasn't enclosed. Adjoining the Lounge on the port side were the Reading and Writing Room and Library.

After the First Class Lounge and its bar, another enclosed corridor and revolving door led to the aft First Class Entrance and the aft Grand Staircase. Located along this corridor were various lounges and bars for the outside decks.

Next was the First Class Smoking Room, followed by the Verandah Café and the Palm Court. The court was divided into two parts, one on each side of the enclosed Second Class Grand Staircase. Finally, on the open deck at the aft end of A Deck were two more of the electrically operated cranes.

BOAT DECK

The Boat Deck, or the top deck, was open to the weather and is where much of the drama of the *Titanic* story would eventually be played out. Most of the deck was either open promenade for the passengers or contained the deckhouse used by the crew. There were, however, two items that dominated the Boat Deck: the ships's four funnels and her 20 lifeboats.

- The Bridge occupied the forward end of the Boat Deck and is where the ship's officers operated and navigated *Titanic*. Glass enclosed the middle third of the Bridge to keep the weather off the crew working there. The telegraphs were located here, which telegraphed instructions to the Engine Rooms, Boiler Rooms and Docking Bridge.

On either side of this enclosed area was the open Bridge, which extended beyond the sides of the ship. Each of the port and starboard ends of this open area had a small room enclosed on three sides with windows. These rooms were called the bridge wings. It was from these little cubes that the ship's officers could look directly down to the water and along the entire side of the ship while docking.

Behind the glassed-off middle section of the Bridge was the Wheel House. Located in here was the huge wooden wheel that the quartermaster turned in order to steer the ship. The Wheel House was completely enclosed because it also contained the compass, the master control to close the watertight doors, and other electrical equipment.

- Behind the Wheel House on the starboard side was the Navigation Room where charts were kept to track the ship's voyage. Following this was the Captain's sitting room, bedroom and bathroom. The Fourth Officer's cabin was next, followed by the Officers Smoking Room, a pantry and finally some storerooms.

- On the port side behind the Wheel House was located the Chief Officer's cabin, followed by the First, Second, Third, Fifth and Sixth Officer's cabins and several other rooms. Located on both sides of the deckhouse was the Officer's Promenade, open deck space reserved for the ship's officers.

- Located on a passageway connecting the officer's cabins on the port and starboard sides, and directly behind the boiler casing for the first funnel, were three Marconi Wireless rooms: an office in the center, a silent room where transmissions were made on one side, and a bedroom for the operators on the other side.

- Behind all of the ship's offices came the grand First Class Entrance with its magnificent Grand Staircase and, above it all, the huge glass and wrought iron dome to let the daylight in. This was also the top deck for the three elevators that carried passengers down to E Deck.

Next came the boiler casing for the second funnel, and on the port side was located the Gymnasium. Next came a long, low flat structure that was actually the raised roof of the First Class Lounge. This roof covered the glass windows that extended around the ceiling of most of the lounge to provide light. There was also a raised skylight in the middle of this roof.

Next in line was the boiler casing for the third funnel, on the port side of which was the Officer's Mess. Located on both sides of the ship, from the closed off Officer's Promenade to the end of the third funnel, was the First Class Promenade.

■ The next deckhouse was reserved for machinery and holding (storage) tanks for water, gravity being used to run fresh water throughout the ship. There was also an engineer's smoking room and the dome over the aft First Class Grand Staircase. Following this was another low structure that was the roof over the First Class Smoking Room with windows that provided sunlight into that room.

On top of this was a deckhouse that housed the casing for the fourth funnel and storage rooms for deck equipment, games, and other miscellaneous items. Surrounding this area was the Second Class Promenade, which was accessible from B Deck via an enclosed room that contained the top of the Second Class Grand Staircase.

■ Just aft of the first and the third funnels were the expansion joints that ran the width of the ship on the Boat Deck and A Deck below. These joints were placed there to allow for the expansion and contraction of the ship as the steel from which it was made heated and cooled due to the weather. In rough seas, the joints allowed the ship to sag or flex as needed. The joints were made of leather and iron.

■ Towering over the Boat Deck were the four funnels, each 60 feet high and 22 feet wide. The first three funnels vented the boiler rooms and the fourth was a dummy for appearance's sake, although it was used to vent a small amount of steam and smoke from the galleys.

Each of the funnels was held in place by several huge cables that ran from the top of the funnel and to the deck. Several of the cables for the funnels were attached to the deck on the opposite side of the expansion joints. Any severe strain on the cables could cause them to snap, allowing the funnels to fall over.

LIFEBOATS, PART I

The most prominent items on the Boat Deck were the objects for which it was named: the 20 lifeboats. There were 14 large and two small lifeboats on *Titanic*, plus four emergency Englehardt Collapsible lifeboats. The 14 large wooden lifeboats were each thirty feet long, nine feet wide, and four feet deep with a capacity of 65 people. The two smaller emergency lifeboats had a capacity of 35 people each.

It is important to note that the sixteen regular wooden lifeboats with a total capacity of 980 people were all the lifeboats required by the British Board of Trade regulations, which are the regulations *Titanic* was licensed under.

However, the builders also added the four extra Englehardt Collapsible lifeboats, each twenty-seven feet long, eight feet wide and three feet deep. Each had a capacity of 49 people, for a total of 196 additional people.

In all, if the lifeboats were filled to capacity, they could carry a total of 1,176 people. Unfortunately, *Titanic* was designed to carry 3,295 people. Fortunately, however, on her maiden voyage *Titanic* would carry only 2,208 passengers and crew. Sadly, that meant that there were still 1,087 more people on the ship than available lifeboat space. Going strictly by the law, however, *Titanic* carried enough lifeboats.

- The lifeboats were numbered 1 through 16 and the collapsibles were lettered A through D. The odd-numbered lifeboats (1, 3, 5, 7, 9, 11, 13 and 15) were on the starboard side. The even-numbered boats (2, 4, 6, 8, 10, 12, 14 and 16) were on the port side, directly opposite the odd-numbered boats.

Lifeboat number 1 on the starboard side and number 2 on the port side were the two small emergency lifeboats. These were located closest to the bridge and were permanently swung out over the water to be ready to lower in case of an emergency (such as someone falling overboard).

All sixteen wooden lifeboats were already attached to falls and davits and each was covered with canvas. Each also had oars, a pole and a sail—but none of them had any sort of supplies except for a gallon tin of water.

- Stored on the deck next to Emergency Lifeboat 1 was Collapsible C, and next to Emergency Lifeboat 2 was Collapsible D. Both of these lifeboats already had their canvas sides made up. On the starboard side roof of the officer's cabin was Collapsible A and on the port side was Collapsible B. These boats were stored right side up but with their canvas sides down. They were securely tied down. Because of their weight, they would not be easy to maneuver off the roof. Since they weren't attached to davits, there was only two ways to get them down: muscle power or water to float them off—the latter being an option the designers never imagined, but in fact happened. It is unknown why they were placed on the roof of the officer's quarters, but for all intents and purposes, these two were useless in an emergency.

Consequently, if you subtract the two collapsible's that were on top of the deckhouse, the final lifeboat capacity was 1,078, or less than one-half the number of people on the ship the night she sank.

OLYMPIC (RIGHT) PLATED, TITANIC FRAMED BUT BARELY VISIBLE *(National Archives)*

TITANIC (LEFT) PLATED, OLYMPIC BEING PREPARED FOR LAUNCH *(National Archives)*

"They just builds 'er and shoves 'er in."

CHAPTER 3

FITTING OUT

The keel of the White Star Line steamship *Titanic* was laid down at Harland and Wolff's Queen's Island North Shipyard in Belfast, Ireland on March 31, 1909, three months after construction of her sister ship *Olympic* had begun. Building two ships at the same time severely taxed the capabilities of Harland and Wolff. Because of their huge size, most of the existing engineering or mechanical equipment could not be used, so everything had to be built specifically for these ships.

■   Construction of the two ships was a citywide event. Most of the residents of Belfast were involved to some extent in their construction. Consequently the ships were the pride of the city. Harland and Wolff had constructed two huge slipways for the ships. Belfast citizens were awed by the size of the 840-foot long, 240-foot wide and 214-foot high gantry that stood over the slipways that was taller than any structure in town and dwarfed every other building in the shipyard. In the harbor near the slipways, a huge 200-ton floating crane was built. It could lift 150 tons, which made it ideal for lifting and installing the engines and boilers.

For almost two years, working twelve-hour shifts six days a week and half a day on Sunday, more than 15,000 Belfast residents worked on the two ships. *Olympic* and *Titanic* were built side-by-side. *Olympic's* hull was painted white and *Titanic's* black so that workers could tell them apart. On April 6, 1910, *Titanic's* hull was framed, and on October 19 the exterior plating was completed.

While construction of the twin ships took place in Belfast, the port authorities in New York City were busy dredging several feet of mud and debris off the bottom of a portion of the Hudson River and extending two of the White Star Line piers another 100 feet into the river to accommodate the ships.

■   Almost 100,000 Belfast citizens turned out to watch the launch of *Titanic's* sister ship *Olympic* on October 20, 1910. On May 2, 1911, the

TITANIC LAUNCHED ON MAY 31, 1911. *(National Archives)*

Olympic started her fitting-out trials in the basin of Belfast's River Lagan, and on May 29 she started two days of sea trials in the Belfast Lough. When the trials were completed on May 31, *Olympic* returned to Belfast and made preparations to steam to Southampton to prepare for her maiden voyage. Something else, however, was taking place in the Harland and Wolff shipyard in Belfast that day, something far more interesting to the 100,000 Belfast residents who turned out to witness it: the launching of the White Star Line steamship *Titanic*.

LAUNCH

Early on the morning of Wednesday, May 31, 1911, the residents of Belfast and the surrounding area started to gather, searching out any vantage point they could find on either side of the River Lagan to watch the launch of *Titanic*. The harbor commissioners reserved the best views and charged a small admission fee with the money going to several local hospitals. A local passenger ferry anchored in the middle of the river served as a platform for those willing to pay more for a better view. Because it was Wednesday and a normal working day for Harland and Wolff employees, the day was declared a holiday so they could all turn out to watch the launching. It was, however, an unpaid holiday.

At 7:30 a.m. the chartered ship *Duke of Argyll* arrived at the Harland and Wolff shipyard with a load of reporters and special guests who were ushered into the yard office. Flying on top of the nearby 214-foot tall gantry were three flags, the British Union Jack, the American Stars and Stripes and, in the center, the White Star Line flag, solid red with a white star in the center.

- At 11:30 a.m. Lord and Lady Pirrie, both of whom were celebrating their birthdays, left the yard office with, among others, J.P. Morgan and J. Bruce Ismay. With some of the Harland & Wolff staff, Pirrie made a final inspection of the launch area and then returned to his guests. Meanwhile, the red launch flag was hoisted on the stern of *Titanic* and a red rocket was fired to warn all nearby boats and ships away from the area.

- Twenty-two tons of soap and tallow coated the 772-foot long launch ramp to help the ship slide stern first into the water. During the morning, workers knocked out and removed most of the huge supports on the bottom and sides of the ship, leaving only just enough supports to hold *Titanic* upright. Several hydraulic rams were positioned to push the hull just enough for it to slide down the launch ramp under its own weight (with the aid of the tons of soap and tallow).

- *Titanic's* hull was almost 883 feet long and the river was only 1,200 feet wide. Steps had to be taken to prevent the hull from grounding itself on the opposite bank as it slid down the launch ramp, including:

FITTING OUT. NOTE CROW'S NEST A QUARTER WAY UP THE MAST, AND THE PRIVATE PROMENADE, THE DARK WINDOW OPENINGS ON B DECK BETWEEN NUMBER 2 AND 3 FUNNELS. *(National Archives)*

1) Three sets of anchors were set in the river and attached to seven-inch cables, which in turn were attached to the ships stern; 2) Two piles of drag cables, each weighing over 80 tons, were attached to the bow. As *Titanic* slid into the water, the drag cables slowed and the anchors stopped the ship within a few feet of the launch ramp.

- At 12:05 p.m. Lord Pirrie gave the order to launch. As whistles blew, workers knocked out the rest of the supports, another red rocket was fired and the hydraulic rams were released.

Just before the ship started to move, a support beam fell on top of a worker. Other workers came to his aid and pulled him out from under the beam. However, 43 year-old James Dobbins died the following day from his injuries. He was the second confirmed fatality during the construction process; the other being 15 year-old Samuel Scott, a rivet catch boy who fell off a scaffold the year before. Contrary to a common myth, no one was sealed up inside the hull during construction.

At thirteen minutes after noon on May 31, 1911, the hull of the White Star Line steamship *Titanic* began to slide stern-first down the soap-and-tallow coated launch ramp while thousands of people cheered. Sixty-two seconds later the anchor chains and drag cables brought the hull to a stop. *Titanic* was afloat for the first time.

Workers removed the anchor chains and drag cables and harbor tugs pushed the hull over to the Harland & Wolff dock, where *Titanic* would be fitted out with the aid of the 150-ton floating crane. Shortly after the launch, Lord Pirrie and his guests left for lunch in Belfast and the thousands of spectators started for home.

- There was no "christening," no breaking of a champagne bottle across the bow, no official speech. A shipyard worker explained to a visitor that the White Star Line philosophy was, *"They just builds 'er and shoves 'er in."*

- After lunch in Belfast, Lord Pirrie, J. P. Morgan, J. Bruce Ismay and a group of guests boarded *Olympic* in Belfast Harbor. At 4:30 p.m. the ship departed, bound for Liverpool, White Star Line's headquarters and *Olympic's* home port. It was *Olympic's* first voyage. It arrived in Liverpool the following day and was opened to the public for tours. The following Wednesday *Olympic* departed Southampton on her maiden voyage to New York.

- RMS *Olympic* began her maiden voyage with a full load of passengers on June 14, 1911, under the able command of Edward J. Smith, White Star Line's senior captain. The voyage was largely uneventful until *Olympic* arrived in New York Harbor. There, harbor tug *O.L. Hollenbeck* was almost sunk by the suction created by *Olympic's* huge propellers.

FITTING OUT

When launched on May 31, 1911, *Titanic* was just a huge hull with absolutely nothing completed other than the shell. The fitting-out process was designed to turn the shell into the most beautiful ship afloat. That, however, was almost a year and tens of thousands of working hours away. During the next ten months, every one of the thousands of finishing touches were added to the ship. A few of these include:

Two huge reciprocating engines and the boilers;
Hundreds of miles of electrical cable;
Thousands of tiles in the swimming bath and the Turkish Bath;
Miles of carpeting and floor tile;
Hundreds of bathroom fixtures;
Tons of furniture were loaded;
Four funnels and 20 lifeboats

■ The Harland and Wolff staff created a book with over 300 pages that detailed the instructions White Star Line and Harland and Wolff had agreed upon for the completion of the ship. Every conceivable item had been included:

"The verandah to have three settees with small square tables in front...the servant's rooms to be finished in dark mahogany and fitted with bed having Pullman over, sofa wardrobe..."

"Bells, 1–23" dia. [diameter] Brass ship's bell for F'csle [Forecastle] on Foremast, 1–17" dia. Brass ship's bell for look-out cage in foremast, 1–9½" dia. Brass ship's bell for Captain's bridge..."

"Twelve rooms to have furniture in oak ("A" design)...14 rooms to have furniture in oak with brass beds ("B" design; six rooms in Adams style, white; four rooms in Louis XVI style, in oak; two rooms in Louis XV style, in gray; two rooms in Empire style, in white..."

■ Sometime in July 1911, J. Bruce Ismay asked Lord Pirrie when he could expect *Titanic* to be completed and turned over to White Star Line. White Star Line still had many preparations to make before *Titanic* could start her maiden voyage: coal ordered and delivered, crew hired, food ordered and prepared, announcements of the maiden voyage made and tickets sold. After some consideration about what Harland and Wolff still had to complete, Pirrie gave Ismay his answer: Wednesday, March 20, 1912. On that date, he declared, *Titanic* could depart Southampton, England, on her maiden voyage.

■ On September 18, 1911, White Star Line announced to the world that the date for the maiden voyage of the *Titanic* would be March 20,

1912. Two days later, however, something happened that would throw the schedule right out the window: *Olympic* was involved in an accident.

THE OLYMPIC AND THE HAWKE

On September 20, 1911, the *Olympic* left Southampton to begin her fifth trip to New York. In the English Channel near the Isle of Wight on a course perpendicular to *Olympic's* was the British cruiser HMS *Hawke*, which was conducting routine engine tests.

- *Olympic*, which weighed over ten times more than *Hawke*, slowed and made a turn to port toward the open sea—and a converging course with the *Hawke*. *Olympic* increased speed and *Hawke* seemed to fall behind. Suddenly *Hawke* changed course hard to port and headed straight for *Olympic's* starboard side. The crew of the *Hawke* vainly tried to slow down and change course, however the backwash created by *Olympic's* massive hull sucked the cruiser into *Olympic's* side.

Hawke, with her concrete filled bow, rammed *Olympic* with a massive thud and ripped open two of the watertight compartments near the stern and damaged *Olympic's* starboard propeller. (The bow of the *Hawke* was filled with concrete because, as a British warship, one of its missions was to ram enemy ships to sink them.)

Hawke limped home to Portsmouth, and the passengers on *Olympic* were off-loaded into tenders and taken back to Southampton. *Olympic* was patched up in Southampton and then steamed back to Belfast and the only drydock in the country large enough to accommodate her. This drydock happened to be the one *Titanic* was currently occupying while she was being completed. En route to Belfast, workers replaced the starboard propeller shaft with the one that was supposed to be installed on *Titanic*.

- Unfortunately, the collision taught a false lesson. *Olympic* survived a major collision with a ship designed to sink it by ramming. Only two of the major watertight compartments were breached and, despite some serious flooding, *Olympic* did not sink. This seemed to convince some people that *Olympic* and her sister ship *Titanic*, were unsinkable.

- Initially the crew of *Hawke* was blamed for the collision because she had rammed the side of *Olympic*. Further investigation, however, revealed that *Hawke*, at 7,500 tons, was drawn into the side of *Olympic* by forces beyond her control. Experts were able to explain that when a ship is moving forward, a large amount of water is pushed away on either side, which rushes back toward the stern of the ship, sucking in any smaller boat in the vicinity. The British Admiralty, responsible for determining who was at fault, found:

"...the collision was solely due to the faulty navigation of the Olympic."

■   The Admiralty Board found George Bowyer, the pilot who was guiding *Olympic* out of port, and not the Captain, was responsible for the accident. White Star Line also found the captain of *Olympic*, who had the ultimate authority to safely navigate his ship, blameless for the accident. He would not be blamed because he was Edward J. Smith, the senior captain and commodore of the White Star Line. Although Bowyer was found responsible, he wasn't formally charged. Eventually, White Star Line's insurance company paid for the damage to both ships.

It was soon discovered that it would take six weeks to repair *Olympic* and that *Titanic* would have to vacate the dry dock it occupied. Repairs to *Olympic* now assumed priority over *Titanic*, both in workers and material. Because of the loss of the dry dock, the maiden voyage of *Titanic* would have to be delayed. A new date was set: Wednesday, April 10, 1912.

■   While *Olympic* occupied the dry dock, work continued on *Titanic*, now tied up to a nearby dock—and the official steaming date grew ever closer. In late November, the repairs to *Olympic* were complete and *Titanic* was returned to the dry dock to continue fitting out.

LIFEBOATS, PART II

In January 1912, the sixteen wooden and two Englehardt Collapsible lifeboats were installed on the Welin lifeboat davits. Alexander Carlisle, the ship's original designer, had requested 32 lifeboats and had ordered davits designed to accommodate them. However, at Bruce Ismay's request, only sixteen wooden lifeboats were installed. By law, that is all that was required at the time. Carlisle had at one time proposed that 64 boats be installed, enough for every person on the ship, but that proposal was never seriously considered.

■   The British Board of Trade created the Merchant Shipping Act of 1894 to deal with lifeboat capacity issues. Capacity was based entirely on the cubic footage of a ship and not how many people the ship would be carrying. For example, a 10,000 ton ship, a total of 9,625 cubic feet of lifeboat space was required, enough for 960 people.

The largest ship considered by the Merchant Shipping Act of 1894 was 10,000 tons (about twice the size of any existing 1894 ship) and the act had not been updated to accommodate larger ships. This meant that once a ship had met this maximum tonnage, (a weight far exceeded by many ships in 1912), no more lifeboats were required by law. For *Titanic*, regulations still only required 9,625 cubic feet of lifeboat space, or enough for 960 people. This was the same amount as required 18 years earlier, when the act was written and the largest ships were still around 5,000 tons.

A few days prior to *Titanic's* departure from Southampton, Board of Trade inspectors noted that *Titanic's* lifeboats exceeded legal requirements. Fortunately, *Titanic's* maiden voyage did not sell out. To accommodate everyone the ship was designed for would have required 63 lifeboats—one less than Alexander Carlisle had originally proposed.

MARCONI WIRELESS SYSTEM

Wireless communication was still a fairly new innovation in the early 1900s. In 1909 its use prevented a major loss of life when the White Star liner *Republic* sank after colliding with the *Florida*, an Italian owned liner. *Republic* had a wireless system and used it to summon help from several nearby ships. As a result, only two people were lost.

By 1912, almost all commercial ships carried wireless set provided by one of several competing companies. Many, including *Titanic*, used the wireless system developed by Marconi, and the Marconi system on *Titanic* and *Olympic* was the most powerful available on any ship at the time.

- Marconi wireless operators were employed by the Marconi Company and *not* by the ship or its owners. The operators were contracted out and reported to their company offices *first* and to the ship's officers *second*. The operators were only required to pass information on to the crew of the ship if the information was related to an emergency, or if it pertained to the navigation of the ship.

- Stretching between *Titanic's* two masts were the four wires of the wireless antenna. The "guaranteed" working range for the Marconi wireless on *Titanic* was 250 miles, but communication could usually be maintained up to 400 miles. Sometimes at night, when weather conditions were just right, messages could be sent and received up to 2,000 miles. In January 1912 *Titanic* was assigned the call letters "MGY", which would identify the ship to anyone who was listening in on its transmissions.

A five-kilowatt generator that received power from the ship's electrical system powered the wireless system. There was a backup generator on the roof of the deckhouse, and another battery-powered backup system in the wireless office.

CONSTRUCTION CONTINUES

From November 1911, when *Olympic* returned to service, until early March 1912, *Titanic* made several moves from the pier to the dry dock in the Harland and Wolff shipyard while construction progressed. In late February, *Olympic* lost a propeller blade on a trip from New York and had to return to Belfast for repairs. *Titanic* had to vacate the dry dock once again. Then on March 6, *Titanic* had to be placed into dry dock to make room for *Olympic's* departure in the restricted waters of the River Lagan.

▪ The constant delays and movement in and out of the dry dock continually squeezed the work time available before the planned April 10 departure. As a result, White Star Line made the decision to forego the planned customary stop in Liverpool to allow citizens to board the ship to view it. Instead, *Titanic* would proceed directly to Southampton to load passengers for its maiden voyage, which was still scheduled to depart on Wednesday, April 10.

J. Bruce Ismay had traveled to New York on the maiden voyage of *Olympic* to see how well the ship performed. Based on that trip, and in conjunction with the Harland and Wolff design team, Ismay decided to make some last minute design changes to *Titanic*. During the last few weeks of March 1912, and only three weeks before its maiden voyage, some noticeable and major modifications were made.

▪ First Class passengers on *Olympic* complained about spray from the bow being tossed up and blowing across the A Deck promenade. To remedy this, the open area in front of and along the sides of *Titanic's* A Deck promenade was enclosed with sliding windows. This change created the only visible difference between *Olympic* and *Titanic*. The windows could only be opened by a special tool, and they would supply their own drama for some of the passengers in a few short weeks.

Another of Ismay's changes to *Titanic* was made shortly before its maiden voyage. Ismay felt that there was too much open deck space on the ship, so he added more First Class cabins and created the two Promenade Suites. Each of these suites had its own private promenade that could be opened to the sea, and each came with a room for a private maid. The suites were huge, had several rooms, and cost a small fortune to reserve.

▪ Time was running out to make the maiden voyage deadline. Painters were falling over carpet layers who were elbowing tile layers for room, who in turn were trying to stay out of the way of the plumbers and electricians. Thousands of fine details were being completed simultaneously. Furniture arrived before the floors were ready or it arrived in the wrong sequence. Bedding arrived before it was needed. Kitchen equipment arrived by the trainload. Thousands of workers crawled all over the ship polishing this, adjusting that, or touching up paint and woodwork. The huge 21-light candelabra arrived to fill the empty space under the huge glass dome over the Grand Staircase. Still material arrived: coat hooks, hangers, 3,560 lifebelts, more furniture, signal equipment, beds, basins, tools and much more.

■ The engineering crew began to arrive in March. Some had been with the ship during construction and many were now living on board. A few of the ship's officers also arrived that month, including Charles Herbert Lightoller, the First Officer of the liner *Oceanic*, which was out of service because of a lack of coal due to a nationwide coal strike. Lightoller would later write,

> "It is difficult to convey any idea of the size of a ship like Titanic, when you could actually walk miles along decks and passages, covering different ground all the time...it took me fourteen days before I could with confidence find my way from one part of that ship to another by the shortest route...there was a huge gangway door through which you could drive a horse and cart on the starboard side aft. Three other officers, joining later, tried for a whole day to find it..."

■ On March 25, the huge center anchor was lowered and then raised, the watertight doors were tested, and all sixteen wooden lifeboats were swung out and lowered, then raised back into position.

On March 26, four additional White Star Line officers met at the company offices in Liverpool to catch transportation to Belfast, where they arrived around noon on March 27. These were junior officers Boxhall, Lowe, Moody and Pitman. When they arrived on *Titanic*, they reported to Chief Officer William Murdoch.

■ While workers continued to add the final touches, a partial load of coal was loaded into the coal bins through the coal chutes located along the side of the ship. There was enough coal for *Titanic* to complete her sea trials and steam to Southampton, England. When coaling was completed, the entire ship had to be wiped down to clean up the coal dust, which had settled everywhere. Then the painters returned and continued their work.

■ On March 29, firemen, stokers, greasers and support crew signed on as part of the crew. There were 79 of them, and each was needed for the April 1 sea trials. Escort tugs from Liverpool arrived in Belfast along with builders, owners and Board of Trade representatives and food for them all.

■   Although finishing touches were being added, on April 1, 1912, the
sea trials for *Titanic* were expected to take place. *Titanic* was only ten days
away from the start of her maiden voyage.

TITANIC DEPARTING FOR SEA TRIALS, BELFAST LOUGH, APRIL 2, 1912. *National Archives*

CHAPTER 4

SEA TRIALS

Olympic had gone through two days of sea trials before her maiden voyage. Because *Titanic* was a copy of *Olympic*, it was believed only one day of trials would be required. The trials were scheduled to begin at 10:00 a.m. on April 1, 1912, in the River Lagan and Belfast Lough. There would also be an extended steaming trial in the Irish Sea before *Titanic* would steam to Southampton to prepare for her maiden voyage to New York.

▪ On the big day, all preparations had been made and the tugboats were along side to maneuver the ship away from the dock. Sometime before 10:00 a.m. the decision was made to postpone the trials because a heavy wind was blowing, which churned up the river and made navigation hazardous. There was very little clearance in the river for a ship the size of *Titanic*, and it was wisely decided to postpone the trials until the next day.

▪ The weather was clear and calm on April 2 as some 200 people boarded *Titanic* to participate in or attend the sea trials. The list of people on the ship that day included:

> Engine room personnel consisting of 78 stokers, firemen and
>> trimmers;
> Other crewmen, including electricians, deck crew, stewards and
>> cooks;
> The officers and other senior crewmen;
> Marconi operators Jack Phillips and Harold Bride, who were
>> setting up their wireless equipment;
> Designer Thomas Andrews, representing Harland and Wolff;
> Harland and Wolff's senior architect Edward Wilding;
> Board of Trade ship surveyor Francis Carruthers, who would
>> sign off on the trials;

Harold A. Sanderson, IMM board member (representing IMM
because Bruce Ismay could not attend);

Mr. Wyckoff Van Derhoef, traveling First Class from Belfast to
New York, was the only paying passenger on *Titanic*;

Finally, there were several other individuals representing various
companies who had supplied equipment or machinery
that might need adjustment during the trials.

▪ By 6:00 a.m., five harbor tugs were ready to assist in getting *Titanic*
away from the dock and into the channel of the River Lagan. The first tug
to attach a line was Harland and Wolff's yard tug *Hercules*, followed by
harbor tugs *Huskisson, Herculaneum, Hornby* and *Herald. Herald* attached a
line directly to the bow of *Titanic* and pulled the giant ship into the river.
Hundreds of spectators turned out to watch as *Titanic* was guided into
the channel and slowly faced toward Belfast Lough.

▪ The stokers built up the fires in the boilers and huge plumes of black
smoke poured out of her funnels while the tugs pulled and nudged
Titanic down the river for more than three miles. Once inside the wide
and deep waters of Belfast Lough, the tugs cast off and returned to
Belfast. *Titanic* was now on her own.

Instructions were passed from the bridge to start the engines, and as
they slowly turned over, the propellers began to churn and *Titanic* was
under way for the first time. On the bridge was *Titanic's* captain, the
senior such officer and commodore of the White Star Line: Edward J.
Smith.

UNDER WAY

The first test including working *Titanic* up to a speed of 20 knots
before stopping the engines and letting the ship coast to a dead stop. The
great ship repeated this pattern throughout the morning. Numerous
rudder, engine and turning tests were also conducted, and the results
were discussed and duly recorded.

During one test, the ship traveled along a straight line at 20 knots
and was set into a hard full circle. The diameter of the circle was
measured at about 3,850 feet, which is 1,283 yards or about 4½ lengths
of the ship.

▪ A stopping test was also conducted. A marker buoy was dropped into
the water and *Titanic* steamed away a couple of miles, and then turned
around to face the buoy. The ship steamed toward it at 20 knots until just
alongside the marker, when the engines were thrown into full reverse to
stop the ship. At 20 knots it took 2,550 feet, or 850 yards, to come to a
complete stop. That was just short of three times the length of the ship

itself. Called a "crash stop," under normal circumstances it would never be tried again because it could potentially cause serious damage to the engines.

- Next came the open water straight run out into the Irish Sea: two hours out averaging 18 knots, then two hours back to the entrance of Belfast Lough. It was late afternoon and the sun was starting to set, but a series of huge "S" turns were made to test the handling of the ship. It was almost dark when the final test was made to drop both anchors.

- Board of Trade representative Francis Carruthers was satisfied that *Titanic* had met or exceeded every one of the Board's requirements, and after dark he signed off the official paperwork with the notation, *"Good for one year from today, 2.4.12."*

Because *Titanic* was going to steam directly to Southampton, those who were not going there were placed on a tender and sent back to Belfast. Sometime during the evening another set of papers was executed: Sanderson signed to accept ownership of the *Titanic*, and Andrews, representing Harland and Wolff as the builders, signed to transfer ownership to White Star Line.

- Around 8:00 p.m. *Titanic* steamed out of Belfast Lough and into the Irish Sea under a tight schedule. The ship had to be at Southampton in time for the midnight tide, which was just 30 hours away.

During the trip, tests of various types were conducted. Everything from the engines to the kitchen stoves and potato peelers were tested.

Wireless operators Phillips and Bride were awake and working during most of the trip, testing their equipment, communicating with other ships, and passing progress reports to the White Star Line offices in Liverpool.

- Around 10:30 a.m. on April 3, *Titanic* steamed into the English Channel and around the south coast of England until she approached the entrance of Southampton harbor in time to meet the high tide later that evening.

A harbor pilot was brought aboard. Once in the harbor, five tugs (*Ajax*, *Hector*, *Hercules*, *Neptune* and *Vulcan*) cast lines onto the ship and guided her up the channel of the River Test. *Titanic* would be departing Southampton on a low tide, and there would not be much room to maneuver. As the ship approached the White Star Line dock, it was turned 90 degrees and pushed in stern first. The trip from Belfast was more than 570 miles. *Titanic* reached a speed of 23-1/4 knots, the fastest she would ever steam. Around midnight *Titanic* was secured to the dock while preparations were made for her brief stay in Southampton.

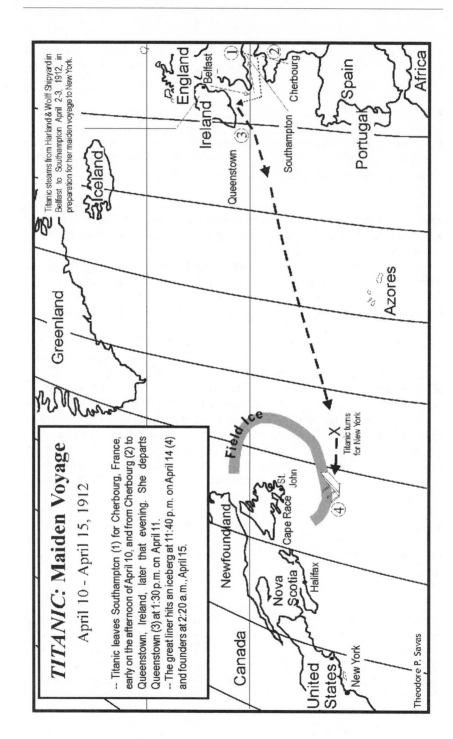

TITANIC: Maiden Voyage
April 10 – April 15, 1912

-- Titanic leaves Southampton (1) for Cherbourg, France, early on the afternoon of April 10. and from Cherbourg (2) to Queenstown, Ireland, later that evening. She departs Queenstown (3) at 1:30 p.m. on April 11.

-- The great liner hits an iceberg at 11:40 p.m. on April 14 (4) and founders at 2:20 a.m., April 15.

Titanic steams from Harland & Wolff Shipyard in Belfast to Southampton April 2-3, 1912, in preparation for her maiden voyage to New York.

Greenland

Iceland

England
Belfast
Cherbourg
Ireland
Southampton
Queenstown
Portugal
Spain
Africa

Field Ice

X
Titanic turns
for New York

Azores

St. John
Cape Race
Newfoundland
Nova Scotia
Halifax

Canada

United States
New York

Theodore P. Savas

"This is a magnificent ship, and I feel very disappointed I am not to make the first voyage."

CHAPTER 5

FINISHING TOUCHES

Southampton, England, is about 80 miles southwest of London and has been a major British seaport since the 15th century. Its location on the English Channel makes it an excellent site for passenger service.

■ The White Star Line was headquartered in Liverpool, which is why that city appeared under the *Titanic* name on the stern. In 1907, passenger service from Southampton to New York was started. Southampton is a short cruise across the English Channel from the French port of Cherbourg, which in turn provided White Star Line a port on the European continent.

From Cherbourg, it is another short cruise back across the channel to Queenstown, Ireland, where White Star Line ships made their third, and final, stop before steaming out into the North Atlantic Ocean en route to their final destinations. By steaming this triangle, White Star ships were able to make a port call in three countries in a convenient steaming pattern.

Several White Star Line ships, including *Adriatic*, *Majestic*, *Oceanic* and *Teutonic*, served Southampton. However, the trio of the *Olympic*-class ships—*Olympic*, *Titanic*, and *Gigantic*—were being built to provide weekly service from Southampton to New York City.

■ In 1911, the White Star Line dock in Southampton was enlarged and the River Test dredged in preparation for the arrival of the three huge ships. The dock was enlarged to six berths with more than 3,800 feet of dock footage, and was 122 feet wide. Berths 43 and 44 were almost 1,500 feet in length and were designed for two of the *Olympic*-class liners to be tied up at the same time. It was into Berth 44 that *Titanic* was placed after her trip from Belfast.

■ Early on the morning of April 4, having just completed her trip from Belfast, *Titanic* was tied up and ready for the next step in her journey. She was due to begin her maiden voyage in six days, and still there were numerous details yet to complete. Her stay in Southampton would be a busy one.

MAKING READY

Because of the national coal strike, which had been ongoing since early January, all the berths in Southampton were full of stranded vessels that did not have enough coal to operate. There were several White Star Line ships stranded in port and their remaining coal, plus coal left behind by *Olympic*, which had just left for New York, was added to what *Titanic* had brought from Belfast.

- Colliers (coal-laden barges) pulled up next to *Titanic's* starboard side. Coal was loaded into buckets, hoisted up the side of the ship and dumped into the hinged coal chutes located all along the side of the ship on F Deck. From there the coal fell into the coal bins along G Deck and the Tank Top. Trimmers, or crewmen inside the coalbunkers, distributed the coal throughout the width of the ship in carts and shoveled it into those bins that didn't have chutes. *Titanic* arrived from Belfast with 1,880 tons of coal on board, and during the coaling phase another 4,400 tons were added. While in Southampton, some of the boilers were kept lit to provide light, power, and heat. During that time 415 tons of coal were consumed.

In all, *Titanic* had enough coal to make the trip to New York, but there wasn't much to spare. Coal for the return trip would be obtained in the New York. In order to conserve fuel, it was decided that instead of steaming at the proposed 23 knots to New York, *Titanic* would maintain an average speed of approximately 22 knots (or 25 miles per hour). There was the real possibility that if *Titanic* steamed too fast for too long, the ship would run out of fuel before she arrived in New York, which in turn would result in a publicity disaster the White Star Line wanted to avoid at all costs.

- In 1912, Southampton was home to over 120,000 people, most of whom were employed by or influenced in some fashion by the shipping industry. The vast majority of *Titanic's* crew came from the small residential districts in and around Southampton.

Because of the coal strike, few ships had left the port during the past several months. Thus, when the time came to sign on a crew for *Titanic*, the enrolling officers could pick and choose from thousands of applicants. For the most part they selected the best from the over 17,000 unemployed men and women in and around Southampton. *Titanic* would be staffed with a premier crew for her maiden voyage.

By Saturday, April 6, most of the crew had been hired, and those not needed prior to departure were sent home so that they could enjoy Easter Sunday with their families. They had secured a good paying job on the world's newest and largest steamship.

- There was also shakeup in the officer assignments in Southampton. Having just come from *Olympic*, Captain Smith decided he needed an experienced officer from that ship to act as his Chief Officer on *Titanic*. White Star Line ordered *Olympic*'s Chief Officer Henry T. Wilde to join *Titanic* for one trip.

Wilde's arrival just a few hours before the start of the voyage caused a domino effect among some of the remaining officers. The current Chief Officer, William M. Murdoch, was bumped down to First Officer and First Officer Charles H. Lightoller became Second Officer.

Lightoller's change bumped Second Officer David Blair, who decided to leave the ship for another assignment. Although he was upset about losing his berth on *Titanic*, the juggling of officers was beyond his control. Although Blair would later say that the decision to leave *Titanic* was one of the best he ever made, he felt badly about being unable to make the trip to New York. *"This is a magnificent ship, and I feel very disappointed I am not to make the first voyage,"* he wrote to his daughter.

▪ In his haste to depart, Blair pocketed the keys to a storage locker in his cabin. When Lightoller moved in, however, he never tried to open it. This was unfortunate, because inside were the binoculars assigned to the lookouts in the Crow's Nest. The lookouts had used them on the trip from Belfast, but by the time the ship was ready to steam out on her maiden voyage, they were safely stored away.

Seven of the eight officers on *Titanic* also belonged to the Royal Naval Reserve, and all had served with White Star Line for various lengths of time. Overall, they were a very capable group. Final officer assignments for *Titanic*'s maiden voyage were as follows:

> Edward J. Smith, Captain
> Henry T. Wilde, Chief Officer
> William M. Murdoch, First Officer
> Charles H. Lightoller, Second Officer
> Herbert Pitman, Third Officer
> Joseph Boxhall, Fourth Officer
> Harold Lowe, Fifth Officer
> James Moody, Sixth Officer

▪ Every officer except Captain Smith stood a "watch." Wilde, Murdoch and Lightoller each stood a four-hour watch with eight hours off. During the off hours, they conducted inspections, did paperwork, ate their meals, and slept. The four junior officers worked four hours on and four hours off, and there were always two of them on watch at the same time along with one of the senior officers. As captain of the ship, Smith did not stand a watch because he was always considered to be on duty.

CAPTAIN EDWARD J. SMITH ON THE DECK OF TITANIC, BELFAST,
APRIL 2, 1912. (*Illustrated London News, April 20, 1912*)

CAPTAIN EDWARD J. SMITH

"When anyone asks me how I can best describe my experience in nearly forty years at sea, I merely say, uneventful," said Captain Smith in 1907, five years prior to *Titanic's* maiden voyage. *"I have never been in any accident . . . or any sort worth speaking about. I have seen but one vessel in distress in all my years at sea. I never saw a wreck and never have been wrecked nor was I ever in any predicament that threatened to end in disaster of any sort."*

■   Smith's record indicates that he was a safe captain, but his 1907 comment was not wholly truthful. During his career he had several mishaps, as noted below:

> 1889: He was captain when *Republic* ran aground off New York and was stranded for several hours;
> 1890: Smith grounded another ship off Rio de Janeiro;
> 1899: *Germanic*, tied up to a dock in New York, capsized due to ice accumulations during an ice storm;
> 1904: There was a serious fire on board *Majestic*;
> 1906: There was a serious fire on board *Baltic*.

After his 1907 statement, Smith was involved in two potentially serious mishaps:

> 1909: The *Adriatic* grounded off New York;
> 1911: He was in command of *Olympic* when she collided with the British cruiser *Hawke*.

In none of these instances was Smith found at fault, although White Star Line paid the penalty in every case, which included the loss of the court case over the collision with *Hawke*, for which White Star had to pay damages incurred by both ships.

■   Known as "E.J." by his friends, Smith was 62 and planning to retire. It is possible that *Titanic's* maiden voyage was supposed to be his last trip. However, there is some indication that he planned to work for a few more years, at least until the third ship of the *Olympic*-class trio, *Gigantic*, was put into service. Smith had been with the White Star Line for 26 years. Since 1886, he had served aboard most of White Star's major ships.

■   As the White Star Line's senior captain, Smith carried the title of Commodore of White Star Line. For many years Smith was given the honor of being the captain of each of White Star's new ships. He had commanded *Olympic*, and was now in charge of *Titanic*.

Smith was an honorary commander of the Royal Naval Reserve and had made two transport runs to South Africa during the Boer War, earning the right to fly the coveted Blue Ensign on any ship he commanded.

One crewman once said of Smith,

> "This crew knew him to be a good, kind-hearted man, and we looked upon him as a sort of father."

Many passengers traveled on ships commanded by captains they liked the most, and Smith had a huge following. Many of *Titanic's* First Class passengers gave up accommodations on other ships that departed on other dates in order to travel with Smith.

- Ocean travel was remarkably safe during this period. Of the millions of passengers who had crossed the sea for thirty years before *Titanic* steamed toward New York, only four had perished in accidents. Smith had never been involved in a collision until the incident with the *Hawke*. This was impressive, but it also meant that he did not have any experience dealing with a serious accident. *Titanic* was over ten times the size of the first ships Smith had served on. Perhaps size and technology had passed him by.

FINISHING TOUCHES

Three major events were taking place in Southampton prior to the arrival of the passengers and crew on April 10: workers were finishing the final touches on the ship, most of the furniture, food, and china arrived, and cargo was being loaded aboard.

- Because of the shortened construction time and the delays caused by the two unplanned dockings of *Olympic* in Belfast, many of the finishing touches to *Titanic* were done enroute to, and while docked at, Southampton.

Painters, plumbers, electricians, carpet layers, tile layers, and drapery hangers got in each other's way as everyone struggled to get the ship ready for the Wednesday departure. Some of the finishing work wasn't completed in time, and plans were made to complete it when *Titanic* returned to Southampton after her first trip to New York. *Titanic* would sail with more than 1,200 empty beds, and many of these rooms would not be finished until she returned to Southampton.

With so much work going on, White Star Line had to cancel plans in Southampton that would allow visitors to board the ship for a tour, the "open house" that most new ships allowed.

- The day before *Titanic* left Southampton and before being displaced by Charles Lightoller, Second Officer David Blair managed to take his sister on a tour. According to Nancy Blair, the visit, *"took several hours and the ship was still a hive of activity with carpets still being laid and decorators busy until the last moment."*

■ Among the people on board for the maiden voyage not counted as passengers or crew were nine senior employees of Harland and Wolff, including Thomas Andrews. Known collectively as the Guarantee Group, they were making the voyage to continue testing equipment and systems.

While workers continued to add finishing touches, the dishes, linen and food arrived.

DISHES, GLASS AND SILVER

All of the following were loaded at Southampton:

BASIN		GLASSES		SHAKER	
SUGAR	400	CELERY	300	PEPPER	2,000
BOTTLE		CHAMPAGNE	1,500	SALT	2,000
WATER	2,500	COCKTAIL	1,500	SPOONS	
BOWLS		LIQUEUR	1,200	DESSERT	3,000
FINGER	1,000	WINE	2,000	DINNER	5,000
SALAD	500	JUGS		EGG	2,000
CUPS:		CLARET	300	MUSTARD	1,500
BREAKFAST	4,500	CREAM	1,000	SALT	1,500
BOUILLON	3,000	KNIVES		TEA	6,000
COFFEE	1,500	BUTTER	400	TUMBLER	
TEA	3,000	DESSERT	4,000	CUT GLASS	8,000
DISHES		FISH	1,500	VASE	
BOUILLON	3,000	FRUIT	1,500	FLOWER	500
BUTTER	400	TABLE	4,000		
CRYSTAL	1,500	PLATES		MISCELLANEOUS	
ENTRÉE	400	BREAKFAST	2,500	TONGS	400
FRUIT	400	DESSERT	2,000	GRAPE SCISSORS	100
MEAT	400	DINNER	12,000	NUT CRACKERS	300
PIE	1,200	ICE CREAM	5,500	SUGAR TONGS	400
PUDDING	1,200	SOUP	4,500	TOAST RACKS	400
SOUFFLÉ	1,500	POTS			
VEGETABLE	400	COFFEE	1,200		
FORKS		TEA	1,200		
DINNER	8,000	SAUCERS			
FRUIT	1,500	BREAKFAST	4,500		
FISH	1,500	COFFEE	1,500		
OYSTER	1,000	TEA	3,000		

TOTAL ITEMS   127,000

With only 2,200 people on board, one must wonder whether any of the 127,000 dishes were washed during the voyage. However, there were several crewmen assigned as dishwashers.

LINENS

CLOTHS		TOWELS		APRONS	4,000
COOKS	3,500	BATH	7,500	BED COVERS	3,600
GLASS	2,000	FINE	25,000	BLANKETS	7,500
TABLE	6,000	LAVATORY	8,000	COUNTERPANES	3,000
SHEETS		ROLLER	3,500	NAPKINS	45,000
SINGLE	15,000	PANTRY	6,500	PILLOW SLIPS	15,000
DOUBLE	3,000			QUILTS	800
				MISC.	40,000

TOTAL ITEMS   199,900

Laundry was not done on the ship. White Star Line maintained a huge laundry facility in Southampton that employed 50 people to process 200,000 items a week.

VICTUALS (FOOD)

DAIRY		VEGETABLES	
CONDENSED MILK	600 GALLONS	ASPARAGUS, FRESH	800 BUNDLES
FRESH BUTTER	6,000 POUNDS	GREEN PEAS, FRESH	2,250 POUNDS
FRESH CREAM	1,200 QUARTS	LETTUCE HEADS	7,000
FRESH MILK	1,500 GALLONS	ONIONS	3,500 POUNDS
ICE CREAM	1,750 QUARTS	POTATOES	40 TONS
FISH		TOMATOES	2¾ TONS
FRESH	11,000 POUNDS	MISCELLANEOUS	
SALT & DRIED	4,000 POUNDS	CEREALS	10,000 POUNDS
FRUIT		COFFEE	2,200 POUNDS
GRAPES	1,000 POUNDS	EGGS, FRESH	40,000
GRAPEFRUIT	50 BOXES	FLOUR	200 BARRELS
LEMONS	16,000	JAMS	1,120 POUNDS
ORANGES	36,000	SUGAR	10,000 POUNDS
MEAT		RICE & BEANS	10,000 POUNDS
BACON & HAM	7,500 POUNDS	TEA	800 POUNDS
FRESH MEAT	75,000 POUNDS	DRINKS	
POULTRY & GAME	7,500 POUNDS	BEER & STOUT	20,000 BOTTLES
SAUSAGE	2,500 POUNDS	MINERAL WATER	15,000 BOTTLES
SWEETBREADS	1,000	SPIRITS	850 BOTTLES
		WINES	1,500 BOTTLES

There was over 200,000 pounds of food on board, so passengers on *Titanic* were certainly going to eat well. Smokers, too, would fare well, for the ship boasted 8,000 quality cigars.

CARGO

While the stewards and cooks managed the loading of the food and eating utensils, other members of the crew were overseeing the loading of the cargo destined for New York. The cargo ranged from common items to highly unique items.

Although this is not a complete list, the cargo manifest included the following:

WINE	300+ CASES	CORK	6 BUNDLES
	3 BARRELS	MUSSELS	225 CASES
	26 HOGSHEADS	WOOD	35 BAGS
WHISKY	1 CASE	OPIUM	4 CASES
LIQUOR	192 CASES	SKINS	100+ BUNDLES
BRANDY	110 CASES	HORSEHAIR	2 CASES
COGNAC	17 CASES	FEATHERS	7 CASES
ANCHOVIES	75 CASES	CALABASHES	16 CASES
WALNUTS, SHELLED	300+ CASES	ARGOLS	33 BALES
CHEESE	480+ BUNDLES	DRAGON'S BLOOD*	76 CASES
LEATHER	100 BUNDLES	EARTH	1 BARREL
BOOKS	HUNDREDS OF BOXES	RABBIT HAIR	15 CASES
PRINTED MATTER	HUNDREDS OF CASES		

*(DRAGON'S BLOOD IS A NATURAL SUBSTANCE. IT COMES FROM A TREE IN ASIA AND WAS USED TO MANUFACTURE STAINS AND VARNISHES.)

▪ Also listed on the general cargo manifest were boots, soap, tennis balls, golf balls, auto parts, tissue, rubber, a load of solid oak beams, five grand pianos, a jeweled copy of *The Rubáiyát* by Omar Khayyám with the binding inlaid with 1,500 precious stones, and passenger William E. Carter's 25 horsepower Renault automobile.

▪ Shippers paid a premium to ship cargo on *Titanic*, but they saved most of the additional cost in their insurance premiums. Insurance companies gave excellent rates because *Titanic* was considered the safest ship in the world.

OLYMPIC (LEFT) ENTERING DRYDOCK WHILE TITANIC (RIGHT) IS BEING MOVED TO A DOCK TO CONTINUE FITTING OUT. MARCH 1912. (National Archives)

CHAPTER 6

THE CREW

Except for the officers, in the early 1900s the crew of a passenger liner was only hired, or "signed on," for one round trip. They had to sign up again for every voyage. They were not guaranteed a job on the next trip. Explained Seaman Alan Fanstone,

> *"When a ship docked in those days the men . . . were paid off. Well, if that ship was in for 2 or 3 weeks they were put ashore and there was no unemployment benefit . . . so they couldn't afford to stay, so they usually jumped on some other ship."*

Some of the crew members, however, managed to sign on for multiple trips, often for several years on the same ship, which gave some sort of continuity and permanence. Some passengers altered their travel plans to make sure they traveled with a favorite steward or waiter regardless of which vessel they were serving aboard.

There were over one hundred different jobs on a ship like *Titanic*, divided into the Deck Department, Engineering Department, and the Victualling and Vendor Department.

DECK DEPARTMENT

The Deck Department consisted of one master and seven mates (Captain Smith was the master and the officers were the mates); two surgeons, two carpenters, one Boatswain, one Boatswain's Mate, 29 Able Bodied Seamen, two seamen, six lookouts, seven quartermasters, two window washers, two mess room stewards, one storekeeper, one lamp trimmer and two Masters-at-Arms.

OFFICERS (OR MATES)

Henry T. Wilde was born in 1872 and went to sea when he was 15. Joining the White Star Line in 1905, Wilde worked his way up from second officer of several White Star Line ships to Chief Officer of *Olympic*, a position he held when it collided with the *Hawke*. Wilde was on the Docking Bridge when it happened, so he had one of the best views of the collision.

When Captain Smith assumed command of *Titanic*, he asked for Wilde to join him as Chief Officer because of his experience handling such a large ship. Wilde joined *Titanic's* crew on April 8 and assumed the Chief Officer's assignment on the morning of April 10—the day *Titanic* left Southampton.

- William M. Murdoch was born in 1873 and was apprenticed to the sea in 1887 when he was only 14. In 1899, he served on a ship with apprentice officer Stanley Lord, who would command the *Californian* the night *Titanic* sank.

In 1900, Murdoch joined the White Star Line as a Second Officer. Ominously, between 1900 and 1910 a total of six of his family members had been lost at sea in various accidents.

In 1905, Murdoch prevented a collision with another ship by countermanding the orders of a senior officer, who had ordered an incorrect change of course. Overruling a senior did not endear him to that man, but it did mark Murdoch as a capable leader willing to make difficult decisions. Murdoch was an extremely capable officer.

- Thirty-eight year old Charles H. Lightoller had been at sea since he was 13. Lightoller joined White Star Line in 1900 and served on several of the company's ships before being assigned to *Titanic* as First Officer two weeks before of her maiden voyage. He served in that position during the trials and the trip to Southampton, but was bumped down to Second Officer with the arrival of Wilde.

- Third Officer Herbert J. Pitman was 35 years old and had been with White Star Line for nine years. He was one of three officers who did not come over from *Olympic*.

- Although only 28 years old, Joseph G. Boxhall had already spent 13 years at sea. He joined White Star Line in 1905, served on *Olympic*, and reported to *Titanic* as Fourth Officer.

- Harold G. Lowe was another officer who did not come over from *Olympic*. Lowe was 29 years old when he joined *Titanic* as Fifth Officer.

- James P. Moody was 24 years old and had just recently graduated from nautical school and passed his Master's Examination. Moody was the third and final officer who did not come from *Olympic*. He signed on as Sixth Officer of *Titanic*.

DECK DEPARTMENT CREW

Surgeon William F. N. O'Loughlin had spent 40 years at sea before transferring over from *Olympic*. One of his jobs was to review the entire crew muster sheet on the day the ship sailed to ensure that a healthy crew was on board. O'Laughlin would not survive the voyage, and would be last seen partaking in a bottle of spirits from his medicine cabinet. J.C.H. Beaumont later stated that,

> *"Whether he had any premonitions about the Titanic...I cannot say, but I do know that during a talk with him, he did tell me that he was tired at this time of life to be changing from one ship to another."*

- John H. Hutchinson from Southampton transferred from *Olympic* as a Joiner. He would die on the voyage.

- Fifty-two year old Alfred Nichols of Southampton signed on as a Boatswain after transferring from *Olympic*. He, too, would not live to see New York.

- Another transfer from *Olympic* was Boatswain's Mate Albert M. Haines from Southampton. Haines was ordered into Lifeboat Number 9, and thus would survive.

- Signing on as quartermasters were Robert Hichens, George T. Rowe and five others, all of whom would survive because they were ordered by the ship's officers to command lifeboats.

- Able Bodied Seaman Edward J. Buley, Thomas W. Jones, George A. Moore, Joseph Scarrott, Frank Osman, Walter T. Brice, William H. Lyons and Robert J. Hopkins all signed on. Each except Lyons would survive the voyage because, once again, they were ordered to command a lifeboat.

- Twenty-seven year old Able Bodied Seaman Frank O. Evans had spent over nine years in the Royal Navy before moving onto merchant ships. On April 10, Evans was one of about 18 sailors who took part in the lifeboat drill. It was a good thing, for he would command one of them after the ship sank.

- John T. Poingdestre was another Able Bodied Seaman, one of twelve children, and had five of his own before he signed up for the maiden voyage of *Titanic*. Only a month earlier Poingdestre had been on another ship, *Oceana*, when it sank. Poingdestre had a lucky star. He would survive *Titanic* and during World War I, survive the sinking of another ship torpedoed out from under him.

- Boarding in Belfast and in Southampton were the six Crows' Nest lookouts, each a resident of Southampton: Reginald Lee, Alfred F. Evans, George K. Hogg, George T. M. Symans, Archibald Jewell, and Frederick Fleet. All six would be drafted as lifeboat commanders and survive the sinking. Jewell and Fleet (who had been at sea since the age of 13) transferred from *Oceanic*.

ENGINEERING DEPARTMENT

The engineering department consisted of 25 engineers, six electricians, two boilermakers, 173 firemen and stokers, 75 trimmers, 33 greasers, six mess stewards, four storekeepers, and two clerks.

- Fifty-one year old Joseph Bell was the Chief Engineer. He had been with White Star Line for 26 years and transferred from *Olympic*. Bell would not survive.

- Chief Engineer Peter Sloan was 31 years old and had worked for White Star his entire professional life. He, too, transferred from *Olympic*. Sloan and the entire electrical department would stay by their equipment to keep the lights working. All of them went down with the ship.

- Firemen William Nutbean, John Podesta, the three Slade brothers (Alfred, Bertram and Thomas), and Trimmer V. Penney signed on and appeared for muster the morning the ship left Southampton. Later, the six headed off to a nearby pub to tip a few ales.

- Fireman Walter Hurst and his father-in-law William Mintram signed on. Mintram would give his son-in-law his own life vest during the upcoming disaster. Hurst would survive; Mintram would not.

VICTUALLING AND VENDOR DEPARTMENTS

The Victualling Department contained 417 employees and was responsible for all customer-related issues. It was divided into the Purser's Staff (which also included the two Marconi operators), First Class, Second Class, and Third Class Stewards and Stewardesses, Kitchen Staff, and Galley Staff.

- Hugh W. McElroy signed on as the Purser. He was not supposed to be on this trip. However, the originally assigned Purser could not make the voyage, so McElroy took his place. His duty, among other things, was to safeguard the passenger's valuables and oversee the Enquiry Office, where First Class passengers paid for their telegrams and fees for the Turkish Bath. After the collision, McElroy remained in the Purser's

Office until he had handed out all of the passenger's valuables. He was last seen on the Boat Deck helping passengers board the lifeboats.

▪ John G. "Jack" Phillips and Harold S. Bride were the two Marconi operators. They boarded *Titanic* in Belfast. They were not employed by the White Star Line, but were employees of the Marconi Company and were contracted to White Star to operate the wireless equipment. They would remain at their stations until the very end. Bride would survive the sinking; Phillips would not.

▪ There were 224 men and women assigned to the First Class Stewards Department, or about one person for every 1.5 First Class passengers. These included saloon stewards and waiters, bedroom, pantry, plate, lift, deck and boots stewards, Turkish Bath, Swimming Bath, Reception Room and Smoke Room stewards, and a host of miscellaneous bellboys, printers, baggage masters, telephone operators, the bugler, gymnasium instructor, and the Squash Racquet Court attendant.

▪ Twenty-four year old First Class Stewardess Violet Jessop supported her mother and five younger siblings. The tips she could expect on each voyage offset the seventeen-hour days and meager salary paid by White Star.
  Jessop had a unique story to tell in later life. She had already survived one White Star Line disaster, having been on *Olympic* when it collided with the *Hawke*. She next survived the sinking of *Titanic*. Then, just a few years later during World War I, Jessop was a nurse on the last ship of the *Olympic* class, the hospital ship *Britannic*, (ex-*Gigantic*) when it was sunk after hitting a mine in the Aegean Sea. She would survive that sinking, too.

▪ P. W. Fletcher was the ship's bugler. Because there wasn't an intercom on the ship, his primary function was to call passengers to meals, which he would do by wandering around the ship in all class areas blowing his bugle. Both Fletcher and his bugle would ride *Titanic* to the bottom.

▪ Frederick Wright was a professional squash player whose job was to provide lessons to the First Class passengers in the Squash Racquet Court. After *Titanic* struck the iceberg, the Squash Racquet Court was one of the first compartments to flood. Wright later commented to a passenger that he guessed they would have to cancel their planned meet. Wright did not survive.

▪ Gym instructor T. W. McCawley was hired to help the First Class passengers make use of the gymnasium on the Boat Deck. One of the surviving photos shows McCawley working out on some of the gym equipment. He would go down with the ship.

STEWARDESS VIOLET JESSOP
AS A NURSE ON BRITANNIC.
(National Archives)

- There were 75 Second Class and 53 Third Class stewards, and 65 galley workers, cooks, and bakers for the two classes.

- Twenty-two people on the ship were not classified as part of the crew although they were gainfully employed. They included five postal employees, eight members of the orchestra, and nine members of the Harland and Wolff Guarantee Staff.

- There were three American postal clerks (William L. Gwinn, Oscar S. Woody and John S. March) and two British postal clerks (John R. J. Smith, and James B. Williamson) whose job was to sort the 3,500 bags of mail carried on the ship. Their respective postal departments employed them, and none would survive the sinking.

   Postal clerk Gwinn was supposed to make the trip on another ship, but he requested a transfer to *Titanic* when he received word that his wife in New York was seriously ill.

   A British postal inspector had recommended changes to the cabins occupied by the postal clerks because, as he noted,

> "the cabins are situated among a block of third class cabins, and it is stated that the occupants of these . . . are mostly low class continentals, keep up a noisy conversation . . . and music."

■ The eight orchestra members, who were employed by the Liverpool firm of C. W. and F. N. Black, were contracted out to the White Star Line. Most had been on voyages on other ships, and all of the musicians were carried as Second Class passengers.

Bandmaster Wallace H. Hartley was 33 years old and highly respected by the rest of the orchestra and those First Class passengers who had seen him on other voyages. Hartley was engaged to be married after the completion of *Titanic's* maiden voyage.

■ The Vendor Department consisted of the 68 employees of the à la carte Restaurant, which was a private concession managed by Mr. Luigi Gatti and staffed with employees from his two London restaurants. A number of his employees were family members. Gatti paid these individuals, although they had signed on as employees and received a token wage from White Star Line. Most of them were asleep down on E Deck when *Titanic* struck the iceberg. They were primarily from France and Italy and considered "low-life continentals" by the British crew. Because some of the crew were afraid they would try to storm the lifeboats, the employees were locked in their cabins. Gatti and all but one of his staff (who was out of his room at the time) went down with the ship. As far as can be determined, this was the only time people were prevented from leaving the ship by being locked into their cabins or behind closed gates.

THE MARCONI WIRELESS OPERATION

Most ships only had one operator and generally the wireless was shut down around midnight so the operator could get some sleep. There wasn't any requirement for the wireless to be manned continuously. Because of the size of *Titanic* and the number of First Class passengers on board, however, two operators were assigned to allow for round-the-clock service. Also, with her nominal range of 250 miles and a night range of up to 2,000 miles, *Titanic* had one of the strongest wireless sets of any ship at sea.

■ The wireless was provided mainly as a service for the passengers. Passengers paid to send or receive messages and tipped the operators for their services. Operators normally took care of passengers' needs before handling official business of the ship unless the ship or another nearby ship was in distress.

Another duty of the wireless operators was to relay messages from one ship to another or to shore because few other ships had a wireless set with enough power to transmit more than a few hundred miles. Thus, a ship with a weak wireless set or out of range would transmit to *Titanic*, which in turn would transmit to another ship or to shore.

▪ One problem with the wireless service was that ships carried service from competing companies. If an operator was asked to relay a message from a ship with a competing service, he might or might not do so, but it normally had low priority. Occasionally, operators from competing companies would turn up the power to drown out the weaker signal of a competitor or actually refuse to respond to signals from them.

Another problem was the informality the operators used to address one another. Operators addressed each other and started their messages with the salutation OM that stood for "Old Man." This was a friendly way to let the recipient know the following message was not "official." Official messages from the captain of one ship to the captain of another was supposed to be addressed, "From Captain (name) of the (ship) to Captain (name) of the (ship)." Messages received by the Marconi operators with this type of salutation were supposed to be delivered immediately to the recipient.

THE CREW

Most of the crew was hired only a few days prior to the April 10 departure date, and did not report for duty until 6:00 a.m. the morning of departure. They were amazed by the size of the ship and most never learned their way around it. In fact, once *Titanic* left Southampton, most of the engine and fire room crew spent the entire voyage in the mechanical spaces and seldom saw daylight again.

Not counting those few who transferred from the *Olympic*, most of the crew, officers included, were totally unfamiliar with the ship and her characteristics.

▪ In all, there were 871 male and 21 female crew members (including the two Marconi operators, but not counting the orchestra, postal workers, the à la carte restaurant staff, and the Harland and Wolff Guarantee Group) on *Titanic* at noon on April 10, 1912, when it steamed out of Southampton harbor. One crewman jumped ship in Queenstown, so there were officially 891 on board when *Titanic* sank.

Of this number, 699 members of the crew called Southampton their home.

"Get off this ship at Cherbourg, if we get that far."

CHAPTER 7

SOUTHAMPTON, ENGLAND

DEPARTURE, NOON, APRIL 10, 1912

Shortly after 5:00 a.m. on Wednesday, April 10, 1912, the sun rose over Southampton for what would be a cool, clear and windy morning. *Titanic* dwarfed the surrounding buildings and was visible for miles around the White Star Line dock on the River Test. Hundreds of the crew began to arrive to spend their first day aboard their new ship.

As the crew began to arrive and assemble on *Titanic's* decks, some of the major players in the events of the day also boarded and headed directly to the bridge. During the next few hours as the crew was making its preparations, the passengers also began to arrive. Berths 43 and 44 on the White Star Line dock would soon be a hive of activity as final preparations for departure were made and hundreds of passengers and visitors gathered on the dock and on board the ship.

■ At 7:30 a.m. Captain Edward J. Smith arrived and headed for his cabin to wait for Chief Officer Wilde to report on the status of preparations. Smith said good-bye to his wife and twelve-year-old daughter who had come with him to see him off.

■ Also at 7:30 a.m., Captain Maurice H. Clarke, the Board of Trade's emigration officer, arrived to oversee the crew muster with the aide of the ship's officers. By 8:00 a.m. the crew had reported aboard and had stowed their gear in time to report to their mustering stations on the various decks.

At 8:00 a.m. the Blue Ensign was raised at the stern. This was a flag the Royal Naval Reserve authorized Captain Smith and certain other RNR officers to fly on commercial ships.

■ As the crew assembled, the ship's articles (or rules and regulations) were read to them while roll was called and then they signed them. Each crewmember had to pass before both a medical officer and Clarke, who signed the crew list as each department was completed.

Additional headcounts were made against a master list as each of the ship's departments checked to make sure there were sufficient crewmembers available, and the master list was then given to Captain Clarke who signed it, indicating his approval. He then arranged to have the original list sent ashore.

- While the crew was being mustered and counted, Clarke ordered the manning and lowering of two of the lifeboats. Fifth Officer Lowe and Sixth Officer Moody supervised the lowering of lifeboats 11 and 15 on the starboard side. Each lifeboat with a crew of eight was lowered into the water, rowed around the ship to the dock, rowed back around the ship and hoisted back up into the davits on the Boat Deck.

- By 9:30 a.m. the crew muster and boat lowering was complete and the crew released for breakfast. Crewmembers on the 8-to-12 watch were sent to their work areas, the 12-to-4 watch was ordered on standby and the 4-to-8 watch was released to do as they wished. Many of these members of the crew went ashore, most of them to their favorite drinking establishment for a final ale before leaving port.

Several of the crewmembers who had signed on earlier in the week did not show up for the morning muster. This was a common occurrence. Consequently, it had been arranged in advance that several additional men for each department would appear at muster to fill in as a substitute for anyone who didn't show. Several substitutes were mustered in at this time while the rest of those who were potential substitutes were asked to remain on board until the ship actually departed in order to replace any other shortages that might occur from those who had gone ashore. This ensured that a full complement would be available for the voyage.

THOMAS ANDREWS, MANAG-
ING DIRECTOR OF HARLAND
AND WOLFF. ANDREWS DID
NOT SURVIVE THE SINKING.
(Author's Collection)

▪ It took a good portion of the morning for the paperwork to be completed by Captain Smith and Captain Clarke. In the end, Clarke signed off that he had observed a boat drill and that *Titanic* had enough coal, 5,892 tons of it, to allow it to steam to New York. This was less than half of what *Titanic* was designed to carry for a round trip, and barely enough for a one-way trip. If Captain Smith wasn't prudent, he could run out of coal before he arrived in New York. But this was all the coal available due to the coal strike, and Smith would have to make do.

▪ A "Report of Survey of an Immigrant Ship" was prepared as required by the Board of Trade and signed by Smith and Clarke. Finally, there was the "Master's Report to the Company":

> *"I herewith report this ship loaded and ready for sea. The engines and boilers are in good order for the voyage, and all charts and sailing directions up-to-date. – Your obedient servant, Edward J. Smith."*

▪ About the time the official paperwork was completed, J. Bruce Ismay and Thomas Andrews arrived on the bridge to greet Captain Smith and wish him a safe voyage. Originally, Lord Pirrie had planned to make the trip to New York but he became ill, so Andrews was sent in his place. Andrews had a First Class cabin on A Deck (A36). This cabin was one of the late additions after Ismay's decision to add more of them after the maiden voyage of *Olympic*.

Andrews' responsibility during the trip was to make sure everything that Harland and Wolff had done was completed satisfactorily and to see what design changes should be made to the third ship of the trio. Andrews was also responsible for the nine-man "Guarantee Group" of Harland and Wolff engineers who were going to make the voyage and whose job it was to assist the crew and correct any problems.

▪ Ismay came aboard about 9:30 a.m. with his wife and three children and took them on a tour of the ship. Ismay was making the trip, but his family was not. Once the tour was completed, his family departed and Ismay settled into his suite of rooms, B52, B54, and B56 with its private promenade, another of the late additions. His manservant John R. Fry had already unpacked Ismay's clothes and had prepared the suite for him.

Ismay was going to New York for the International Mercantile Marine Directors' meeting, and his private secretary, William H. Harrison, accompanied him. Although carried as First Class passengers, neither Fry nor Harrison would survive the voyage.

▪ One item not mentioned in any of the reports or to the Board of Trade representative was the fire that had been smoldering for almost a week in a coalbunker in Boiler Room Number 5 next to the watertight bulkhead adjoining Boiler Room Number 6. The fire had started during the coaling process in Belfast, and had been smoldering ever since.

Smith, Andrews, and the Guarantee Group were aware of the fire, but until it could be put out, little could be done to check for any potential damage to the Tank Top deck or the bulkhead.

Stokers in Boiler Room Number 5 had been working for a week trying to move enough coal to get to the bottom of the pile to put out the fire. However, it wasn't until a full complement of crew was on board that serious headway could be made to reach the bottom of a pile of almost a thousand tons of coal—one shovel full at a time.

Even though chief engineer Bell was not able to examine the bulkhead, he believed that there was little cause for worry that the fire had damaged either the Tank Top or the bulkhead. Also, *Titanic* did not have enough coal to dump any of it, so there might be less waste just to let it burn. With this assurance, Smith never said anything to the Board of Trade inspector. Although coal fires were fairly common, if the inspector had known about the fire he might have delayed the voyage. The fire was still smoldering at noon when *Titanic* left Southampton.

THIRD AND SECOND CLASS PASSENGERS

At 7:30 a.m. the boat train carrying the Second and Third Class passengers left London's Waterloo Station for the two-hour trip to Southampton. Upon arrival, Second Class passengers immediately began to board through the Second Class entrance, aft on C Deck, while Third Class passengers entered near the bow on the Well Deck or further aft on C Deck.

THIRD CLASS PASSENGERS

There were 497 Third Class passengers boarding in Southampton, many of them (124 adults and 16 children) were emigrants from various Scandinavian countries. Most of these emigrants had purchased passage on "the first available ship" and, for these seemingly lucky people, the first available ship was *Titanic*.

■ There were 134 Third Class passengers from Britain, including the Goodwin and the Sage families, with a total of 19 people between them; all 19 would be dead in four days.

Loading the Third Class passengers proved an extremely chaotic affair. In some respects it was a preview of things to come. Many did not speak English. In conjunction with a crew who had been on the ship only a few hours, it was difficult to get the foreign passengers sorted out and to their proper accommodations.

No one attempted to help Third Class passengers find the public rooms, show where the corridors and stairs led, or where the exits were located. They were allowed to wander aimlessly, up and down staircases, down blind corridors, careening off walls and each other, looking for lost children, lost luggage, and lost cabins, and often running into locked doors and gates with signs that read "First Class" or "Second Class passengers only."

Prior to boarding, Third Class passengers were checked by a health inspector who also reviewed their identification cards. For the most part, British or American subjects were quickly approved, but foreigners were closely checked. White Star Line did not want to carry anyone to New York only to have him or her denied entry into the United States. If this happened, White Star Line would then have to carry them back to Britain at their expense.

- Third Class passengers were often referred to as "steerage" because historically that is exactly where they were quartered: in the holds of the ship and most often at the stern where the steering mechanism was located. There was a time when human passengers traveled in one direction and livestock on the return trip, all occupying the same areas. Until the late 1800s there were often signs posted asking First and Second Class passengers not to throw food or money to steerage passengers because it could cause a disturbance.

Although there had been dramatic improvements in the quality of accommodations for Third Class passengers, American immigration laws required that gates be placed between Third Class and other passengers. The gates were to be locked at all times to keep the classes from mixing and to prevent the spread of infectious disease. American law also required that Third Class passengers be given 20% more space per passenger than what the British Board of Trade mandated. Although American law superseded Board of Trade requirements for passenger comfort, it did not require more lifeboats than what the Board of Trade set forth.

Third Class single men were sent to their accommodations on several decks in the bow of the ship while the single women and families were sent to their cabins on D, E, F and G decks closer to the stern. This helped prevent the mingling of the single male and female passengers. It also consigned the Third Class passengers to the bow and stern, the worst riding portions of the ship.

- Traveling from Sweden to Worcester, Massachusetts, was 40-year-old Carl and 38-year-old Selma Asplund and their five children, ages 13, 9, 5, 4 and 3. Mr. Asplund and three of the children would not survive this trip. The senior Asplund's body was recovered and he is buried in Worcester. As of the date of this revised edition, Lillian Asplund, who was five years old when the *Titanic* went down, was still alive.

■   Twenty-three year old Miss Wendla Heininen was traveling alone from Finland to New York. She would not survive either, but her body was recovered and she is buried in Halifax.

■   Mr. Karl Backstrom, 32, was returning to the United States from Finland with his wife Maria, 33, along with her two brothers, 37 year-old Anders and 28-year-old Johan Gustafsson. Of the four, only Maria would complete the trip. Anders' body was recovered and he was buried at sea.

■   Mrs. Belia Moor, 27, and her six-year-old son were from Russia and traveling to Canada. They had purchased passage on *Adriatic,* but because of the coal strike were transferred to *Titanic.* Both survived.

■   Mr. Ernst Danbom, 34, was born in the United States and worked as an emigrant recruiter in Iowa. He had traveled to Sweden with his bride and infant son for a vacation, and the family was now returning to the United States, along with family friends Alfrida and Anders Andersson, their five children, and 22-year-old Anna Nysten. Of these 11 people, only Anna Nysten would survive, and only Ernst Danbom's body was recovered. His final resting place is Stanton, Iowa.

■   Mrs. Stanton (Rosa) Abbott, 35, was from Rhode Island and was the wife of former middleweight champion Stanton Abbott. Rosa and her two sons Rossmore, 16, and Eugene, 13, traveled to England on *Olympic* in August, 1911, and were now heading back to Rhode Island. Rosa would survive the trip but her sons would not.

■   Eighteen-year-old Leah Rosen Acks was from Russia and was en route to Norfolk, Virginia, with her infant son to meet her husband Sam Acks. Leah and her son would survive the trip, but it would be a very trying experience.

■   Mrs. Maria Panula, 41, was married to John Panula and lived in Pennsylvania. She returned to Finland in 1910 to sell the family farm and convince the rest of their family to emigrate. John Panula was in the United States, but Maria and her five children and 23-year-old Sanni Riihivuori, the daughter of a neighbor, all boarded in Southampton. All seven would perish on the voyage, and only the body of two-year-old Urho (Eino) was recovered. He is buried in Halifax.

■   Jules Van Der Planke, 31, and his wife Emilie, 31, were newlyweds from Ohio who had traveled to Belgium before Christmas. Two other family members, Jules' sister Augusta, 18, and brother Leon Van Der Planke, 16, accompanied them back to the United States. All of them would die on the trip, and none of their bodies were recovered.

- Ernst Persson, 25, was emigrating to Indiana from Sweden along with his sister Elna Strom and two-year-old niece Selma Strom. Also traveling was friend Agnes Sandstrom and her two young daughters, who were returning home to San Francisco. Ernst, Agnes and her two children would survive, but Elna and Selma would not. Although he ended up in the freezing water, Ernst survived because he managed to get onto Collapsible Lifeboat B after the ship sank.

- Mr. Olaus Abelseth, 26, emigrated from Norway in 1902 and lived in South Dakota. He left New York in late 1911 to visit his family in Norway, and he was now returning home with five friends and family members: 19-year-old Peter Soholt, a cousin; 25-year-old Sigurd Moen, his brother-in-law; and friends 42-year-old Adolf Humblen, 21-year-old Anna Salkjelsvik and 16-year-old Karen Abelseth, not related but the daughter of a close friend. Peter, Sigurd and Adolf would perish, but the rest would make it to South Dakota. Sigurd's body was recovered and is buried in Norway.

- Twenty-two year-old Hilda Hellstrom was traveling to Evanston, Illinois, to help her widowed aunt. Hilda would survive the voyage.

- Miss Berta Nilsson, 18, was traveling from Sweden to Montana with her fiancé, 22-year-old Edvard Larsson-Ronsberg. Berta would survive; Edvard would not.

- Miss Carla Jensen, 19, was traveling to Portland, Oregon, with her uncle Niels Jensen, 48, her brother Svend Jensen, 17, and her fiancé Hans Jensen, 20. Carla alone survived.

- Brothers Alfred, 24, John, 21, and 17-year-old Joseph Davies and their uncle James Lester were traveling together to Pontiac, Michigan. None of them would survive.

- Miss Elizabeth Dowdell, 30, was traveling as a nurse, escorting five-year-old Virginia Emmanuel to her grandparents in New York City. They shared a cabin with 24-year-old Amy Stanley, who was traveling to New Haven, Connecticut, to become a children's maid. All three would survive.

- Another 24-year-old passenger was Mrs. Elisabeth Johnson, who was traveling back to St. Charles, Illinois, with her two children after a visit to Sweden. All of them would make it back to St. Charles.

- Nils Johansson, 29, traveled to Sweden after having spent eight years in Chicago. He was returning with his fiancé, 23-year-old Olga Lundin, and three friends, 20-year-old Paul Andreasson, 23-year-old Albert Augustsson, and 32-year-old Carl Jonsson. Olga and Carl would survive but the rest of the men would not; none of the bodies were recovered.

- Traveling to Los Angeles, California, was 32-year-old Thure Lundstrom and his fiancé, Elina Olsson, age 31. Lundstrom was the de-facto leader of a group of ten people traveling to California. Thure would tell many versions of how he survived, but witnesses would claim that he saved himself and left Elina behind to die. Thure was the only survivor of the entire group.

- Helga Hirvonen, age 22, and her infant daughter were traveling to Monessen, Pennsylvania, to meet her husband. Traveling with them were her 20-year-old brother Eino Lindqvist and friend August Abrahamsson. All but Eino would survive.

- Frederick Goodwin and his wife and six children from Wiltshire, England, were traveling to Niagara Falls, New York. Frederick was set to begin a new job at a power station there. All eight members of the family perished, and none of their bodies were ever recovered.

- Oscar Hedman, 27, was leading a group of 17 Swedish emigrants to Sioux Falls, South Dakota. Most of them could not speak English. Oscar would live to see the United States, but most of the rest would not.

- Thirty-two year-old Oscar Olsson was a sailor on a Swedish ship. He was returning to New York with friends, 32-year-old Karl Johansson and 28-year-old Samuel Niklasson, to sign on with another ship. Oscar would live to do so; the other two would not.

- Twenty-seven year old August Andersson, a radical socialist and journalist from Sweden, was under threat of arrest if he left his home country. As a result, he traveled to New York under the name "Wennerstrom" with two friends, 21-year-old Carl Jansson and 25-year-old Gunnar Tenglin. All would survive the sinking.

- Adolf Dyker, 23, and his wife Elisabeth, 22, were returning home to New Haven, Connecticut, after having traveled to Sweden to arrange the final effects of his recently-deceased father. Elisabeth would soon be attending another funeral, only this one would be for her husband.

- Miss Aina Jussila, 21, and her sister Katriina, 20, were en route to New York to obtain work with their uncle who owned an employment agency. Both sisters would perish.

- Anton Kink, 29, his wife and four year-old daughter, his sister Maria, 22, and brother Vincenz, 26, were traveling from Zurich, Switzerland, to Milwaukee, Wisconsin. Neither Maria nor Vincenz would survive.

- John Sage, 44, his wife Annie and their nine children from Peterborough, England, were emigrating to Jacksonville, Florida. None survived, and only the body of 11-year-old William Sage was recovered. He was buried at sea.

- These and hundreds of other Third Class passengers continued to board: August Abrahamson from Finland traveling to Hoboken, New Jersey; Mrs. Johanna Ahlin and her brother, 25-year-old Johan Petterson from Sweden, traveling to Minnesota; 25-year-old Josef Arnold, his wife Josephine, 18, and friend 24-year-old Aloisia Haas traveling from Switzerland; Mrs. William Coutts and her two children traveling to Brooklyn, New York. Of all of these souls, only August Abrahamson, Mrs. Coutts, and her children would complete the voyage.

SECOND CLASS PASSENGERS

As the Third Class passengers were boarding *Titanic* and sorting themselves out, 234 Second Class passengers also began to board. There was somewhat less chaos and better organization for these passengers, befitting their more expensive accommodations and fewer numbers.

- Percy A. Bailey was 18-years old, traveling to Akron, Ohio, to visit his uncle. Bailey was accompanied by two friends, Harry Cotterill, 21, and R. George Hocking, 23. None of them would ever see Ohio.

- Reverend Ernest C. Carter, 54, and his wife Lilian, 44, were en route to New York City. Mrs. Carter befriended 26-year-old Marion Wright and 36-year-old Kate Buss during the trip. On the last night aboard, Carter led the hymn service in the Second Class dining saloon. Marion sang a solo. Neither of the Carters would set foot in New York.

- Marion Wright was traveling to Cottage Grove, Oregon, to join her fiancé. She reported the collision with the iceberg as a *"huge crash of glass."* She is also one of the survivors who reported that the last song the orchestra played was *"Nearer, My God, To Thee."*

- Kate Buss was traveling to San Diego to meet her fiancé. Kate didn't want to watch as the lifeboats were being loaded, and she decided she didn't have a chance to get into one. At some point, though, she managed to climb in one. She lived to be 96, but she was never able to discuss the sinking without becoming very emotional about it.

■ The only Japanese passenger on the voyage was 42-year-old Masabumi Hosono, a civil servant from Tokyo. He was found almost frozen to death lying on top of a piece of wreckage, and was picked up by a passing lifeboat. Despite being almost frozen, he survived and helped row. However, he was ostracized in his own country for surviving when so many others had died. He lost his job, Japanese newspapers called him a coward, schoolbooks cited his shameful behavior, and he was labeled immoral. Although he died in 1939, he was still being cited as a coward even in 1956, when Japanese newspaper articles referred to him after the sinking of the *Andria Doria*.

■ Mrs. Arthur H. Wells, 29, was en route to Akron, Ohio, with her two children to meet her husband, whom they had not seen for two years. All would survive, but the lifeboat they were on was so overcrowded they had to stand up until they were rescued.

■ Thirty-four year-old Lawrence Beesley was a science teacher in London and was planning on making a lengthy tour around the United States. He had specifically chosen *Titanic* because it was the maiden voyage. Beesley wanted to *"stand some distance away to take in a full view of her beautiful proportions, which the narrow approach to the dock made impossible."* He decided that he would have to wait until *Titanic* arrived in New York to get his view of the ship.

■ Mrs. Allen (Nellie) Becker, 36, was traveling from India to Benton Harbor, Michigan, with her three children Ruth, 12, Marion, 4, and Richard, 1. Mr. Becker was a missionary and was still in India, but Mrs. Becker and the children were traveling to the United States for treatment of a disease Richard had contracted. All would survive. Ruth would live to be 90 years old, and was often interviewed about her experiences.

■ Father Thomas R. D. Byles was a highly respected member of the clergy who was traveling to New York to officiate at the wedding ceremony of his brother.
By many accounts, Father Byles was a hero to the very end, hearing confessions and praying with those who could not escape. His body was not recovered. His brother in New York had his wedding as planned, and then the couple went home, changed into their mourning clothes, and returned to the church for a memorial mass.

■ Mrs. Elizabeth Nye, 29, had already suffered through appendicitis, the loss of her first fiancé, the loss of two children, and the death of a husband. She was returning to New York after a visit to Britain, and was supposed to travel home on *Philadelphia*. Because of the coal strike, however, she was transferred to *Titanic*. She was loaded into a lifeboat and while waiting for the boat to be lowered, caught an object flying through the air she thought was some luggage. It turned out to be baby Frank Acks, who was tossed down by a crewmember. She wrapped him in a steamer blanket to keep him warm and did not know who his mother was until Leah Acks was found aboard the rescue ship *Carpathia*.

- William H. Harbeck, 44, was a successful cinematographer who had taken the earliest movies of the San Francisco earthquake in 1906. He had been in Europe making films to show American audiences and was hired by the White Star Line to film the maiden voyage. Traveling with Harbeck was his mistress, Henrietta Yrios. Harbeck was carrying over 100,000 feet of exposed motion picture film with him on *Titanic*. Both Harbeck and Yrios died, and his film went down with them.

- John and Elizabeth Chapman, both 28, were recently married and traveling to Spokane, Washington, to celebrate a belated honeymoon. Both died on the trip. John's body was recovered and buried in Halifax. They would be but one of the four newlywed couples lost that night.

- Benjamin and Esther Hart, 43 and 45, respectively, were traveling with their daughter Eva, 7, to Winnipeg, Canada. Esther was so afraid the ship would sink that she slept during the day so she would be awake at night while her husband and daughter slept. Benjamin would not survive.

- Louis Hoffman of Nice, France, boarded in Southampton with his two children, two-year-old Edmond and three-year-old Michel. The Hoffman's were en route to an unknown destination in the United States and were traveling under fictitious names. Hoffman was really Michel Navratil, and he was kidnapping his two children from his estranged wife in France, who had no idea where he or the children were.

- Thirty-one year old Harvey Collyer, his wife Charlotte, 31, and their daughter Marjorie had sold their home in Britain and were traveling to Payette, Idaho, with everything they owned. Harvey would never see his new home.

- Six-year-old Annie (Nina) Harper was traveling to Chicago with her widowed father, Reverend John Harper and his adult niece, Miss Jessie Leitch, age 32. One of the more memorable photographs that survive of the voyage show Reverend Harper and his daughter taking a stroll on the Boat Deck. Jessie and Nina would survive, but John would not.

- Mrs. Elizabeth Hocking was moving to Akron, Ohio, with her son Richard, 23, daughters Nellie and Emily, sister Ellen Wilkes and her

(Left) Michel (3) and Edmond (2) Navratil. They were kidnapped by their father and traveling under the name Hoffman. Michel died in 2001, the last of Titanic's male survivors. *(Harper's)*

(Below) Father Thomas Byles heard confessions and gave absolution to the doomed as the ship sank. *(National Archives)*

grandsons George and William Richards, plus two of her son George's good friends, Percy Bailey and Harry Cotterill. Richard, Percy and Harry would perish.

■   Henry Morley, 39, told his friends he was traveling to Los Angeles when, in fact, he was eloping with 19-year-old Kate Phillips. They were traveling under the names of Mr. and Mrs. Henry Marshall. Henry would perish; Kate would not. It would take a long time for family and friends to sort out what happened because the couple traveled under assumed names.

■   Three single women ended up sharing the same cabin: 27-year-old Edwina "Winnie" Troutt, 36-year-old Susan Webber, and Nora Kean. Their cabin adjoined that of the orchestra. The musicians were willing to perform special musical requests for the ladies and the other nearby passengers during their off-duty hours. All three women survived. Winnie lived to be 100.

■   Father Francis M. Browne was making a short trip, traveling only to Queenstown, *Titanic's* last stop before crossing the Atlantic for New York. During the short overnight voyage, Browne took dozens of photographs of the ship, passengers and crew, including the image of John and Nina Harper strolling on the Boat Deck. The famous photos that appear in many books are the only photos taken during the voyage that survived.

FIRST CLASS PASSENGERS

The train carrying most of the 193 First Class passengers left Waterloo Station in London at 9:45 a.m. and arrived at the White Star Line dock in Southampton at 11:30 a.m., thirty minutes before *Titanic's* scheduled departure. They boarded the ship via the First Class main entrance on B Deck, where they were met by Chief Steward Andrew Latimer and his staff, and escorted immediately to their cabins. This was First Class—these passengers wouldn't be aimlessly wandering the corridors looking for their cabins.

■   Confronting the First Class passengers as they entered the B Deck entrance was the huge 16-foot wide, 60-foot (six deck) tall Grand Staircase, complete with a massive glass and iron dome overhead and a huge 32-light chandelier.

■   Because of her size, luxury, and the tremendous amount of publicity concerning *Titanic*, sailing on the maiden voyage was, to the rich and famous of 1912, what some of the significant media events would be to

FATHER JOHN HARPER AND DAUGHTER NINA ON THE SECOND CLASS PROMENADE,
BOAT DECK, IN QUEENSTOWN. NINA SURVIVED, HER FATHER DID NOT. LIFEBOAT 13
CAN BE SEEN TO THE RIGHT, AND TIP OF LIFEBOAT 15 AT FAR RIGHT. NOTE WELIN
DAVITS DESIGNED TO HOLD TWO LIFEBOATS EACH. AT FAR LEFT IS NUMBER 4 (DUMMY)
FUNNEL AND THE RAISED ROOF OVER THE FIRST CLASS SMOKING ROOM. (*Cork Examiner*)

their counterparts in the latter part of the century. Many of the biggest
names in politics, business or entertainment had booked passage in
order to be seen, some even adjusting the length of their stay in Europe
in order to secure passage on *Titanic*. In 2003 dollars, a "cheap" First
Class cabin cost about $2,700 and the two First Class parlor suites with
the private promenade cost $74,000 each—one way.

After the final port call in Queenstown, there would be 324 First
Class passengers on board. Most of the First Class male passengers were
captains of industry or politics, and just 12 of them alone were worth
$3.4 *billion* 2003 dollars. Taken together, they were worth an estimated
$8.8 *billion!*

- Major Archibald W. Butt, 45, was a close personal friend of
President William H. Taft. He was a journalist in the Army during the
Spanish-American War in Cuba and the Philippines. Later he became
military aide to Presidents Theodore Roosevelt and Taft. He tried,
unsuccessfully, to remain neutral during the personal quarrels between
the two men. In need of a rest, Butt took leave and traveled to Europe
with close friend Francis D. Millet. They were returning to Washington
D.C. Neither would complete the voyage.

■ Twenty-nine year old Thomas Pears was a very successful businessman who owned manufacturing sites all across Europe. He was an avid sportsman and had participated in automobile and motorcycle races. Pears was traveling to the United States to scout new business locations with his wife of two years, Edith. Pears would not survive, but his wife would finish the trip. Within five years, three of Edith's four brothers would die in combat during the First World War.

■ Sixty year-old Colonel John Weir was president and owner of several silver mines in the western United States and had also served during the Spanish-American War. He was well respected and gave generously to various charities. Weir had sent a letter to friends on April 6 stating he was going to be coming home on *Philadelphia*. Because of the coal strike, he was transferred to *Titanic*, but his friends didn't know this until he was listed as lost in local newspapers.

■ Mr. Charles M. Hays, 55, was the former president of the Southern Pacific Railway and the president of the Grand Trunk Railway. The Hays party included Hays' wife Clara, 52, his assistant Vivian Payne, Clara's maid Mary Anne Perreault, their daughter Orian, and her husband Thornton Davidson. Hays was returning to the United States after having wrapped up a business deal with the White Star Line to transport, via rail, European emigrants from White Star Line ships to their final destination in America and Canada. The Hays group members were traveling as the guests of J. Bruce Ismay. Charles Hays, Vivian Payne and Thornton Davidson would all die when the ship sank. Hays' body was recovered and he is buried in Montreal, Canada.

■ Mr. Hudson J.C. Allison, 30, was a successful Canadian businessman and breeder of horses. Allison's wife, 27-year-old Bess, their two children Helen, 3, and Hudson Trevor, 1, were traveling back to Canada with Mrs. Allison's maid Sara Daniels, young Hudson's nurse Alice Cleaver, and two servants, Mildred Brown and George Swane. Young Trevor, Alice, and Mildred would survive. Mr. Allison's body was recovered and is buried in Ontario, Canada. The Allison family saga would be one of the most tragic stories to come out of a long night full of tragedy.

■ George Bradley was traveling under the alias George A. Brayton. He was a professional gambler who made a livelihood traveling the circuit of First Class passengers on various steamships. His luck would hold out.

■ Miss Elisabeth Allen, 29, was returning to her home in St. Louis with her aunt, Mrs. Edward Robert, her 15-year old cousin Georgette Madill, and Mrs. Robert's maid Emilie Kreuchen. Miss Allen was engaged to a

Isador and Ida Straus. They decided to remain together and went down with the ship. *(National Archives)*

British physician and was returning home to gather her belongings. All four would survive the loss of the great liner.

■   Isador and Ida Straus usually traveled on German liners whenever possible. For their return to New York City, however, they decided to travel on *Titanic* and occupied parlor suite C55. Isidor, 67, was involved in blockade running for the Confederate States during the Civil War, had been a Congressman from New York, and was the owner of Macy's Department Store. Traveling with the Straus's were Mr. Straus' manservant John Farthing, and Ms. Ellen Bird, Mrs. Straus' maid. After having spent a lifetime together, the Straus's preferred to go down with the ship rather than be separated. Among them, only Ellen Bird would survive.

■   Canadian Army Major Arthur Peuchen, age 52, was president of Standard Chemical Company, had a military career in the Queen's Own Rifles and was Vice-Commodore of the Royal Canadian Yacht Club in Toronto. Major Peuchen would survive, but $300,000 in securities he was carrying with him went down with the ship. Because he survived, he was called a coward in the Canadian newspapers and eventually lost his business because of it. Later, after fighting and surviving the trenches in World War I, he was again ostracized and called a coward. Why? Because he survived the war when so many others did not.

■   Another of the several professional gamblers on this trip was Charles H. Romaine, traveling as Harry Romain. He was planning to make some money off the affluent First Class passengers. His luck would hold out—he would survive this voyage, but he would meet his end in 1922, when he was run over by a New York City taxi.

- Miss Kornelia Andrews, 63, was vice-president of the Hudson City Hospital in Hudson, New York, and was returning to New York with her sister Anna Hogeboom and niece, Gretchen Longley. All three of them would survive the terrifying ordeal.

- Mrs. Edward Appleton and her sisters, Mrs. John M. Brown and Mrs. Robert C. Cornell, had gone to England to attend the funeral of another sister, and they were returning home to New York. During the voyage they met up with old friends Archibald Gracie and Miss Edith Evans. All but Miss Evans would survive. Gracie escorted Mrs. Brown and Miss Evans to one of the last lifeboats. There was only room for one of them to get in, so Edith Evans stepped back and told her friend, "*You go first, you have children waiting at home.*"

- Mr. Mauritz Bjornstrom–Steffansson, 28, was the son of the owner of a major Swedish paper company and was living in Washington D.C. while completing his law studies. During the voyage back to the United States, he befriended passenger Hugh Woolner and the two of them took it upon themselves to be the personal escort of Mrs. Edward Candee, a young and beautiful widow. All of them survived.

- Mrs. Lucien P. Smith was only eighteen, but she was traveling to Huntington, West Virginia, with her 24-year-old husband. They were on their honeymoon. Although Mrs. Smith would survive, her husband went down with the ship. Mrs. Smith would eventually marry fellow survivor Robert Daniel.

- Traveling home to Scituate, Massachusetts, was famous 37-year-old fiction writer Jacques Futrelle and his wife Lily May, 35. His books may have been an inspiration for the Agatha Christie novels. Mrs. Futrelle would make it home, but her writer-husband would not.

- Lucy Noel Martha Dyer-Edwards, the Countess of Rothes, 33, whose home was at Kensington Palace in England, was traveling to Vancouver, British Columbia, with her cousin Gladys Cherry and her maid, Roberta Maioni. All would survive, the Countess spending her night on the lifeboat manning the tiller while Gladys and Roberta helped with the rowing.

- Forty-six year old Herbert Chaffee was a multi-millionaire businessman from North Dakota. The Chaffee holdings included 42,000 acres of farmland, dozens of grain elevators, and several company towns. Chaffee and his wife Carrie were returning home from a

LUCY NOEL MARTHA DYER-EDWARDS, THE COUNTESS OF ROTHES AND RESIDENT OF KENSINGTON PALACE. *(New York Times)*

FAMOUS FICTION WRITER JACQUES FUTRELLE ON TITANIC'S BOAT DECK. LIFEBOAT 7 IS IN THE BACKGROUND, FIRST CLASS ENTRANCE TO THE LEFT. *(National Archives)*

European vacation. Mrs. Chaffee would complete the trip home but Mr. Chaffee would not.

■   William Thomas Stead, 62, was a world famous and controversial journalist and author. He was en route to New York City to speak at a peace congress at the request of President Taft.

In the 1880s he was editor of a liberal publication, the "Pall Mall Gazette," and in 1883 was elected to parliament. In 1885, Stead published a controversial book exposing child prostitution.

Starting in the 1890s Stead devoted himself to pacifism and became interested in spiritualism. Ironically, in 1886 Stead wrote a fictional article titled *"How the Mail Steamer Went Down in Mid-Atlantic, by a Survivor,"* in which a steamer collides with another ship and there is large loss of life because of a shortage of lifeboats.

In 1892, he wrote a fictional story titled *"From the Old World to the New,"* about an accident involving a ship that collided with an iceberg. The White Star Line ship, *Majestic,* arrived to rescue the survivors.

On this trip, Stead would have the opportunity to witness first hand what he had written about. However, he did not survive to write about it.

- Henry B. Harris and his wife Rene were world famous Broadway theater owners and producers. Mrs. Harris would survive the trip, and in later years help young actresses get a start on Broadway, including Judith Anderson and Barbara Stanwyck.

- Dr. and Mrs. Washington Dodge were traveling to San Francisco with their four-year-old son; all three would make it.

- Mr. Washington A. Roebling, II, age 31, was the president of the Roebling Steel Company, grandson of John A. Roebling, the designer of the Brooklyn Bridge and nephew of Washington A. Roebling who actually built the bridge. He was returning to New York after a business trip to Britain. Roebling would perish.

- Mr. Alfred G. Rowe and his brothers owned 100 sections (100 square miles) of land in Texas, and Rowe was making his annual trip to check on his holdings. He would not survive.

- Counted among First Class passengers was J. Bruce Ismay. Ismay occupied Promenade Suite B52, which was one of two such suites and the one designed especially for J.P. Morgan. Pittsburgh steel magnate Henry C. Frick had reserved the suite, but had to cancel his trip when his wife sprained her ankle. Morgan planned to use the suite, but had to cancel because of business. Mr. and Mrs. J. Horace Harding reserved the suite, but they too canceled and transferred to *Mauretania*. And so Ismay occupied the lavish quarters.

DEPARTURE

At 11:15 a.m., harbor pilot George Bowyer boarded *Titanic*. Within a few minutes his red-and-white striped pilot flag was raised while Bowyer made his way to the bridge. By noon, just about everyone who was going to depart Southampton on *Titanic* was aboard.

Bowyer had been a harbor pilot for over 30 years and was the White Star Line pilot of choice for ship movements in Southampton. Bowyer had been the pilot commanding *Olympic* the day it collided with *Hawke*, but he wasn't held responsible for that collision.

After reaching the bridge, Bowyer conferred with Captain Smith and the ship's officers prior to their returning to their various stations and duties associated with the departure.

- Chief Officer Wilde was assigned to the forecastle, far forward, to oversee the mooring lines and tugboat hawsers.

First Officer Murdoch was on the Poop Deck at the stern, in charge of the mooring lines and tugboat hawsers there.

JAMES BRUCE ISMAY, CHAIRMAN OF THE WHITE STAR LINE AND SON OF ITS FOUNDER. ISMAY TRAVELED AS A FIRST CLASS PASSEN-GER. HE WAS RESPONSIBLE FOR THE DECISION NOT TO INSTALL MORE LIFEBOATS. *(National Archives)*

Second Officer Lightoller was at the aft end of the forecastle to assist Wilde, as needed.

Third Officer Pitman was on the Docking Bridge above the Poop Deck, assisting Murdoch and passing orders along to him that were telegraphed from the bridge.

Fourth Officer Boxhall was on the navigating bridge, passing orders via the Engine Room and Docking Bridge telegraphs, logging every order, command, or maneuver into the scrap log (a temporary place to write orders before they are written into the official log), and taking his orders directly from Smith and Bowyer.

Also on the bridge with Boxhall was Fifth Officer Lowe, who worked the ship's telephones and communicated directly with all departments.

Overseeing late arrivals at the gangway was Sixth Officer Moody. The gangway remained open until the last minute in order to allow back on board anyone who might have gone ashore.

■   Less then one minute before noon, Smith gave the order and the two huge whistles blasted the surrounding waters, thrilling the estimated

50,000 people who were perched on every piece of available space to watch the departure of the world's largest ship from their port.

- Two more times the whistle blew and Sixth Officer Moody began to lower the gangway. As he did so, two stokers, John Podesta and William Nutbean, came running up and jumped the few inches between the end of the gangway and the open hatch.

Podesta, Nutbean, the three Bertram brothers, Tom and Alfred Slade, and three other crewmen had been at one of the local pubs and were returning to the ship when they were held up on the dock by a passing train. Podesta and Nutbean managed to cross the tracks but everyone else waited.

Podesta and Nutbean jumped aboard *Titanic*. Their eight drinking buddies came running up behind them, but Moody made the decision to continue retracting the gangway, thus preventing them from boarding. Moody immediately passed the word and eight substitutes waiting at the aft entrance, which was still open, were signed onto the ship. The remaining substitutes were allowed to go ashore.

The three Slade brothers and their friends were obviously upset over this action, but within a few days their disappointment would change to relief. Somehow Podesta and Nutbean would survive the voyage (few stokers did so), but none of the eight substitutes would be so fortunate.

- Three other brothers scrambled to get on the ship at the very last minute. Alfred and Percy Pugh actually made it, but a third brother literally missed the boat. Alfred would be saved; Percy would not.

- As Sixth Officer Moody was lowering the gangway, the five tugs (*Ajax, Hector, Hercules, Neptune* and *Vulcan*) began to pull the ship sideways away from the dock. All of the mooring lines were dropped into the water and then hauled onto the dock by the dock hands.

The tugs pulled the ship away from the dock and then out into the newly-dredged turning circle in the middle of the River Test. After *Titanic* was towed into the turning circle, the tugs pushed and pulled it 90 degrees to port so it was facing down the channel.

It was just a few minutes after low tide and *Titanic* drew 35 feet of water, so extreme caution had to be used to prevent damaging the hull. It was for this reason that *Titanic* had been backed into the berth at Southampton. Once the turn was completed, orders were telegraphed to the engine room to move "Ahead Slow" and the two huge wing propellers began to turn.

The lines to the tugs were dropped and they pulled away, the *Vulcan* moving around the stern to the open door on E Deck to pick up the last of the standby crew who were not needed, but were waiting to be taken to shore.

A CLOSE ENCOUNTER

As *Titanic* picked up speed and the tugboats began to drop behind, the forward motion of the ship combined with the low tide caused a surge of water in the channel.

On the starboard side, this surge flowed into the River Test and the low ground beyond, but on the port side the wave rolled toward the docks and had nowhere to go. Because of the coal strike, two idle passenger ships, *Oceanic* and *New York*, were tied up in tandem at Berth 38, facing downstream with *New York* on the outside.

The surge of water lifted *New York* up and her mooring ropes slackened. Then, as *Titanic* passed by, the volume of water decreased and *New York* dropped back to her old level, bobbing up and down like a cork. These movements caused too much of a strain on the mooring ropes, and each one snapped. The stern ropes broke first with a loud bang, and the ropes flailed across the decks of the two ships and the bystanders on the dock. Fortunately, no one was hit.

The stern of *New York* was now loose, and *Titanic's* increasing speed was drawing both water and the *New York* toward her. *New York* was sucked within four feet of colliding with the *Titanic's* stern. All of this happened within a very few moments.

■ Quick action by the captain of the tug *Vulcan* prevented a collision. *Vulcan* was able to get ropes on the stern of *New York* to try to hold it in check. At about the same time, a quick-thinking Captain Smith ordered *"Full Astern!"* which stopped the forward motion of *Titanic*. The back wash of water now forced *New York* away from *Titanic's* stern.

Titanic backed past Berth 38 and the stern of *New York*. As a precaution, Smith had the starboard anchor lowered part way so it could be dropped immediately if required. At that point, Captain Smith and *Titanic* waited on other developments.

■ Meanwhile, with all of her mooring lines broken, *New York* started to drift downriver, controlled by the tugs that had managed to get more ropes on it. Her forward progress was finally halted after *New York* had drifted past the end of the docks. The ship was moored to an open dock while additional ropes were attached to *Oceanic* to prevent the same thing from happening to her. It was later discovered that a large sunken barge in the river had been dragged nearly half a mile by the suction created by *Titanic*.

■ Finally, now over an hour late, Captain Smith was given permission to continue *Titanic's* twenty-four mile journey down the River Test to the English Channel, this time a little slower and with more caution. Halfway down the river, *Titanic* passed the spot where *Olympic* and *Hawke* had collided in a situation very similar to what *Titanic* had just encountered.

Captain Smith gave four blasts on the whistle as *Titanic* passed the Royal Yacht Squadron to acknowledge all of the people lined up to see the ship, in particular one photographer named Frank Beken who was watching in a boat with his camera. As *Titanic* passed, Beken took some of the most remarkable photographs of the ship ever captured.

■ While Beken was taking his photographs, another amateur photographer, Father Francis M. Browne, was taking pictures on the ship. Father Browne spent most of the daylight hours searching for good camera angles, and he took several pictures of the near collision with *New York* and later of life aboard the ship. Browne was a transit passenger. He was only going as far as Queenstown, Ireland, *Titanic's* last port call before heading out into the Atlantic for New York. Browne's photographs are some of the most famous ones that exist of the ship and her passengers.

■ As *Titanic* approached the English Channel, it slowed long enough to drop pilot Bowyer off onto a waiting pilot boat, then picked up speed for a routine crossing of the Channel to Cherbourg, France, 67 miles away and her next port of call.

■ The April sun was dropping lower in the sky at 3:00 p.m. when the passengers were called for dinner (or, more correctly, the ships bugler P. W. Fletcher went from deck to deck announcing meal call with his bugle), and they began to settle in for their first meal on the great ship *Titanic*.

Probably much of the dinner conversation centered around the near collision that most of the passengers had witnessed. Mrs. Henry Harris remembered speaking to a stranger who asked her, *"Do you love life?"* *"Yes, I love it."* she replied. *"That was a bad omen,"* said the stranger. *"Get off this ship at Cherbourg, if we get that far. That's what I'm going to do."*

Mrs. Harris laughed about the episode, probably thinking, as many others did, that the ship was unsinkable. However, she never saw the stranger again after Cherbourg.

■ The American flag fluttered from the mast of the ship, announcing her final destination of New York. Cherbourg was just a few hours away.

TITANIC DEPARTING SOUTHAMPTON, APRIL 10, 1912. NOTE MASS OF THIRD CLASS PASSENGERS ON THE FORWARD WELL DECK AND FIRST CLASS PASSENGERS ON A DECK. HALF OF THE A DECK PROMENADE IS NOW ENCLOSED, THE ONLY VISIBLE DIFFERENCE BETWEEN TITANIC AND OLYMPIC. (Author's Collection)

CHAPTER 8

CHERBOURG, FRANCE

WEDNESDAY AFTERNOON, APRIL 10, 1912

White Star Line had been using Cherbourg as a port of ready access to the continent since it began using Southampton as a port in 1907. Cherbourg has an outstanding deep water harbor and a prime location only 75 miles from Southampton. What Cherbourg did not have was docking facilities for large passenger ships. Consequently, *Titanic* had to anchor about a mile offshore. To overcome this problem, White Star used tenders to ferry passengers out to the ship from the passenger terminal on shore.

- Built at the same time as *Olympic* in Harland and Wolff's Belfast shipyard, and actually steaming along with *Olympic* on her sea trials, were *Nomadic* and *Traffic*, White Star Line's two newest passenger tenders. They had been built specifically for use in Cherbourg.

    Nomadic was designed to carry 1,000 First and Second Class passengers and their luggage, while *Traffic* was built to carry 500 Third Class passengers, freight, and luggage. It was also equipped with conveyers to load mail onto the liners.

- About the same time that the First Class train was leaving Waterloo Station in London for Southampton, another train was leaving Paris bound for Cherbourg carrying 274 First, Second, and Third class passengers, destined for an afternoon rendezvous with *Titanic*.

    At 3:30 p.m., about six hours after leaving Paris, the train pulled into the Gare Maritime station in Cherbourg. The passengers were notified that because of the near collision with *New York* in Southampton, *Titanic* would not depart at 4:30 p.m., but would leave at least an hour later.

    Most of the 102 Third Class passengers were emigrants from eastern European countries like Syria and Croatia, and few could read or understand English or French. Normally they would have been routed through a Mediterranean port, but for some unknown reason they had instead been routed through Cherbourg onto the first available ship: *Titanic*.

- At 5:30 p.m., the passengers were gathered up from around the station and escorted onto the two tenders where they could await the arrival of *Titanic* under cover and out of the cold air.

- Now two hours behind schedule, at 6:30 p.m. the passengers watched *Titanic* slowly enter the harbor. Everyone commented on what a beautiful sight she made with her lights on as the last glow of sunset appeared behind her. One observer wrote the following:

> *"Perhaps then, more than at any other time, she was the lovely ship that people thought her to be. Her outline was etched clearly in light, with each porthole gleaming like a star."*

The trip across the English Channel had taken more than four hours steaming at 15 knots. There had not been any attempt to make up time, and in fact *Titanic* lost another hour.

- At 6:35 p.m. *Titanic* came to a stop about one mile from the dock and dropped anchor with her starboard side facing it. The passenger shuffle at Cherbourg was about to begin. Before passengers were allowed to board, 15 First and nine Second Class passengers traveling only to Cherbourg were allowed to board *Nomadic* with their baggage.

THIRD AND SECOND CLASS PASSENGERS

Among the 102 third class passengers boarding in Cherbourg was 14 year-old Miss Banoura Ayoub, who was traveling from Syria to Ontario, Canada. Her cousin, Mrs. Shawneene George, age 38, and three other male cousins were traveling to Youngstown, Ohio. Banoura and Shawneene would survive the trip, but the three men would not.

- Mr. Said Nackid, 20, was en route to Waterbury, Connecticut, with his 19-year-old wife Mary and their 18-month-old daughter Maria. All three would be rescued, but young Maria would die of meningitis three months later. She will carry into history the unfortunate distinction of being the first *Titanic* survivor to die.

- Mrs. Solomon Baclini, age 24, together with her three daughters aged five, three, and nine months, and Adele Najib, the 15-year-old daughter of a friend, were en route from Syria to Brooklyn. They had already missed another ship because of illness, so they decided to take the next available—*Titanic*. All five would survive the sinking. Mrs. Baclini's husband did not even know they had been on *Titanic* until they arrived in New York. Tragedy struck, however, when the three-year-old daughter died four months later . . . the second *Titanic* survivor to die.

- Another Syrian traveling to Ottawa, Canada, to meet up with his wife was Joseph Elias and his two 17-year-old sons Tannous and Joseph Jr. Three other children remained in Syria. Joseph would perish with his sons, and their bodies would not be recovered. It would take months before the three remaining children would be reunited with their mother, who traveled from Canada back to Syria, and then only with the assistance of the American Red Cross.

- There were 30 Second Class passengers boarding in Cherbourg, including 28-year-old engineer Joseph LaRoche from Haiti, his French born wife, and their two daughters, aged one and three. Mrs. LaRoche was pregnant. Since Joseph was black, he had sustained racial discrimination in France, and the family was moving back to Haiti so he could find a high paying engineering job. They had planned to take a French liner to New York, but French liners would not allow the children to eat their meals in the dining room with their parents. The decision to take *Titanic* would cost Joseph his life, but the rest of his family would survive. Joseph was the only black person on the ship. His body was not recovered.

- An interesting individual boarding in Cherbourg was a German named Alfred Nourney, age 20. Nourney traveled under the name "Baron von Drachstedt," a name he picked up from a local newspaper. Upon boarding he decided he didn't like his accommodations, so he demanded First Class accommodations and was upgraded to First Class. He and two card playing friends, William Greenfield and Henry Blank, survived by getting into the first lifeboat launched. Nobody seems to know why he was traveling under that name. When the list of survivors was published in Germany, the von Drachstedt family was surprised to discover someone was traveling under their name.

- Samuel Ward Stanton was a well-known American marine artist returning home from Spain after making sketches for murals he would paint back in New York. Stanton would not survive the voyage.

FIRST CLASS PASSENGERS

April was the end of the high-travel season in Europe and some of the most interesting individuals to board *Titanic* did so in Cherbourg. In addition to regular business travelers, there were many who were socially prominent among the 142 First Class passengers that boarded in Cherbourg.

RICHEST MAN ON TITANIC. JOHN JACOB AND MADELEINE FORCE ASTOR, RE-TURNING FROM THEIR HONEYMOON. MRS. ASTOR WAS PREGNANT AND SUR-VIVED. HE DID NOT. *(National Archives)*

MARGARET TOBIN (MRS. JAMES JOSEPH) BROWN, ALSO KNOWN AS "MOLLY." SHE TOOK COMMAND OF LIFEBOAT 6. *(Daily Mirror)*

MILLIONAIRE'S BENJAMIN GUGGENHEIM (LEFT) AND JAMES CLINCH SMITH. GUGGENHEIM DRESSED IN HIS BEST AND AWAITED THE END. NEITHER SURVIVED THE DISASTER. *(National Archives)*

■ By far, the wealthiest passenger on board was 48-year-old Colonel John Jacob Astor, IV, of New York City and Rhinebeck, New York, and about a dozen other residences. Estimated to be worth $100 million at that time (or about $1.8 billion today), Astor managed the family fortune while writing novels and inventing mechanical devices like bicycle brakes.

In 1897, Astor built the Astoria Hotel in New York, which was later joined with its neighbor, the Waldorf Hotel, and was renamed the Waldorf-Astoria (currently the site of the Empire State Building). Astor also owned the St. Regis and Knickerbocker hotels. During the Spanish-American War, Astor was appointed colonel in the U.S. Volunteers. He was married and had two children. In 1909, he did something that was so socially unacceptable that he would spend the rest of his life dodging the gossip it created: he divorced his wife.

In the late Victorian era, socially prominent men did not divorce their wives. They had mistresses—sometimes many and often very public mistresses. Having a mistress was fine, but divorce was not. However, Astor did divorce his wife Ava and two years later, in 1911, married an 18-year-old girl named Madeleine Force, who was one year younger than his son.

The gossip and rumormongers had a field day with Astor's decision. In order to create some stability in their lives, the Astor's decided to spend the winter in Egypt and Paris, and travel home to the United States on board *Titanic*. They occupied suite C62-C64 on the port side. Traveling with the Astor's were Victor Robbins, Astor's manservant, Miss Rosalie Bidois, Mrs. Astor's maid, and Miss Caroline Endres, a private nurse hired because young Mrs. Astor was pregnant. Rounding out the Astor clan was Kitty, Astor's pet Airedale. Madeleine Force Astor and the other two women survived. John Jacob Astor, his servant, and Kitty, would not.

■ A friend of the Astor's, boarding at Cherbourg, was 44-year-old Mrs. James J. (Molly) Brown, wife of a rich Colorado gold miner who had made and lost several fortunes. Molly had to change her reservations from another ship in order to travel with the Astor's. She would spend an interesting evening on a lifeboat, but she would survive.

■ At least millionaire Benjamin Guggenheim had his social priorities in order. He was en route home to his wife in New York with his mistress Madame Leontine Aubert from Paris. Guggenheim was also accompanied by his valet, Victor Giglio, and his chauffeur Rene Pernot. Miss Aubert would survive the sinking, but the rest of the group would perish.

Guggenheim and his valet took part in one of the more memorable final acts played out as the ship sank beneath them. The men returned to their rooms and dressed in their most formal attire. So outfitted, they camped out in the First Class Smoking Lounge and awaited their end. When asked by

Bruce Ismay why he wasn't trying to get onto a lifeboat, Guggenheim replied, *"We are dressed up in our best and are prepared to go down like gentlemen."*

- Mrs. James W. M. Cardeza, 58, from Germantown, Pennsylvania, was traveling with her son Thomas D. M. Cardeza, 36, her maid Anna Ward, his manservant Gustave Lesueur, and fourteen trunks, four suitcases, and three crates of baggage. They occupied the other Promenade Suite, B51-B53-B55, on the starboard side. All four would survive the trip, but the luggage is still at the bottom of the North Atlantic. Mrs. Cardeza would later file a claim for $177,352 (in 1912 dollars) for the lost luggage and clothing.

- Colonel Archibald Gracie IV, age 54, was the son of a Confederate general killed during the Civil War. He lived in New York and Washington, D.C. and had four daughters, all of whom died very young. One of Gracie's ancestors built Gracie Mansion, which is the official residence of the mayor of New York City.
    A graduate of the United States Military Academy, Gracie was colonel of the U.S. Army's Seventh Regiment and an amateur historian. He spent several years researching and writing a book titled *The Truth About Chickamauga*, an examination on the Civil War battle of the same name, and one in which his father had participated. Gracie decided it was time to relax after the book was published, so he took a trip to Europe aboard *Oceanic* and made friends with one of that ship's officers, Herbert Pitman. During his trip he had taken notes and did considerable research for a new book he was going to write about the War of 1812. Gracie would survive *Titanic's* final plunge, but his notes would not.
    Once aboard *Titanic*, Gracie formally offered his service to several "unprotected ladies" (women traveling alone). It was a custom for gentlemen at this time to do so. Accepting his offer were three sisters returning from a funeral in England: Mrs. E. D. Appleton, Mrs. R. C. Cornell, and Mrs. John M. Brown and their friend, Miss Edith Evans. Of this group, only Miss Evans would not survive. She stood back to let her friend and a mother of small children, Mrs. Brown, enter a lifeboat ahead of her.

- George D. Widener, 50, was from Elkins Park, Pennsylvania. He was also very wealthy. George was the son of P. A. B. Widener, a board member of the Fidelity Trust Company in Philadelphia, which controlled the International Mercantile Marine, which owned the White Star Line. George was heir to the largest fortune in Philadelphia. He was traveling home from a vacation with his wife Eleanor, son Harry E. Widener, and two servants.
    Neither George, his son Harry, nor his manservant would survive the collision with the iceberg. George and Harry helped Mrs. Widener and the maid into a lifeboat, then stepped back to await their fate. To honor

her son, Mrs. Widener donated the money to design and build the Harry Elkins Widener Memorial Library at Harvard University.

- Arthur L. Ryerson, 61, was en route home to Cooperstown, New York, for the funeral of his eldest son who had been killed in an auto accident. He was traveling with his wife Emily, their three other children (Suzette, 21, Emily, 18 and John, 13), and their maid. Unbeknownst to them, also on board was distant cousin William Ryerson, a steward in the dining saloon. Arthur would not survive the trip, but William and the rest of the family lived to see New York again.

- Sir Cosmo and Lady Lucille Duff Gordon were an interesting couple. There isn't any information that Sir Cosmo ever held a job, and he essentially lived off the family wealth after graduating from Eton (England's premier men's academy). Lucille was a famous fashion designer in London, Paris, and New York. Sir Cosmo represented Britain in the 1908 Olympics as a fencer, and beyond that did little else. The couple occupied staterooms A16 and A20, which were not connected and across the hall from each other. For a reason that remains unexplained, they had booked their trip under the names of Mr. and Mrs. Morgan. Their actions the night of the sinking would cause them a lifetime of grief.

- James Clinch Smith, 56, was the brother of Bessie Smith White and the brother-in-law of the late architect Stanford White (another person who did not have his social house in order). White also had a mistress, Evelyn Nesbit. In 1906, Harry Thaw, until recently married to Evelyn, murdered White on the roof of Madison Square Garden while Clinch Smith looked on. This horrific deed set the stage for the first "trial of the century."
  Clinch Smith and Archibald Gracie were good friends. Smith would die in the icy Atlantic; his body was not recovered.

- Dickinson H. Bishop, 25, was a widower from Dowagiac, Michigan, who had recently married Sturgis, Michigan, resident Helen Walton. The Bishops were returning from a four-month honeymoon in Europe and had delayed their return so they could travel on *Titanic*. Helen was also pregnant. The Bishops were unique: most of the honeymooning couples on *Titanic* lost one or both of their partners, but both of the Bishops survived. Their tragedy would come later.
  The child Mrs. Bishop carried died two days after birth. In 1916, the Bishop's divorced and Helen passed away on March 16, two days after Dickinson remarried. Notice of her death in the local newspaper appeared on the same page as his marriage announcement.

- William E. Carter, 36, from Byrn Mawr, Pennsylvania, was traveling home from vacation with his wife Lucile, 36, their two children, 11 and

SIR COSMO AND LADY LUCILLE DUFF GORDON WERE TRAVELING UNDER ASSUMED NAMES. THEY WERE ON LIFEBOAT 1, WHICH CONTAINED 12 PEOPLE BUT COULD HAVE HELD 40. THEY WERE LATER FALSELY ACCUSED OF PAYING OFF THE LIFEBOAT CREW TO NOT GO BACK TO PICK UP SWIMMERS. *(National Archives)*

THE DUFF GORDONS AND SURVIVORS OF LIFEBOAT 1 SMILING FOR THE CAMERA. THIS PHOTO WAS TAKEN ON BOARD CARPATHIA. LADY DUFF GORDON IS IN THE CENTER, SIR COSMO TO HER LEFT. THE PHOTO ADDED A CIRCUS ATMOSPHERE TO THE PROFOUND GRIEF FELT BY THE OTHER SURVIVORS WHO LOST FAMILY AND FRIENDS. *(Daily Mirror)*

14, a maid, Auguste Serraplan, a chauffeur Charles Aldworth, a manservant Alexander Cairns, their two dogs, and Mr. Carter's 25 horsepower Renault automobile. This was another rare case of an entire family and the maid surviving the trip. However, Aldworth, Cairns, the automobile and the two dogs were not as fortunate.

- Twenty-four-year old Margaret B. Hays, a resident of New York City, was touring Europe with friends Lily Potter and Olive Earnshaw, and Margaret's Pomeranian dog. They, too, had a self-appointed "escort" named Gilbert Tucker, who had met the three ladies while traveling in Europe with his parents. Tucker decided to return home with them because he had fallen madly in love with Miss Hays.

After the collision with the iceberg, Tucker helped get the three women up to the boat deck, where he helped them into their life jackets. Margaret was holding onto her dog, which was wrapped up in a blanket. At some point James Clinch Smith walked by and commented, jokingly, *"Oh, I suppose we ought to put a life preserver on the little doggie, too."*

Margaret, Lily, Olive, Gilbert Tucker and the dog survived. Although Tucker and Margaret remained friends for years, she married someone else.

- Mr. Arthur W. Newell, 58, from Lexington, Massachusetts, had been on a trip to the Middle East with his two daughters Madeleine, 32, and Marjorie, 23. After the collision, Newell went to the girl's room and told them to get dressed in their warmest clothes and to follow him to the boat deck. Once there, he helped them get into Lifeboat number 6, commenting, *"It does seem more dangerous for you to get into that boat than to remain here with me but we must obey orders."*

Newell continued to help load passengers into other lifeboats, and he died when the ship went down. His body was later recovered and identified and he was buried in Cambridge, Massachusetts. The watch he was wearing was returned to his wife, who never remarried and lived until 1957, passing away at the age of 103. She spent the rest of her life in mourning, usually wearing black and sleeping with his watch under her pillow. She never allowed mention of *Titanic* in her presence. Ironically, daughter Marjorie would also live to be 103 years old, dying in 1992. She was the last of the First Class passengers to pass away.

- Englehart Ostby, 65, was the owner of the world's largest supplier of gold rings. The Providence, Rhode Island, resident was returning home from vacation in Europe with his daughter Helene and a bag full of gems he had purchased in Paris.

After the collision, Ostby managed to get to the Boat Deck with his daughter, but he went back to his room to get warmer clothes. Meanwhile, Helene was placed into Lifeboat number 5. She never saw Ostby again. His body was recovered, and he is buried in Providence.

■ The Spedden family—Frederick, 45, wife Margaretta, 40, six year-old son Douglas, plus two servants, Helen Wilson and Elizabeth Burns—were another success story: All of them would escape death on April 15. Frederick would place his wife and child into a lifeboat and step back after saying good-bye, but before the lifeboat would be lowered, about 20 men would be allowed to enter because there were not any more women or children around. One of the more endearing *Titanic* photographs taken by Father Browne is of young Douglas spinning a top on the Promenade Deck while his father looks on.

■ Mr. Ramon Artagaveytia, 72, was returning to Argentina. He survived the fire and sinking of the ship *America* in Uruguay in 1871, something only 65 of the 205 passengers could claim. Most of the dead had died of burns. Ramon had nightmares throughout his life, and had written a relative two months before sailing on *Titanic* that he kept hearing the words *"Fire! Fire! Fire!"* and said he often wore his lifebelt when he was on a ship.

Artagaveytia thought that wireless communication would prevent large scale sea disasters because help could now be called. He was wrong. His body would be recovered and he would eventually be buried in Uruguay.

YOUNG DOUGLAS SPEDDEN SPINNING A TOP ON THE PROMENADE DECK AS HIS FATHER WATCHES. (*Daily Mirror*)

- Manuel E. Uruchurtu, 40, was from Mexico City but had been exiled to France because he was too rich and had too much money. With government permission, he was returning to Mexico City to arrange for his wife to join him in France. He would not survive.

- Eighteen-year-old Victor and 17-year-old Maria Penasco y Castellana had already been married for two years. Wealthy beyond their dreams due to family fortunes, the newlyweds were on a two-year honeymoon, having traveled throughout Europe and Russia. Because of their age, his mother controlled the money, sending money drafts as they sent her postcards showing what they had seen.
  Forbidden by mom to go to the United States, as a lark they decided to make the trip anyway, leaving one of the servants in Paris to send the weekly pre-written postcards. Several postcards were mailed after Victor died before the servant knew his fate. By law, Victor could not be declared dead without a body, and Maria, who would survive the sinking, would not inherit his money for 20 years. Eventually, one of the unidentified bodies buried at Halifax was declared to be Victor just long enough for Maria to collect the inheritance.

- Mrs. Walter Stephenson, 52, from Haverford, Pennsylvania, had already survived the 1906 San Francisco earthquake. She was now returning home from a vacation in Europe with her sister Elizabeth Eustis. Both women would survive this disaster as well.

- Mrs. Louis (Ida) A. Hippach and her 16-year-old daughter Jean were returning to Chicago from a European vacation. They were trying to recover from the loss of two of Mrs. Hippach's sons in the famous 1903 Iroquois Theatre fire in Chicago. Both would survive *Titanic*, but a cruel fate continued to dog Ida. Less than two years after *Titanic* sank, her third son was killed in an automobile accident.

- It was completely dark at 8:00 p.m. when the loading process was completed. In ninety minutes the 274 embarking and 24 departing passengers had been taken care of, and at 8:10 p.m. *Titanic* got underway. The ship and all aboard were now heading west into the night, across the English Channel again to make the next and last port call at Queenstown, Ireland, the following afternoon.

- *Titanic* was still two hours behind schedule.

TITANIC AT SOUTHMAPTON, EASTER SUNDAY, APRIL 7, 1912. NOTE CROW'S NEST, THE BRIDGE (DARK ROW OF NINE WINDOWS ON THE BOAT DECK IN FRONT OF THE FIRST FUNNEL, AND THE NOW ENCLOSED PROMANADE ON A DECK. *(Author's Collection)*

"I still don't like this ship. I have a queer feeling about it."

CHAPTER 9

QUEENSTOWN, IRELAND

THURSDAY AFTERNOON, APRIL 11, 1912

Before *Titanic* left Cherbourg, P. W. Fletcher made his second round of the ship, blowing his bugle to announce the evening meal. Most of the passengers took advantage of the opportunity to make their way to the various dining saloons.

After the evening meal, many of the passengers began "the grand promenade" or "the big search," fancy expressions for exploring their floating palace. The sea that evening was somewhat rough, but several passengers remarked at how smoothly *Titanic* handled the waves. There was little notice of any rocking or motion, and many commented that the only sense of movement came from the distant, hollow thumping of the engines.

■ While the passengers were settling into the routine they believed would last until they arrived in New York, the crew settled into their own routine. The stokers, firemen, trimmers, greasers and other members of the engineering department stood their four hour shifts. In the Victualling Department, stewards and stewardesses, cooks, bakers, and anyone else responsible for running the hotel portion of the ship prepared for their twelve and eighteen-hour days. Some stewards were on call twenty-four hours and would only get to rest early in the morning when their passengers no longer needed their services.

All of the ship's officers except Captain Smith stood normal four-hour deck watches, but they had other duties as well. Each had various rounds to keep and duties to attend. Each had his own cabin and would retire there whenever possible to catch up on his rest, but the normal routine was eight to ten hours on duty, and two to four hours off.

■ Marconi operators Phillips and Bride settled on their own watch schedule prior to leaving Southampton. Phillips took the 8:00 p.m. to 2:00 a.m. watch, and Bride the 2:00 a.m. to 8:00 a.m. stretch. During the

A TYPICAL FIRST CLASS SUITE (TOP). DOOR AT FAR LEFT LEADS TO A CORRIDOR, THE
OPEN DOOR AT NEAR LEFT LEADS TO A RESTROOM. THE DOOR TO THE RIGHT LEADS TO
ANOTHER ROOM OF THE SUITE. THE CAFÉ PARISIEN (BOTTOM) ON THE STARBOARD
SIDE OF B DECK, LOOKING TOWARD THE BOW. WINDOWS ON THE RIGHT GIVE A VIEW TO
THE OCEAN. BOTH PHOTOS ARE FROM THE OLYMPIC, WHICH WAS AN EXACT COPY OF
TITANIC. *(National Archives)*

rest of the time—the busiest on the ship—both men were usually on duty, although they did manage to take time off to rest when the work load allowed it.

■   The Harland and Wolff Guarantee Group was up and about offering their services to the various departments, but for most of the voyage there was little for them to do except enjoy the journey.

■   Down on F Deck near the Third Class Dining Saloon and close to where the butchers prepared the meals were the dog kennels. On this night the animals, too, were settling in for a long trip. These four-legged passengers would be almost as well treated as their masters up in First and Second Class.

■   What the roaming passengers discovered in their travels through the magnificent ship was almost beyond belief for most of them. The First Class travelers were used to the finest accommodations, but most of the rest of the passengers had never seen anything like the luxury offered on the *Titanic*. Most of them would never see it again.

AMENITIES FOR THE FIRST CLASS PASSENGERS

First Class passengers boarded the ship through the main entrance on B Deck, and the first thing they saw was the magnificent Grand Staircase towering two stories above them, topped off by a huge glass and wrought-iron dome that allowed light to flood into the enclosed First Class entrance on the Boat Deck. This stairway had a landing and a right-angle turn between the decks on each level, so that passengers descending the stairs would have a view of the entire room they were about to enter. There were also two wells, or light shafts, that went all the way from the Boat Deck down to the bottom of the stairwell on D Deck so that light from the dome penetrated deep into the ship.

The stairway and the landings were fully carpeted in light beige, the banisters were of carved wood and iron, and the walls were adorned in light oak. One crewman wrote,

> "Carpet . . . you sank in it up to your knees . . . furniture so heavy you could hardly lift it . . . she was a beautiful, wonderful ship."

There was a second smaller Grand Staircase aft of the third funnel that also had a dome and a light shaft. This stairway also extended all the way down to D Deck.

Most of B Deck contained First Class suites, including the two Promenade Suites with their own private decks. Further aft on B Deck was the reception room for the à la carte restaurant at the base of the aft

OLYMPIC'S FIRST CLASS GRAND STAIRCASE, LOOKING AFT. UPPER STAIRS LEAD TO THE BOAT DECK, LOWER STAIRS TO A DECK. THE CENTER PIECE IS HONOUR AND GLORY WATCHING OVER TIME. GLASS AND WROUGHT IRON DOME CROWN THE STAIRCASE. OPEN AREAS ON EITHER SIDE ALLOW LIGHT ALL THE WAY DOWN TO D DECK. *(National Archives)*

Grand Staircase, and further aft was the restaurant itself. The Café Parisian was on the starboard side, and many of the younger adult passengers gathered here during the trip.

- The Grand Staircase led up from B Deck to A Deck, where the partially enclosed and fully covered promenade ran almost two-thirds of the length of the ship on both sides. This promenade surrounded several rooms: the First Class Lounge, which was finished in green velvet and dull polished oak; the reading and writing room with its huge fireplace, finished with plush carpeting done in old rose; the Smoking Room, done in dark Georgian style surrounded by the finest mahogany, mother of pearl inlay work, and stained glass windows; and the Verandah and Palm Court Café, with their floor-to-ceiling windows that opened to let the air in, finished with thick heavy carpeting and surrounded with live plants.

The corridors were oak paneled and revolving doors helped keep the cold air out. Mirrors and cut glass abounded.

■ Passengers walking up the Grand Staircase toward the boat deck saw the beautiful wood carving of Honour and Glory Crowning Time on the wall of the landing.

■ Once on the Boat Deck, people could look up through the huge dome and then go outside to the deck, which contained both the First and Second Class promenade. Noticeable on this deck were the abundance of chairs and benches for the passengers to sit on, as well as the four funnels and 20 lifeboats.

The enclosed entrance had a linoleum floor, which was a new invention and very expensive. The walls were covered in dark oak, and there were several electric heaters to keep the room warm.

■ A First Class passenger who entered the ship on B Deck and went down the main Grand Staircase to C Deck would find the majority of the First Class cabins (as opposed to multi-room suites on B Deck).

■ Continuing down one more level to D Deck, a First Class passenger would find more First Class cabins and the huge First Class Reception Room that extended the width of the ship and had large floor-to-ceiling windows. Thick Axminster carpet covered the floor. Wicker chairs and Chesterfields were placed for the passengers comfort. A huge grand piano waited in the room.

Passing from the reception room through two large iron and wooden doors brought passengers into the First Class Dining Saloon, the largest single room on the ship. It was so large that the room could seat every First Class passenger on this voyage in one sitting—comfortably.

After a lavish meal, if someone wished to return to the Boat Deck for some air or exercise but didn't want to climb back up five levels, he simply stepped into one of the three elevators located behind the stairway, each manned by an attendant.

■ Down one more level of the Grand Staircase were the First Class accommodations on the starboard side of E Deck. Running the length of E Deck on the port side was the corridor called "Scotland Road" by the crew. It was used by the crew and the Third Class passengers to move from one end of the ship to the other.

■ The First Class accommodations were designed to emulate the best hotels of the world—and they were fabulous. All were decorated in various styles popular at that time: Louis XIV, Louis XVI, Italian

Renaissance, Queen Anne, Modern Dutch, Old Dutch, and Georgian. Each room boasted the finest brass, wood, cloth, and carpeting. Many of the fixtures cost hundreds of dollars each, and all were fully authentic to the period.

▪   More than 400 live plants in five-inch or larger pots were loaded in Southampton for placement in the First and Second Class portions of the ship. Climbing ivy was brought aboard for use in the Palm Court and the Café Parisian. Thousands of fresh flowers and roses were loaded for use in the First Class cabins and dining rooms.

▪   In an age when some of the best hotels did not have private rest room facilities, most of the suites on the *Titanic* had such facilities that included full size bathtubs. The suites also had storage areas for trunks and closets for clothes, and each room had call buttons to summon attendants. Most of the First Class accommodations were not suites but individual rooms. About half of these had restroom facilities, and the rest used shared facilities. You got what you paid for.

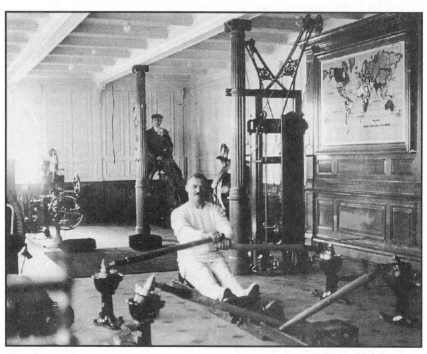

PASSENGER LAWRENCE BEESLEY (REAR) AND GYM INSTRUCTOR T. W. McCAWLEY IN THE GYMNASIUM PRIOR TO THE DEPARTURE FROM SOUTHAMPTON. *(National Archives)*

Many of the suites also came with separate rooms for servants and maids, and all came with electric heaters, four-foot wide brass bedsteads, wicker armchairs, ceiling fans, marble fixtures in the bathrooms, thick carpeting, and heavy drapes to block the outside light.

All of the cabins were connected by long corridors, painted white and carpeted, and the corridors led to one of the two huge Grand Staircases. Cabins came with one, two, three, or four beds.

There was a barbershop, a dark room for amateur photographers, a library, a separate dining room for personal maids and valets, and a hospital equipped with a modern operating room.

- To keep the idle rich occupied, *Titanic* was equipped with a heated 30 x 14 foot indoor saltwater swimming bath, a Turkish and electric bath with adjoining cooling room, a Squash Racquet Court (30 x 20) with spectator areas. On the Boat Deck was the gymnasium, which measuring 44 x 18, and containing several pieces of exercise equipment including cycling, rowing, and horse-riding equipment.

The Turkish and electric baths were forward on F Deck. They were open to ladies between 10:00 a.m. and 1:00 p.m. and to gentlemen from 2:00 p.m. to 6:00 p.m. The cost to use the baths was $1.00.

The swimming bath was across the corridor from the Turkish Bath, and it was open the same hours in addition to being open for gentlemen from 6:00 a.m. to 9:00 a.m. The cost was twenty-five cents if you didn't buy a ticket for the Turkish Bath. The pool was not filled with water until *Titanic* left Queenstown because it was filled directly from the sea and the water too close to shore was considered too dirty to use for this purpose.

Located on the Boat Deck next to the First Class Entrance was the gymnasium. It was open the same hours as the swimming pool, but children were allowed only between 1:00 p.m. and 3:00 p.m.

Located forward on G Deck was the Squash Racquet Court. Open by appointment only during the day, the cost was $1.00 per hour and included the service of racquet professional Frederick Wright. In addition to Wright, there was an instructor for the gymnasium and assorted attendants for the swimming and Turkish Baths.

SECOND AND THIRD CLASS PASSENGERS

Passengers who did not have the funds or the social stature to travel in First Class traveled Second Class. Those who were emigrants or who wanted to travel cheaply chose Third Class.

- Second Class accommodations on *Titanic* were said to be better than First Class on most other ships, and even Third Class was supposed to be better than First Class on some of the liners of the day.

Second Class passengers had their own grand staircase leading down six decks from the Boat Deck. *Titanic* and *Olympic* were the first ships to have an elevator for Second Class passengers. There was a separate library, smoking room, enclosed promenade, and a huge dining saloon. The Boat Deck had a separate open promenade area.

- Third Class passengers did not get all of the amenities and trappings of the other two classes, but they were well taken care of. Instead of the usual dormitories that other ships had, *Titanic* provided individual rooms with anywhere from two to six beds. All restroom facilities were common, but many of the Third Class passengers had never seen or used indoor plumbing. The food was exceptional by their standards and there was a lot of it. Most Third Class passengers had more to eat on the voyage than they had ever had in their life.

In this era Third Class passengers knew their social status, and they were not upset by locked gates or by segregation from upper class passengers. Few had ever had the opportunity to take charge of a serious situation, and they were used to being told what to do. This, in large part, is why so many of them would not survive the sinking. There was not anyone to tell them what to do or where to go, and they perished while waiting for instructions.

- While First Class accommodations were located in the center of the ship (the most stable portion ride-wise), Second Class cabins were mainly aft of the First Class areas and the Third Class passengers were in the bow or stern areas. Third Class families and single women were placed in the stern, while single men were placed in the bow, and their only route of communication was down Scotland Road, the wide corridor down on E Deck.

- The crew's quarters were jammed into just about every available nook and cranny. Separate cabins or dormitories were provided for complete departments: postal clerks, the band, the bakers, and the cooks. The quartermasters had their own cabin, while the larger crews such as the stokers, firemen, and trimmers all had a bunk in a dormitory, some of which held over 50 men. Most of the different departments had their own mess areas. The only crew members who had private rooms were the officers and some of the stewards and stewardesses who were on call for the First Class passengers.

QUEENSTOWN

Throughout the night and into the morning of April 11 *Titanic* steamed toward her final port call at Queenstown, Ireland. Breakfast was served and the passengers started to congregate on the decks watching for landfall in the form of the southern coast of Ireland.

- Around 6:45 a.m. Father Francis Browne walked up on the Boat Deck and began taking pictures, including one of six-year-old Robert Spedden spinning a top while his father Frederick looked on.

Browne snapped a lot of pictures that morning, including images of passengers and crew. One shows that *Titanic* was not steering in a straight line but in broad curves because the officers were making course changes to test the compass.

- Near the Cobh Harbor light vessel, *Titanic* slowed to a stop and picked up the pilot who would guide the ship into the harbor. At 11:30 a.m. *Titanic*, now three hours behind schedule, stopped in the harbor about two miles from shore because once again, the harbor did not have facilities for a ship the size of *Titanic*. Normally *Titanic* would anchor about one mile out, but because of the three-hour delay and low tide, *Titanic* had to anchor about a mile further than usual.

- Ferried out on a half-hour run from the dock in Queenstown on the tenders *Ireland* and *America* were seven Second Class and 113 Third Class passengers and 1,385 sacks of mail. Seven First Class passengers disembarked, including Father Browne, who was clutching his photographic plates. While waiting on the tender, Father Browne took more pictures, including one of Captain Smith looking over the side of the starboard bridge wing.

- While the loading and unloading process was going on, a flotilla of merchants in small boats, called bumboats, pulled up next to the tenders. The merchants started showing off their wares by hanging them all over the sides of the boats. Many of the owners of these boats (the respectable looking ones, at least) were allowed to board *Titanic* with their goods by crossing over the decks of the tenders. One enterprising bumboatman got lucky when John Jacob Astor approached him and bought a lace jacket for Madeleine on the spot for $800. At today's rate, that jacket would cost more than $13,000.

- One unauthorized departure in Queenstown was stoker John Coffey. His home was in Queenstown and he probably signed on in Southampton to get a free trip home. In any event, he managed to get off the ship and onto one of the tenders and hide behind some of the cargo destined for shore.

Since leaving Southampton the day before, many of the passengers and crew had taken the time to write letters or address some of the many

CAPTAIN EDWARD J. SMITH LOOKING OVER THE SIDE FROM THE STARBOARD BRIDGE WING (TOP). LIFEBOAT 1 HANGS ON ITS DAVITS. A CREWMAN AND A FIRST CLASS PASSENGER ON A DECK ARE LOOKING OVER THE EDGE AS ARE THIRD CLASS PASSENGERS ON THE FORWARD WELL DECK. PHOTO TAKEN BY FATHER FRANCIS BROWNE, WHO WAS GETTING OFF IN QUEENSTOWN. HE TOOK THE PHOTO FROM THE DECK OF THE TENDER IRELAND. THIS IS THE LAST KNOWN PHOTO OF SMITH. *(National Archives)*

Titanic postcards provided them, so there was a lot of outbound mail to take ashore.

Little is known about Chief Officer Wilde, but he did mail a letter to his sister from Queenstown. In it he included this observation: *"I still don't like this ship. . . . I have a queer feeling about it."*

■ Loading the Third Class passengers was less hectic here. The stewards and the crew knew their way around now, and, *"At least this lot spoke English,"* one steward said.

■ At some point during the boarding process one of the highlights of the stop in Queenstown took place. An unnamed stoker, totally covered in black soot, climbed up the 165-foot ladder inside the aft funnel to get a look outside and some fresh air. The appearance of his black head popping out of the funnel scared a number of people, and many took it as an ill-omen.

■ At 1:30 p.m., two hours after *Titanic's* arrival, the huge whistle blew again and the propellers started to churn the water. As preparations were being made to close the gangway door, a local photographer took a photo of First Officer Murdoch and Second Officer Lightoller standing in the door opening. This was the last known surviving photograph taken of anyone on the ship. The anchor was hauled up and Father Browne, now standing on the tender, took one last photo of the stern of *Titanic* as the tender moved away. Because *Titanic* had been forced to anchor an extra mile from shore, she lost yet another hour. The great ship left Queenstown four full hours behind schedule.

■ On the stern of the ship, newly arrived Third Class passenger Eugene Daly propped himself up on a bench and began playing the dirge "Erin's Lament" on his Irish pipes as the green hills of Ireland began to fall away from the ship. There was another brief stop to drop off the pilot, and then *Titanic* picked up speed. The sun was beginning to drop into the western horizon when a French fishing boat edged so close to *Titanic* that it was splashed with water, but nothing serious happened and as the boat fell astern, so too did the Irish coast. The next stop would be New York City in six days.

■ *Titanic* was now steaming west into a setting sun and into history.

THE LAST PHOTOGRAPH OF FIRST OFFICER MURDOCH (CENTER) AND SECOND OFFICER LIGHTOLLER (RIGHT) LOOKING OUT THE GANGWAY DOOR PRIOR TO CLOSING IT FOR THE LAST TIME. PHOTOGRAPHED FROM THE TENDER IRELAND IN QUEENSTOWN, APRIL 11, 1912. *(Cork Examiner)*

"God himself could not sink this ship."

CHAPTER 10

DESTINY

APRIL 11-APRIL 14, 1912

There were 2,208 people on *Titanic* as it steamed west into the afternoon sunset on April 11, 1912. One of the many questions that has not been fully answered, and may never be, is exactly how many people were really on board.

Researchers use their own methods of tracking and counting people, and the numbers range from a low of 2,202 up to 2,230. This author believes that the most accurate accounting to date is 2,208. Regardless of which number is used, more than two-thirds of the people on *Titanic* that April afternoon would never see land or home again.

- There were accommodations for 1,024 Third Class passengers. Some 710 were on board, which was 69% of capacity.

- In Second Class, there were accommodations for 674 passengers and 283 were on board, which was 42% of capacity.

- First Class accommodations for 735 passengers existed, yet only 324 were traveling on the maiden voyage, or 44% of capacity.

- In addition to the 1,317 passengers were the 891 crewmembers.

- There were accommodations for 2,433 passengers, so *Titanic* was steaming westward at just 54% of capacity.

FIFTY-FIVE VERY LUCKY PEOPLE

For various reasons, fifty-five ticketed passengers did not make the trip on *Titanic*. Several canceled because they didn't like their accommodations. Most of these had booked First Class passage on another ship but were transferred to *Titanic* because of the coal strike.

There, they were offered Second Class accommodations for the same price they had paid earlier for First Class, and thus declined the honor.

Several more cancelled because they had premonitions of disaster or didn't like to travel on maiden voyages, and several cancelled for business or personal reasons.

- Mr. and Mrs. E. W. Bill were planning to make the trip but a few nights before they were supposed to leave Southampton, Mrs. Bill had a nightmare about a sinking ship. They cancelled their trip.

- Millionaire George W. Vanderbilt and his wife also cancelled the day before their departure because his mother talked them out of the trip; she, too, did not like maiden voyages. Since their huge collection of luggage (even more than the Cardeza's haul) was already aboard the ship, their servant Frederick Wheeler was sent on with it as a Second Class passenger to collect the luggage in New York. Neither the luggage nor Wheeler survived the trip.

- Robert Bacon, United States Ambassador to France, had to cancel because his replacement was late arriving in Paris.

- Then there were the Frick's, the Morgan's, and the Harding's. Each couple had booked a Promenade Suite and each cancelled for various reasons, which in turn allowed Bruce Ismay his opportunity to occupy it.

- In addition to the fifty-five passengers who cancelled, there were about 20 crewmen who missed the boat, as the saying goes, for various reasons.

- Lucky also were the more than 1,100 people who could have booked passage on *Titanic*, but did not.

LIFE AT SEA, PART I

Other than meals and Sunday church services, there were no organized activities for the passengers. They were expected to provide their own entertainment.

- Meals were scheduled at:

>   8:30 a.m. to 10:30 a.m. for breakfast
>   1:00 p.m. to 2:30 p.m. for lunch
>   6:00 p.m. to 8:00 p.m. for dinner

The à la carte restaurant was open to First Class passengers from 8:00 a.m. to 11:00 p.m. daily for anyone wanting a snack or not wanting to partake in the regular daily meals.

- The First Class Library on A Deck was open from 8:00 a.m. to 11:00 p.m. There was also a library for Second Class passengers. Third Class passengers could spend their time in the great general room on C Deck, where a piano was to be had and where dances were held.

A large selection of card and board games were available to all classes, and each class had its own outside promenade where chairs and tables were available.

Most people spent their time reading or writing letters, playing card games, or visiting with friends. In the days before radio, television, or slot machines, there was little else to do.

There were always high stakes card games going on in the First Class areas, and there were also several professional gamblers who were doing their best to part the rich from their money. White Star Line had given all of the passengers a written warning about the possibility of the gamblers' presence.

- One thing that occupied the minds of many of the First Class men was the large board in the Smoking Lounge that listed the number of miles in the previous day's run, posted from noon one day until noon the next:

> Thursday to Friday, 386 miles
> Friday to Saturday, 519 miles
> Saturday to Sunday, 546 miles

It looked like *Titanic* was due for an early morning arrival in New York City on Wednesday. Many of the passengers were taking bets on Monday's and Tuesday's runs and the time the ship would arrive in New York on Wednesday.

- Several passengers had overheard conversations or rumors that an attempt was going to be made to try to set a speed record on the run, but that was neither possible nor practical. *Titanic* wasn't designed to beat *Mauretania's* current 26-knot record on the transatlantic run. Because of the coal strike there wasn't a full load of coal on the ship. Finally, the fire in the coalbunker in Boiler Room 5 had consumed an unknown amount of coal. Steaming at high speed for too long could have consumed so much coal that there was a chance *Titanic* would run out before making port. Running out of coal in the middle of the Atlantic would have been a marketing disaster for White Star Line. The fastest *Titanic* ever steamed on her maiden voyage was a short run of 23 knots on Saturday.

Titanic probably could have beaten its sister ship Olympic's maiden voyage record if it hadn't been four hours behind schedule. To accomplish that record would have put Titanic outside New York harbor in the middle of the night. Titanic might have tried to make up some of the four hours, but there wasn't any attempt to do so. Even if there had been sufficient coal, given the problems of getting the ship out of Southampton in the middle of the day, docking Titanic in New York in the dark would have been out of the question. About all that could have been done is to have the ship wait outside the harbor until morning, which wouldn't have set any records and would not have made much sense to the passengers. Many of the passengers didn't have any arrangements to get picked up any earlier, so they wouldn't have been overly excited about an early arrival.

MEALS

Meals were the only organized activity of the voyage and for the First Class passengers, evening meals were signature events.

- The First Class Dining Saloon could seat 532 people in one sitting, so the 324 First Class passengers on this voyage could all eat at the same time. All 283 of the Second Class passengers could also be seated at one time in the Second Class Dining Saloon, which could hold 394. The two Third Class Dining Saloons could hold 473 in one sitting, so the 710 passengers on this voyage had to be accommodated in two meal sittings.

Before Titanic left Southampton, more than 200,000 pounds of fresh food was loaded on board, along with 35,000 bottles of beer, wine, and spirits, and 9,000 cigars. Nobody on this trip would go hungry or thirsty.

- Lunch served to the First Class passengers on April 14 included: Consommé Fermier, Cockie Leekie, Fillets of Brill, Egg A L'Argenteuil; Chicken A La Maryland, Corned Beef, Vegetables, Dumplings, Grilled Mutton Chops, Custard Pudding, Apple Meringue, Salmon Mayonnaise, Potted Shrimps, Norwegian Anchovies, Souses Herrings, Plain and Smoked Sardines, Roast Beef, Veal and Ham Pie, Bologna Sausage, Corned Ox Tongue, and eight types of cheese.

- First Class dinner on April 14 was a seven-course meal. There was a large selection of hors d'oeuvres, two soups, sauté of chicken Lyonnaise or stuffed marrow, lamb, duckling or sirloin of beef, salmon, filet mignon, various vegetables, several special dishes including asparagus vinaigrette and pâté de foie gras, and four desserts including Waldorf pudding and French ice cream. A meal in the First Class Dining Saloon was strictly a formal affair. In an era when gentlemen always wore a coat, tie, and a hat, mealtime didn't provide an opportunity to dress down.

Captain Smith had a small personal table in the Dining Saloon, but he usually ate his meals in his own room.

- While First Class passengers were being pampered with an almost limitless meal selection, Second Class passengers also fared quite well.

The Second Class dinner meal on April 14 included: Consommé, Tapioca, Baked Haddock, Sharp Sauce, Curried Chicken and Rice, Spring Lamb and Mint Sauce, Roast Turkey, Cranberry Sauce, various vegetables, and assorted desserts.

- Many of the Third Class passengers ate better on this voyage than they ever had or ever would again. While the selection was not as bountiful as the other classes, the amount of food was more that they were used to having. No one complained about the quantity or quality.

Third Class breakfast included: oatmeal porridge with milk, smoked herring and potatoes, ling fish with egg sauce, fried tripe and onions, boiled eggs, fresh bread and butter, marmalade, tea, and coffee.

Dinner was served at midday, and a typical Third Class dinner included: soup, beefsteak and kidney pie, boiled mutton and caper sauce, various vegetables, and desserts.

The evening meal for the Third Class passengers was called "tea," and included: cod fish cakes, cheese and pickles, fresh bread and butter, and plum and apple jam.

While much of the menu might seem rather unappetizing to us today, it was more than acceptable to the passengers of *Titanic*.

- In addition to the dining saloon and the Café Parisian, First Class passengers could take their meals at the à la carte restaurant up on B Deck, adorned with French walnut paneling and two-tone Dubarry rose carpeting. Luigi Gatti was the operator of the restaurant and had recruited most of his staff from his employees at the two London restaurants he owned, Gatti's Adelphi and Gatti's Strand.

Gatti brought his own staff of chefs, waiters, and manager. All of them were French or Italian, and ten of them were Gatti's cousins. Although not counted as part of the crew, all 68 of Gatti's employees signed the ship's articles indicating that they would take orders from the ship's officers.

Gatti had been on *Olympic* when it collided with *Hawke*, and Gatti's wife did not want him to go on *Titanic's* maiden voyage. He told her not to worry because . . . he was an excellent swimmer.

THE ORCHESTRA

While the First Class and Second Class passengers were enjoying their meals or relaxing in the lounges and smoking rooms, they were entertained by the ship's orchestra.

- The leader of the orchestra was Wallace Hartley, a 33-year-old violinist who had been recruited from the *Mauretania*. There were a total of eight members of the orchestra, which was divided into two sections. One section with three members performed in the Second Class Lounge and Dining Saloon. The remaining five, led by Hartley, played in the First Class Dining Saloon during meals and at after-dinner concerts.

Their cabins were down on E Deck, and they would often take musical requests from the passengers who had cabins near theirs. They played from a published list of 352 musical selections. Each member was expected to know all of the selections and its assigned number so that Hartley could call for the next selection by number only.

Titanic's orchestra was not employed by White Star Line, but contracted by the Liverpool Company of C. W. and F. N. Black. The men held Second Class tickets and also signed the ship's articles.

WIRELESS

Next door to the First Class Purser's Office on C Deck was the Enquiry Office, where passengers could pay for tickets to the Turkish Bath or the Squash Racquet Court. However, most passengers would use the Enquiry Office to arrange for the transmission of wireless messages to friends, family, or business partners.

- For a small fee based upon a flat rate of ten words (each extra word cost more money), passengers could give a handwritten message to the clerk who would send it by pneumatic tube to the wireless office up on the Boat Deck. There, the wireless operator would arrange to transmit the messages in the order they were received.

BANDMASTER WALLACE HARTLEY (LEFT) LED THE ORCHESTRA UNTIL THE VERY END. HE DID NOT SURVIVE. FIRST CLASS PASSENGER ARCHIBALD GRACIE ENDED UP IN THE WATER, BUT SURVIVED TO WRITE ABOUT HIS ADVENTURES. *(National Archives)*

Incoming messages were handled in reverse, being sent down another pneumatic tube to the Enquiry Office, where they were given to a courier for delivery to the recipient.

▪ Incoming messages for the ship were given directly to the officer on duty on the bridge, which was just down the corridor. Messages concerning navigation were supposed to be handled immediately, but because the wireless operators didn't work for the ship but for the Marconi Company, and the majority of their pay came from tips, there were times when navigation messages would pile up if one of the operators wasn't available to take them to the bridge. However, at least, with two operators on *Titanic*, the wireless office was never allowed to be unoccupied.

▪ Wireless operator John ("Jack") Phillips was the senior wireless operator and had spent several years on various ships. Junior operator Harold Bride assisted Phillips. Both were more than competent. Between them *Titanic* had two excellent wireless operators who managed a large volume of messages. Many of the First Class passengers delighted in sending dozens of messages to tell their friends and family about their trip on *Titanic*.

▪ On Friday night, the wireless set blew a circuit and shut down. Both Phillips and Bride worked on it all night and had it running again on Saturday morning, but now they had more than ten hours of incoming and outgoing messages to catch up on, something they hadn't completed by Sunday night.

Shortly before dark on Sunday night, the wireless land station at Cape Race, Newfoundland, came into Marconi range. Bride and Phillips knew they would have to spend the entire night catching up on both the incoming message backlog and the huge number of outgoing messages that had been received during the day from passengers who knew that Cape Race would be in range that night. Messages sent to Cape Race would be forwarded via wireless or phone line to Montreal for distribution to the rest of North America.

LIFE AT SEA, PART II

Although there was supposed to be a lifeboat drill on Sunday morning, it was not conducted. Nor were there any lifeboat drills held during the entire voyage, and no instructions were issued about who was to report to what lifeboat in case of an emergency. Furthermore, there weren't any instructions posted about how to use the life belts. It was not uncommon at the time to cancel lifeboat drills or to fail to post instructions.

As was customary, Captain Smith and his officers made a complete inspection of the ship every day at 10:00 a.m. to check on the safety of the crew and passengers and the operation of the ship.

- Some Second Class passengers complained that the heat didn't work in their cabins and only part of the fixtures in some of the washrooms were installed. Due to the haste in preparing the ship for departure, much of the finishing work was not complete.

- Down on G Deck, the five postal inspectors, three American and two British, worked fourteen-hour days sorting and bagging 3,430 bags of mail and hundreds of packages.

- Second Class passengers Benjamin and Esther Hart were traveling with their seven-year-old daughter Eva. Eva and her father seldom parted company and spent a good portion of the trip touring the ship and meeting with the other passengers. Before leaving home, Eva's mother had a premonition about the ship sinking and she seldom left her cabin except for meals. In addition, she slept during the day and sat up at night so she would be awake if something happened while her family slept.
    On Sunday night, Benjamin and Eva were sleeping while Mrs. Hart

Senior Marconi wireless operator John (Jack) Phillips (left) sent his last message three minutes before Titanic disappeared beneath the waves. Junior operator Harold Bride stayed with him. Phillips was lost, Bride survived. *(National Archives)*

performed her nightly vigil. Before the night was over, Esther and Eva would be on a lifeboat and Mr. Hart would be dead.

■   Second Class passenger Nellie Hocking of Cornwall told several friends that she heard a rooster crowing late one night. According to Cornish folklore this was a sign of pending disaster. Her friends didn't believe her. A rooster on *Titanic?* After the ship sank, passenger Mrs. J. S. White filed a claim for lost property that included . . . roosters and hens. It is entirely possible that Nellie Hocking did indeed hear a rooster on *Titanic.*

■   The Second Class Purser's Clerk assured Mrs. Ruth Becker,

> *"You don't have to be afraid at all. If anything should happen to this ship the watertight compartments would keep it afloat until we get help."*

■   Second Class passenger Mrs. Albert Caldwell asked a deck hand, *"Is this ship really non-sinkable?"* His reply was, *"Yes, lady. God himself could not sink this ship."*

■   On Saturday morning it was reported to Captain Smith that the coal fire in Boiler Room 5 had finally been put out. All the coal in the bunker had been moved out and watered down. The fire had burned for two weeks.

■   Religious services for all classes were held in the First Class Dining Saloon at 10:30 Sunday morning. This was the only opportunity Third Class passengers would have to see the First Class sections of the ship.

■   First Class passenger and author William T. Stead had written about a ship that collided with an iceberg and sank. Stead also believed in mysticism and spiritualism, and had been advised by mediums to avoid ocean travel.
    During dinner on Sunday evening, Stead told a story about an Egyptian mummy that carried a curse that caused death and destruction to all who viewed it. The mummy itself was on display in a London museum.
    Passenger Fred Seward was so impressed by the mummy story that he told it to a reporter of the *New York World* after his rescue. The story was written that the mummy was actually being transported on *Titanic* and its spell had caused the disaster. There was no mummy aboard.

■ Sometime Sunday, Mrs. Henry Harris tripped and fell down one of the stairwells and broke a bone in her arm. The ship's surgeon set her arm in a plaster cast.

■ In the First Class section, many of the unaccompanied male passengers engaged in the tradition of formally offering their services to "protect" the "unprotected" ladies, mainly, those that were single, widowed or otherwise traveling alone. Usually the services provided didn't involve any more strain than to call a steward to bring something for the lady, and it often provided the gentleman with a dinner companion. There wasn't any pretext for romance in offering one's services.

One of the busiest passengers involved in protecting the ladies was Colonel Archibald Gracie, who offered his services to at least six women, among them the widow Mrs. Helen Churchill Candee. Mrs. Candee was an independent, strong-willed woman and a successful author. She was so popular, in fact, no less then six gentlemen offered to "protect" her during her voyage to the United States. She was traveling home to meet her son who had been injured in an airplane accident, a rather unique event in 1912.

Colonel Gracie called Mrs. Candee and the six gentlemen, "our coterie," and they all got along so well that several of the passengers later commented on the closeness of the group. On Sunday, Mrs. Candee and one of her "protectors," Hugh Woolner, spent an hour in the gymnasium on the Boat Deck where instructor T. W. McCawley let them use the new equipment, including the stationary bicycles and mechanical horse. Afterwards they had tea in the First Class Lounge.

■ Reverend Ernest Carter, traveling Second Class, spent much of Sunday preparing for Sunday night's hymn singing in the Second Class Dining Saloon.

■ Third Class passenger Eugene Daly spent a good portion of Friday, Saturday, and Sunday out on the aft well deck playing his bagpipes.

■ Down in the Third Class common areas there was some sort of dance every night with music provided by the many musically inclined passengers.

■ The passengers followed pretty much the same routine every day. When weather permitted, many spent much of the daylight hours out on the open decks. Whatever event was occupying their time would give way to meal call, when P. W. Fletcher made his appearance with his trusty bugle.

ICE WARNINGS

The winter of 1912 was one of the mildest in more than thirty years, and this warm weather caused huge chunks of ice to break off Greenland's ice fields and drift south into the North Atlantic shipping lanes. These shipping lanes were routinely moved further south at this time of year because of the potential for icebergs, but this year even ships steaming in the southerly lanes reported an increasing amount of ice.

Some of the ice resembled huge buildings or mountains, and icebergs 100 feet tall were not uncommon. There were also miles of sheet ice (also called field ice) ten or twenty feet thick. No ship afloat could penetrate into these fields without constant low speed maneuvering. Most ships had to steer miles out of their way to get around this ice—and only in the daylight. "Growlers," or smaller icebergs that broke off from the larger ones, were also plentiful.

All in all, the huge ice pack that was floating down from Greenland that April extended more than 70 miles north-to-south and was sitting right in the middle of the main shipping lanes. The ice pack was so extensive that ships either had to stop at night or steam further south to go around it. The first option wasn't even considered by Captain Smith. His decision was to go around the ice field.

- Wireless operators Phillips and Bride received ice warnings even before *Titanic* left Southampton. Between Thursday and Saturday more than twenty ships reported ice in the area *Titanic* would be steaming. At night, most of these ships were forced to stop once they entered the area of the ice field. This was pretty much standard practice for ships of the time.

On Friday morning the *Empress of Britain*, eastbound from Halifax to Liverpool, reported ice. That afternoon, *La Touraine*, also eastbound from New York to Le Havre, reported the same thing. These and future ice warnings were picked up by *Titanic's* wireless operators, either directly or passed on from another wireless station. Wireless operators would then pass the messages to the ship's officers.

In all, there were ten warnings on Friday alone about ice in the area of 42° to 44° north latitude, an area north of where *Titanic* was supposed to cross on Sunday evening.

- On Saturday, more than a dozen ice warnings were received by Phillips and Bride, who were now fully occupied in trying to work through the backlog of messages created when the wireless broke down the night before.

- Sunday, April 14 was a beautiful day to be steaming across the North Atlantic. The weather was perfectly clear and the seas calm. The outside temperature was such that many passengers spent much of the day on the promenade decks to enjoy the sun. The air temperature wasn't overly warm, rising only to the mid-50's during the day, but for the passengers coming from the winter months in the colder climates of Europe, the temperature was almost perfect.

There was a White Star Line requirement that all liners conduct a lifeboat drill on Sunday morning after Services. For reasons that will probably remain unknown, Captain Smith decided not to hold it.

- **9:00 A.M.:** The day's first ice warning was received from the *Caronia*, eastbound from New York to Liverpool. This message was directed to *Titanic* instead of the usual general warning directed to all ships: "*Captain, Titanic—West-bound steamers report bergs, growlers and field ice in 42° N, from 49° to 51° W, April 12. Compliments, Barr.*" This warning was passed to Captain Smith, who posted it for his officers to read and take note. This message, with information two days old, had the ice in the vicinity of 42° north.

- **10:30 A.M.:** Religious services were held in the First Class Dining Saloon for all passengers, including those from Third Class.

- **11:40 A.M.:** *Noordam* signaled to *Titanic*, "*Much ice.*" No position was given.

- **12:00 NOON:** The ship's officers gathered to "shoot the sun" and take the noon position bearings. They also calculated the previous 24-hour distance of 546 miles. This information was posted in the First Class Lounge for all those taking bets on the previous day's progress.

- **1:42 P.M.:** *Baltic*, eastbound from New York to Liverpool, relayed a message:

> "*Greek steamer Athinai reports passing icebergs and large quantities of field ice today in lat[itude] 41°51' N, lon[gitude] 49°52' W. Last night we spoke German oiltank steamer Deutschland...not under control, short of coal, lat[itude] 40E42' N Lon[gitude] 55E11' W. Wishes to be reported to New York and other steamers. Wish you and Titanic all success. Commander.*"

This message was handed to Captain Smith, who in turn handed it to Bruce Ismay, with whom he was speaking at the time. Ismay put the message in his pocket instead of passing it to the bridge officers. A look at the map would have shown that *Titanic* was headed right into the center of this ice field, which by now had moved south twenty or so miles from the Friday sightings.

Another important part of this message was the phrase "not under control." It meant that the *Deutschland* was out of fuel and could not maneuver to avoid a collision with another ship, in other words it was a derelict ship in the middle of the shipping lanes, an area *Titanic* would be transiting after dark. The *Deutschland's* captain wanted it reported to all ships that he was drifting. He did not want to be run over by a passing ship in the dark.

- **1:45 P.M.:** A private message was relayed from *Amerika* through *Titanic's* wireless to the US Hydrographic Office that *Amerika* had passed several large icebergs in the same area reported by the *Athinai*. This message was not passed to the bridge.

During the afternoon the temperature had steadily declined to 43 degrees at 5:30 p.m., but between then and 7:30 p.m. it dropped another 10 degrees to 33 degrees. Because of the rapid drop in temperature, most of the passengers moved inside for the remainder of the afternoon.

- **5:20 P.M.:** There was a planned change of course that was to be made at this time to bring the ship to a more westerly direction from its current generally southwesterly direction. This imaginary spot in the middle of the North Atlantic was known as the "corner." Captain Smith held off making this turn for 30 minutes in order to bring *Titanic* about eight miles further south of its planned route in order to avoid the ice that was reported to be in the area of *Titanic's* original course. This would still put *Titanic* north of the area in which the *Deutschland* was supposed to be stopped.

- **5:50 P.M.:** Captain Smith ordered the delayed course change that the officers thought would put *Titanic* south of any of the reported ice. Although Smith did not know it, the course change would still send *Titanic* into the area of the ice field.

- **6:00 P.M.:** Lightoller relieved Wilde on the bridge. Sixth Officer Moody shared the watch with him.

- **7:15 P.M.:** Earlier during dinner, Ismay had shown the *Baltic* ice warning message to several passengers. By this time, however, Captain Smith had retrieved it and posted it in the chart room.

- **7:15 P.M.:** It was dark outside and very cold, just a couple of degrees above freezing. First Officer Murdoch ordered lamp trimmer Samuel Hemming to secure the forward forecastle hatch and the skylight over the crew's galley. This was to prevent light from reflecting up into the eyes of the lookouts in the crow's nest. They were now on alert to spot any ice.

- **7:30 P.M.:** A message was intercepted from *Californian* to *Antillian*: "*To Captain, Antillian: Six-thirty p.m...latitude 42° 3' N, longitude 49° 9' W, Three large bergs, 5 miles to the southward of us. Regards. Lord.*" The message was delivered by Marconi operator Bride to one of the officers on the bridge. Later, he could not remember which officer had received the message.

This message wasn't passed on to Captain Smith, either. He was down in the à la carte restaurant having dinner with the Widener's and several other First Class passengers. Although Smith's delayed course change was supposed to take *Titanic* south of the ice, the ship was still steaming directly into it, and the ice was only 50 miles away.

- **7:30 P.M.:** Lightoller "shot the stars" and gave the information to Boxhall, who updated the plot. If anyone had remembered to mark *Californian's* warning on the chart, it would have been obvious that *Titanic* was entering dangerous waters. *Titanic* was steaming at 266°, or almost due west. Remaining on this course, *Titanic* would encounter ice about eight miles north of the extreme southern edge of the 70 mile long ice field.

- **8:00 P.M.:** Lightoller decided to check Moody's navigational skills by having him plot the estimated time *Titanic* would enter the area of the ice field. Moody estimated around 11:00 p.m., but Lightoller wasn't happy with that answer. He had already figured the time to be around 9:30 p.m. Lightoller based his assumptions on experience and knowledge that wherever there was an ice field, individual icebergs would extend out for miles in all directions.

Titanic was still running four hours behind schedule. Had it been on time, *Titanic* would not have begun encountering ice in the dark at 9:30 p.m. but in the early evening twilight around 5:30 p.m.

- **8:40 P.M.:** While Reverend Carter was conducting his evening hymn singing down in the Second Class Dining Saloon, the temperature continued to drop. Lightoller ordered the ship's carpenter to check the fresh water supply because there was a good chance that it might freeze.

- **8:55 P.M.:** Captain Smith returned to the bridge after his dinner with the Widener's and engaged Lightoller in a conversation, speaking about the weather. Lightoller later reported:

> *"There is not much wind,"* said Captain Smith.
> *"No, it is a flat calm, as a matter of fact,"* I replied.
> *"A flat calm. Yes, quite flat,"* replied Smith.

> *"I said that it was a pity the wind had not kept up with us whilst we were going through the ice region. Of course he knew I meant the water ripples breaking on the base of the berg. . . I remember saying, 'Of course there will be a certain amount of reflected light from the bergs,' with which the Captain agreed. Even with the blue side toward us, we both agreed that there would still be the white outline."*

- **9:00 P.M.:** Captain Smith updated the chart to reflect the 7:30 p.m. position fix Lightoller had taken. This should have allowed Smith to see the location of the ice field that *Titanic* was rapidly approaching. Whether he realized it or not is unclear.

- **9:30 P.M.:** Captain Smith retired to his cabin, telling Lightoller,

> *"If it becomes at all doubtful let me know at once. I shall be just inside."*

- **9:30 P.M.:** Lightoller sent another message to the crow's nest to keep a sharp lookout for ice. It was now about the time that Lightoller figured they would be entering the area of the ice field. It was extremely dark. Had the lookouts and ship's officers been able to see them, they would have seen dozens of icebergs filling the horizon to the north, south and west of them.

- **9:40 P.M.:** Message received by Jack Phillips in the wireless room:

> *"From Mesaba to Titanic. In latitude 42° N to 41° 25' N, longitude 49° W to longitude 50° 30' W, saw much heavy pack ice and great number large icebergs, also field ice, weather good, clear."*

This message did not get delivered to the bridge. Phillips was working alone because Bride had gone to bed to rest for a while before he relieved Phillips at midnight. *Titanic* had just recently come within range of the Cape Race land station, and Phillips was extremely busy with all of the commercial traffic to be sent to them. The ice message was laid on a desk by the door of the wireless office and a weight placed on top of it to keep it from going astray. Unfortunately, *Titanic* was already inside the area described in *Mesaba's* message, and Captain Smith knew nothing about it.

- **10:00 P.M.:** Murdoch replaced Lightoller on the bridge for the next four-hour watch. Before returning to his cabin to sleep, Lightoller made his rounds through the ship. He observed that the temperature was continuing to drop and it was now 31 degrees. Down in the First Class Lounge, he found many of the passengers listening to Wallace Hartley and the orchestra while others were engrossed in one of the several card games.

- **10:00 P.M.:** High up in the crow's nest on the foremast, lookouts Frederick Fleet and Reginald Lee replaced George Symons and Archie Jewell. Word was passed to Fleet and Lee to watch for icebergs.

The crow's nest was an open platform, exposed to the wind and the cold. The air temperature by this time had dropped to 31 degrees and, combined with the 22.5-knot speed of the ship, the lookouts had a real problem keeping their eyes open as the cold air stung and burned them. The lookouts were probably spending as much time trying to keep warm as looking for icebergs.

The binoculars the lookouts should have had with them had been unknowingly locked up in Lightoller's cabin by David Blair. In his haste to depart the ship before leaving Southampton, Blair had taken the keys to the cabinet with him. Normally, the lookouts would not have been using the binoculars in the dark anyway. They were only used once the lookouts had spotted something that required additional attention, because the narrow view of the binoculars makes them useless when you are trying to scan the entire horizon at night.

There was no moon, no haze and the sky was completely full of stars. The water was absolutely flat. Anything ahead of the ship would be difficult to see because there would be no wave action against the object to provide a warning.

Ironically, the worst place to try and detect an iceberg ahead of the ship under these conditions was from the crow's nest. Located more than 100 feet above the surface of the water, the lookouts would have had the disadvantage of looking down at the sea, and any object would be even harder to spot because it would tend to blend into the dark background of the water. A much better location for the lookouts would have been from the bow of the ship, looking straight ahead and up to try to see any break in the pattern of the stars in the background.

- **10:15 P.M.:** Somewhere northwest of *Titanic*, at a position logged as 42° 5' N, 50° 7' W, Captain Stanley Lord of the steamship *Californian* noticed a glow along the western horizon and concluded it was caused by an unseen ice field. Lord ordered *"All back emergency"* and turned his ship hard a port to turn the ship to starboard. Within moments *Californian* slowed to a stop with its bow facing east-north-east, or almost opposite the direction it had been steaming. *Californian* had almost run headlong into the ice—and then with the turn to starboard, she had almost skidded into it. Lord ordered the engines stopped but had steam kept up all night just in case the ship had to move to keep from bumping into the ice surrounding the ship on three sides.

- **10:30 P.M.:** A visual message by signal lamp was received from *Rappahannock* that it had just passed through a huge ice field, in the dark. What *Rappahannock* did not report, however, was that she had collided with an iceberg and damaged her rudder.

- **10:30 P.M.:** Before leaving the bridge of *Californian*, Captain Lord thought he saw the light of an approaching steamer from the south and east, but it was so far away Third Officer Charles V. Groves thought the light was from a star.

- **10:35 P.M.:** *Parisian* warned *Titanic* of ice, and then its wireless operator shut down his system for the night.

- **10:55 P.M.:** Captain Lord on *Californian*, still thinking he had seen the lights of a steamer to the southeast, asked his wireless operator Cyril Evans if there were any other vessels in the vicinity. *"Only the Titanic,"* replied Evans. *"That's not the Titanic,"* replied Lord, *"she's a vessel close to us in size. You'd better contact Titanic, however, and let her know we're stopped in ice."*

- **10:55 P.M.:** Cyril Evans of *Californian* sent a message to *Titanic*, using the more familiar 'old man' introduction instead of the official address of 'Captain, Titanic': *"We are stopped and surrounded by ice."*

- **10:55 P.M.:** Before the message was completed, Jack Phillips on *Titanic* broke in with *"Keep out! Shut up! You're jamming my signal. I'm working Cape Race."* Having been rebuffed, Evans made no further attempt to contact *Titanic*.

- **11:30 P.M.:** As far as the passengers on *Titanic* were concerned, the evening hours passed quietly. Most of the passengers were now in their cabins and asleep. Up in the First Class Lounge and Smoking Room, a large group of men were involved in card games, reading, or conversation. It was now 30 degrees outside and the water temperature had dropped to 28 degrees. Except for a few diehard passengers who were walking the decks, the two lookouts up in the crows nest, and Murdoch on the bridge, everyone was inside keeping warm.

- **11:35 P.M.:** Cyril Evans on *Californian* listened to some of Phillip's messages to Cape Race. Extremely tired after another eighteen-hour day as *Californian's* only wireless operator, Evans shut down his wireless for the night and did not bother to rewind the detector system, figuring he would do that in the morning. Without the detector being rewound, there would be no way to detect incoming messages or to determine if anyone was sending messages to *Californian*. After his fourth 18-hour day in a row, he might be forgiven for not resetting the detector. Most operators did not reset their detector before going to bed because the resulting noise prevented them from getting any sleep.

■   **11:35 P.M.:** High up in the crow's nest, lookouts Fleet and Lee were bitterly cold and they were looking forward to being relieved in twenty-five minutes. Then, off in the distance and directly ahead they detected a slight haze on the horizon. Both men strained to see what was behind the mist. For several crucial minutes they tried to determine what the haze indicated. Binoculars at this time would have been of great use.

■   **11:40 P.M.:** Still staring into the mist, Fleet finally saw something. His reflexes took over. Fleet grabbed the cord for the crow's nest 16-inch warning bell and gave it three sharp tugs. He grabbed the phone connecting the crow's nest to the phone on the starboard side of the bridge and urgently rang its bell. Sixth Officer Moody picked it up. The brief conversation must have chilled his blood:

> *"Are you there!"* shouted Fleet.
> *"Yes. What do you see?"* replied Moody.
> *"Iceberg right ahead!"* shouted Fleet.
> *"Thank you,"* was Moody's polite reply.

■   Disaster would strike *Titanic* in less than thirty seconds.

"CQD...MGY, CQD...MGY. 41° 46' N, 50° 14' W."

CHAPTER 11

ENCOUNTER

750 MILES SOUTHEAST OF HALIFAX, NOVA SCOTIA

Nine-tenths of an iceberg's mass is under water.

What can be seen of an iceberg is only about 10 percent of its actual size. As this underwater mass melts, the iceberg gets top heavy and turns over, exposing the portion that had been underwater. When this happens, the water in the newly-exposed portion makes the iceberg very dark—and almost black. This phenomenon is called "blue ice." In the dark, blue ice is virtually impossible to see.

It only takes a few hours for the water in the exposed portion to either drain out or freeze, at which time the portion above water turns white again. The various spurs protruding from the iceberg below the surface are rock hard—harder than the side of any ship that might brush against it.

The iceberg that Fleet and Lee saw ahead of *Titanic* was apparently one that had recently turned over. And it was directly in the ship's path.

■ Fleet and Lee looked on in horror at the iceberg, which seemed to grow larger by the second as *Titanic* steamed toward it at more than 22 knots. To the lookouts, the mountain of ice looked like a black mass surrounded by a white mist. It appeared to be slightly taller than the crow's nest.

In almost the same instant that Moody said, *"Thank You,"* to Fleet, he turned to Murdoch, who had just come in from the starboard bridge wing. Moody repeated Fleet's message, *"Iceberg right ahead!"*

In an instant Murdoch was fully aware of pending disaster. He rushed to the engine room telegraph and ordered the engines stopped and then reversed, while at the same time ordering quartermaster Robert Hichens to turn the rudder *"Hard-a-starboard!"* Murdoch obviously hoped his prompt action would prevent a head-on collision with the iceberg.

Hichens turned the wheel as fast as he could until it stopped turning, and waited for the bow of the ship to begin her long swing to port. Time, at least for Fleet, Lee, Murdoch, and Hichens, had suddenly stopped.

- Murdoch did not order the engines reversed. Instead, he ordered them to stop, and then go into reverse, which consumed additional time. To reverse the engines while they are running, which is called a "crash stop," would in all likelihood have ruined them. (A modern, though not completely perfect, analogy would be throwing the transmission of your automobile into reverse while moving forward.) At this point, Murdoch was trying to miss the iceberg, not destroy the ship's engines.

- Up until 1928 when the rules were changed, turning directions were based upon the direction a rudder tiller would have to be moved to make a vessel go in a given direction. Turning the tiller to starboard (or right) would make the rudder go to port (or left), which would turn the vessel to port. Thus, the command "Hard-a-starboard" meant to turn the tiller to the starboard in order to make the rudder and ship turn to port. To further confuse matters, in order to turn *Titanic* to port, the command "Hard-a-starboard" was given, but Hichens actually had to turn the wheel to port. After 1928, this process and command were reversed, so in a similar situation today, the order would have been "hard-a-port" to turn the ship to port.

- While Hichens was turning the wheel, Murdoch hurried over to the aft wheelhouse bulkhead to the switches that closed the watertight doors. He briefly pushed the warning bell to provide an alarm for anyone who might be near the doors, switched on the power, and then turned the lever to activate the iron doors. Just above the tank top, far down inside the ship, the fifteen electrically operated watertight doors began to close.

- With the rudder hard over and the engines slowing first to a stop and then into full reverse, *Titanic* began her slow turn to port. The ship turned two points of the compass, or 22.5 degrees, and it seemed that she would miss the ice. At least Fleet and Lee thought so. The iceberg kept growing in size, but the bow was now pointing away from it.

- The huge mass of ice passed silently by the bow and then slipped beyond the crow's nest platform, where the top of the iceberg towered 25 feet above Fleet's head. Within a few second it disappeared down the starboard side. There was absolute silence on the deck as the iceberg slid past, soon followed by the sound of ice falling on the deck. Several large chunks of it fell onto the forecastle and forward Well Deck, where it shattered into hundreds of smaller pieces.

- Some thirty-seven seconds ticked off the clock from the time Fleet first spotted the iceberg until it passed his crow's nest position. During those few seconds, *Titanic* traveled about 446 yards, or 1,338 feet. Had Fleet seen the iceberg just five seconds sooner, or had *Titanic* been steaming just two knots slower, the encounter with the ice would likely have been nothing more than a near miss—and maybe Captain Smith would have ordered his ship to stop for the night.

- The iceberg bumped and scraped its way along several hundred feet of the forward portion of the starboard side of the ship as *Titanic* grounded her iron-plated hull along a protruding shelf of rock hard ice.

- Another rock hard protrusion below the water caused the riveted plates to separate at their joints, popping the rivets as the hull scraped by. The ship was still moving forward at about 21 knots because not enough time had passed for Murdoch's "stop and reverse" order to take effect. At this speed, Titanic would have bumped her way along 300 feet of rock hard ice in about 10 seconds.

As the bow approached the iceberg, Murdoch ordered the wheel turned hard to port (turn the bow to the starboard, or right) in order to try to get the ship to "port-around" the iceberg, a movement similar to trying to fishtail an automobile around an object. Had Murdoch not done this, *Titanic's* initial turn to port would have caused the hull to scrape along the iceberg for the entire length of the ship. This may have flooded all of the compartments instead of just the first five. Flooding them all would have sent the doomed *Titanic* to the bottom within less than an hour.

As *Titanic* began scraping against the iceberg, the turn to the starboard meant the bow of the ship was now turning toward it. Although this does not sound like something you would want to do, in fact this maneuver prevented all of the watertight compartments from being flooded simultaneously.

To those few men now paying close attention, it looked as though the ship was going to miss the iceberg completely. The bow, after all, had turned 22 degrees to port. Ships, however, are steered by the stern and not the bow. While the bow was drifting to the left, the stern was still moving toward the right—heading toward the iceberg. This is why the port-around order issued by Murdoch was so vitally important. In all likelihood, his quick thinking may have saved hundreds who would otherwise have perished.

- The weight of *Titanic* sliding across an ice shelf caused the iceberg to tilt toward the ship, which is why there was damage below the waterline and there was a large amount of ice from the top of the iceberg dumped onto the ship's deck.

Sliding across the ice shelf also caused a considerable amount of damage to the bottom of the ship, which was protected by the watertight double bottom. Reports of damage by the crew indicated that the Tank Top deck was bent and twisted far out of shape by the collision, which clearly indicates damage to the double bottom.

- The iceberg passed the bridge and disappeared into the darkness off the stern. As it went by the crow's nest, Fleet and Lee finally saw a tip of white high above their heads at the very top of the iceberg. Forty-seven seconds had elapsed since the iceberg was spotted. Murdoch had the time logged. It was 11:40 p.m., April 14, 1912. *Titanic* would only live for another two hours and forty minutes. Fifteen hundred people were about to perish.

- In addition to the damage to the sealed compartments below the Tank Top deck in the double bottom, *Titanic* suffered an intermittent gash, or rippling of the plates, about 300 feet long and about 1/2" wide along the riveted seam some twelve feet above the keel. The total area actually opened to the sea was probably less then twelve square feet, which was enough to allow several tons of water to enter the ship every minute.

The gash opened the forepeak, number one, two and three holds, number 6 Boiler Room, and extended for about four feet into number 5 Boiler Room. *Titanic* was designed to survive flooding in four forward compartments and remain afloat, or five forward compartments with enough time to reasonably affect the evacuation of the passengers and crew. However, six compartments were flooding, although the four-foot gash in Boiler Room number 5 was small enough that the engineers could pump the water out as fast at it came in. In any case, the flooding of five compartments was more than *Titanic* was designed to withstand and remain afloat.

The great liner was doomed, though no one yet realized that fact.

A THOUSAND MARBLES

Depending on where they were at the time, survivors would tell some interesting stories about how the collision felt and sounded.

- In the First Class Dining Saloon on D Deck, several stewards were sitting around a table talking when a faint grinding sound came from somewhere deep within the ship. Not much of a jar, but enough to rattle the silverware that was being set for breakfast the next morning.

- First Class passenger James B. McGough had the porthole in his stateroom open. As the iceberg passed by, chunks of ice fell into his room.

- Mauritz Bjornstrom-Steffansson, a First Class passenger having a drink in the First Class Smoking Room, felt a slight jar but not enough to cause him to get up and investigate its cause.

- Colonel Archibald Gracie was asleep in his cabin, C51, which was six decks directly above Boiler Room 6. The jolt awakened him, and he climbed out of bed and opened his cabin door. He did not see anyone. More ominously, he could no longer hear the faint thump of the giant ship's engines. All he heard was the sound of escaping steam.

- A *"ripping sound"* awakened Mrs. Walter Stephenson and her sister Miss Elizabeth Eustis. When they heard noise in the corridor, they decided to get fully dressed and go up to the Boat Deck.

- Third Class passenger 14-year-old Miss Jamila Nicola-Yarred was asleep and felt a slight bump. Her 12-year-old brother Elias was still asleep, but she woke him up and had him investigate. Before too long they left their room and followed several others up to the Boat Deck—pretty smart for a couple of children. They were traveling, without any adult supervision, from Lebanon to Jacksonville, Florida.

- Miss Margaret Hays was in bed and did not feel anything until the engines stopped running. The absence of the "thumping" sound from the engines awakened many people who had not felt the collision.

- Third Class passenger Victor Sunderland felt a slight jar and heard a noise *"similar to that a basket of coal would make if dropped on an iron plate."* Victor and some of his cabin mates made their way up onto the forward Well Deck, where they saw ice on the deck. The mystery solved, the men walked back to their cabin several decks down near the bow because they did not think anything serious was wrong. Their room was only two decks directly above the forward hold—which at that moment was rapidly filling with water.

- When the ship struck the iceberg, Quartermaster George Rowe was on duty high on the Docking Bridge at the stern of the ship, trying his best to stay warm. He felt a change in the motion of the engines, and then thought he saw the sails of a windjammer passing along the starboard side. Another glance showed it to be an iceberg more than 100 feet tall. It vanished into the dark night as quickly as it had appeared.

- Third Class passenger Miss Carla Jensen was sharing a cabin with three other single women. They all felt a bump, but after some discussion about it they went back to sleep. Carla's uncle, Niels Jensen, later awakened her, told her dress, and she followed him up to the boat deck.

The other three ladies opted to stay in bed. Neither they nor Niels Jensen were ever seen again.

■   Marjorie Newell felt the collision, but before she and her sister Madeleine could get dressed to investigate, their father knocked on their door and told them, "*Get up, girls and get dressed. Put on your warmest clothes and follow me.*" They did, and they survived; their father did not.

■   Mrs. Ida Hippach heard someone say they had hit an iceberg, so she decided to go out on deck to take a look. One of the officers saw her and told her to, "*Go back to bed. You'll catch cold.*" Ida ignored the command and she and her daughter Jean went up to the Boat Deck; both survived.

■   One seaman on duty outside the seaman's mess said it felt like a heavy vibration, a rumbling noise that continued for about ten seconds.

■   Several crewmen thought an anchor had been dropped and the chain was dragging along the hull. Others believed the ship had thrown a propeller.

■   Passenger Lawrence Beesley, who was down in cabin D56, later reported that,

> "*No sound of a crash or of anything else; no sense of shock, no jar that felt like one heavy body meeting another. . . nothing more than what seemed to be an extra heave of the ship's engines and a slight dancing movement of my bunk mattress.*"

■   According to Mrs. J. Stuart White in cabin C32, "*It was as though we went over about a thousand marbles.*"

■   First Class passenger Henry Blank was in the First Class Smoking Room when he felt "*a slight jar.*" Someone called out to the men in the room, "*Hey boys, we've just grazed an iceberg!*" The men went out on deck to see it, but the iceberg had already disappeared into the darkness. Disappointed, they went back to their card game.

■   Miss Sarah Daniels, maid to Mrs. Hudson Allison, felt a bump and got up and dressed to see what was happening. She never went back to her cabin. Instead, the smart young woman marched straight to the Boat Deck and climbed into Lifeboat 8.

■   Miss Caroline Bonnell and relative Natalie Wick felt the collision and went up on deck. Caroline said to Natalie, "*Well, thank goodness, Natalie, we are going to see our iceberg at last!*"

■ Third Class passenger Edward Dorking was playing cards down in the public room, only a few decks away from the site of the collision. *"We were thrown from the bench on which we were sitting. The shock was accompanied by a grinding noise."*

■ Third Class passenger Gunnar Tenglin felt a thud and, having just removed his shoes, went out on deck to check out the source. He never went back to his room to get his shoes; he climbed into a lifeboat without them.

■ Third Class passenger Carl Jansson also went out on deck without his shoes. When he went back to his cabin to get them, the cabin was already filling with water. He, too, made do without his shoes that night, and suffered severe frostbite as a result.

■ Mrs. Arthur Wells awoke to a tremendous jolt. She heard someone yell, *"Dress quickly: there's some trouble I believe, but I don't know what it is."* She did dress, then dressed her two young children, and went up to the Boat Deck, where they climbed into a lifeboat.

■ Miss Marion Wright said the collision sounded like a *"huge crash of glass."*

■ Crewman Albert M. Haines heard air escaping from the forepeak tank and reported to Chief Officer Wilde that the tank was filling with water.

■ Steward Alfred Theissinger was on C Deck when the collision occurred. He saw a fireman running past, shouting, *"There is water forward!"* and someone else shouted, *"All watertight doors shut!"* Thessinger went to his station near the mailroom, where he could look down and see water pouring in while the mail clerks struggled to move the mail sacks out of the way.

■ Steward James Johnson thought they had dropped a propeller blade, and told his friends that this would certainly mean *"Another Belfast trip!"* in reference to *Olympic's* two trips back to the shipyard. Second Class steward Walter Williams later reported, *"The joker [Johnson] went down with the ship."* This was not true. James Johnson survived.

■ Night baker Walter Belford noticed the collision because several pans of freshly baked rolls were knocked off the top of a cabinet and went crashing to the deck.

▪ Second Officer Lightoller and Third Officer Pitman were just going to sleep when they felt the collision. Both went out on deck, but neither man saw any alarm on the bridge, and so both went back to their rooms where they knew they could be found if needed.

▪ Harland and Wolff manager Thomas Andrews barely felt the collision and did not know there was a problem until Captain Smith summoned him to the bridge.

▪ Bruce Ismay also felt the jolt and decided to head up to the bridge to see what caused it.

▪ Fireman George Beauchamp was on duty in Boiler Room 6 when he was told to shut the dampers to the boilers in order to cut off the air supply. He was still performing his duty when the icy water reached his waist. Someone told him to leave the room, and he was just able to go through the watertight door before it closed.

▪ Leading fireman Frederick Barrett was also in Boiler Room 6 when the side of the ship was opened up and a flood of ice water poured in. Within moments there was eight feet of water in the compartment, six feet of which was below the iron grating he was standing on. The watertight doors started to close and two crewmen (including George Beauchamp) squeezed through, but Barrett had to climb the emergency escape ladder up to E Deck and then down a similar ladder into Boiler Room number 5. En route he ran into chief engineer Bell and told him what happened. There were no other survivors from Boiler Room 6.

▪ Esther Hart felt a bump, as did her husband. He dressed and went out on deck, returned a short time later, and told Mrs. Hart to dress herself and little Eva.

▪ Moments after the ship struck the iceberg, Boxhall stepped onto the bridge in time to see Captain Smith arrive, and address Murdoch,

> *"What have we struck?"* Smith asked Murdoch.

> *"An iceberg, Sir. I hard-a-starboarded and reversed the engines and I was going to hard-a-port around it, but she was too close. I could not do any more. I have closed the watertight doors."*

> *"The watertight doors are closed? And you have rung the warning bell?"* asked Smith.

> *"Yes, sir!"* was the reply.

DAMAGE CONTROL

Smith and Murdoch walked to the starboard bridge wing and looked aft to have a look at the iceberg, but it had already disappeared into the darkness.

Smith then sent Boxhall below to check on passengers and crew down in the bow area, and to see if there was any damage. Boxhall returned quickly and reported that he had gone down a few decks and had seen no injuries or sea water. Since Boxhall had only gone down to E Deck, he was correct on both counts. The news was good, and probably triggered a sigh of relief from the captain. Unfortunately, it was also wrong. Boxhall's report was the last time in his life that Smith would hear good news.

While Boxhall was away, Smith (still unaware of any major damage) conferred with Murdoch on the bridge. If there was significant damage to the ship, the best course of action would be to steam toward Halifax, the closest port. From there, the passengers could be sent by train to New York City. By this time *Titanic* was fully stopped and facing northeast because of the port-around move Murdoch had ordered.

- Although Murdoch had ordered "stop" and then "full astern," by this time the propellers had just begun turning in reverse, and so the ship had not yet begun moving backward.

Cavitation, the effect of air bubbles caused when a propeller is stopped and then reversed, had set in. The reversing of the propellers and forward motion of the ship had caused a dead space in the water and millions of bubbles, which prevented the propellers and rudder from doing their work.

It is very possible that Murdoch's order to reverse the engines did more harm than good. The bubbles created did not allow for the reversing propellers to slow the ship down significantly, and also prevented the rudder from performing its vital function. If Murdoch had simply ordered "Hard-a-starboard" and NOT reversed the engines, *Titanic* might have missed the iceberg because the rudder would have been more effective.

- Chief engineer Bell next reported to the bridge, and Smith ordered him to sound the ship (check for damage). When Bell left, Smith went into the Marconi office and told Phillips and Bride, as Bride later reported,

> "We've struck an iceberg and I'm having an inspection made to tell what has been done to us. You had better get ready to send out a call for assistance, but don't send it until I tell you."

■   After Smith returned to the bridge, the next to arrive was carpenter John H. Hutchinson. His news was not good: the ship was taking water fast. He was followed by postal clerk John R. J. Smith, who reported that the mailroom was flooding.

■   Captain Smith dispatched Boxhall on another tour, and as he was leaving, Ismay and Andrews showed up on the bridge. After conferring with Ismay, Smith ordered that the engines started and the ship to move forward at 'Half Ahead.'

■   The decision to move the ship was one of the most crucial, and perhaps *the* most crucial, commands spoken by Smith that night. Almost certainly it had the most effect on the stability and rapid sinking of *Titanic*.

By the time the ship had finally coasted to a stop, with her bow facing northeast, tons of water were pouring into the hull. Some of the watertight compartments on the starboard side of the double bottom were ruptured because of the slide across the ice. In Boiler Room 5, however, the pumps were pumping the water out as fast as it came in. The pumps in the other ruptured compartments helped neutralize the flooding. *Titanic* was going to sink, make no mistake about it. But it was going to sink slowly enough for help to arrive in time to save her passengers and crew.

■   We will never know for sure because this point was specifically avoided in the court hearings yet to be held. But the conversation between Smith and Ismay ended with the order by Smith to steam forward again. This decision was made before the full extent of the damage was known, and Smith likely would not have made the decision to begin the move without someone—perhaps Ismay—making the decision for him.

■   After Smith ordered *Titanic* to move "Half Ahead," the forward motion of the ship helped 'scoop' water into the forward compartments and the pressure ruptured some of the Tank Top decking. The result was a rapid increase in the amount of water that poured into the ship.

Although we do not know why Smith or Ismay made the decision to steam ahead, it probably had something to do with getting the ship underway to calm the passengers and make some progress toward Halifax. If so, it was not fully thought through. It was also a fatal decision.

■   At this point Smith decided to conduct his own tour with Andrews and Hutchinson, so they set off, using the crew passageways so they would not alarm the passengers. The trio returned within ten minutes with enough information to enable them to predict the worst. When he returned to the bridge, Smith ordered the engines stopped for the last time.

- Fifteen minutes after he started on his second trip, Boxhall returned to the bridge with more information about the damage he had seen. Smith and Andrews had also just returned. Smith ordered Boxhall to work out the ship's exact position. Ismay asked, *"Do you think the ship is seriously damaged?"* Smith replied, *"I'm afraid she is."*

- Smith, Ismay, and Andrews huddled in the chart room behind the bridge to discuss the deteriorating situation. Six compartments were flooding. In less then ten minutes, fourteen feet of water had poured into the first five compartments. There was nothing that could be done to save the ship. The pumps would keep the water out of the sixth compartment, Boiler Room 5, but eventually the bow of the ship would sink so low that the water would lap over the top of the watertight bulkhead between Boiler Rooms 6 and 5, which would then flood Boiler Room 5. This process would be repeated from compartment to compartment until the ship sank. *Titanic* was doomed. And by now, some of the time *Titanic* had left had been squandered away because of the decision to restart the engines.

    In the company of Ismay, Smith asked Andrews, *"How long have we?"* Andrews replied, *"An hour and a half. Possibly two. Not much longer."*

- Boxhall worked out the ships' current position. Using the 7:30 p.m. stellar position, his own guess of the ship's speed at 22 knots, and the course *Titanic* had been on since 5:50 p.m., he figured the position to be 41° 46' N, 50° 14' W.

    There were some errors in Boxhall's calculations. First, *Titanic's* speed had been 22.5 knots. Second, it is unknown if Boxhall had allowed for the one knot speed of the current *Titanic* had been passing through since the last star sighting. These and other errors could have placed the ship as much as four miles south and six miles east of the reported position. This error would cause many problems when the issue of the position of *Californian* relative to *Titanic* was debated.

- Boxhall handed Smith a piece of paper with the position on it, and the captain walked down to the wireless office and gave it to Marconi operator Jack Phillips. He asked Phillips to send out a call for assistance. As Bride would later report, Smith said, *"Send a call for assistance . . . [send] the regulation international call for help, just that."*

    While Phillips sent the CQD (the distress signal), Harold Bride reported,

"We joked while he did so. All of us made light of the disaster. . . . The humor of the situation appealed to me, and I cut in with a little remark that made us all laugh, including the captain. Send 'S.O.S.' I said, it's the new call, and it may be your last chance to send it. . . "

■ **12:05 A.M., MONDAY, APRIL 15, 1912:** Just 25 minutes after the collision with the iceberg and 30 minutes after Cyril Evans on *Californian* shut down his wireless system and went to bed, the first call for assistance was sent out by Phillips:

CQD . . . MGY, CQD . . . MGY. 41° 46' N, 50° 14' W.

(CQD was the international distress signal, and operators said it stood for "Come Quick, Danger." Although the present day SOS was also in use in 1912, having been adopted just a few years earlier, it was not yet universally used. Phillips began with the universal CQD. MGY was *Titanic's* call sign.)

Several ships and the land station at Cape Race heard the message, but each heard a different location due to atmospheric interference. All of them, however, got the correct location on subsequent transmissions.

CARPATHIA

At noon on Thursday, April 11, about the time *Titanic* was steaming into Queenstown, the Cunard Liner *Carpathia* departed New York bound for several Mediterranean ports with 743 passengers.

■ *Carpathia* had only one wireless operator, twenty-one year old Harold Cottam. He worked whatever hours were required to keep up with the messages inbound or outbound from the passengers. By midnight Sunday, he had been on duty for seventeen hours with only a short lunch break. Cottam was tired and ready to go to bed, but he was waiting for confirmation of a message he had sent to the liner *Parisian*. While waiting for the reply through his headphones, Cottam removed his shoes and some of his clothes.

Still waiting for *Parisian*, Cottam switched over to the Cape Cod land station to see if there was anything interesting going on, and heard Cape Cod transmitting some commercial messages to *Titanic*. Because *Titanic* wasn't responding, Cottam copied several of the messages, figuring he would transmit them to *Titanic* in the morning.

It was now more than thirty minutes after Cottam had planned to shut down for the night, but because he was still waiting for a reply from the *Parisian*, he switched over to *Titanic's* frequency. Hearing nothing being transmitted, he sent the following message, using *Carpathia's* call letters MPA:

> *"I say, old man, do you know there is a batch of messages coming through for you from MCC (Cape Cod)?"*

Phillips: (MGY), *broke into Cottam's message:*

> *"Come at once. We have struck a berg. It's a CQD, OM [Old Man]. Position 41° 46' N, 50° 14' W."*

Cottam: *"Shall I tell my captain? Do you require assistance?*

Phillips: *"Yes. Come quick."*

Carpathia was 58 miles from *Titanic*.

■ Cottam grabbed his jacket, ran up to the bridge, and reported the message to the watch officer, First Officer H. V. Dean. Dean, pushing Cottam ahead of him and down the stairs, burst into Captain Arthur H. Rostron's cabin without knocking.

Rostron, who had just gone to bed and was irritated by the intrusion, demanded to know what was happening. Dean ordered Cottam to repeat the message.

> Cottam: *"Sir, I have just received an urgent distress call from Titanic. She requires immediate assistance. . . . She has struck an iceberg and is sinking. Her position is Position 41° 46' N, 50° 14' W."*

Rostron: *"Are you certain?"*

Cottam: *"Yes, sir."*

Rostron went to the chart room and quickly figured out the course, distance and time to *Titanic. Carpathia* should be at *Titanic's* side in about four and one-half hours, or around 4:45 a.m. if she steamed at her maximum rated speed of 14.5 knots.

■ **12:05 A.M.:** On the bridge of *Titanic*, Smith, Ismay, Andrews, and some of the officers were discussing the status of the ship. In the 25 minutes since striking the iceberg, all five of the forward holds were almost full of water, and water was already appearing on F Deck, coming up through the open stairways from G Deck.

- Down in the mailroom on the Orlop Deck, the five postal clerks struggled to move some of the 3,300 sacks of mail up one deck to the post office on G Deck. Once the water started flooding that deck, they gave up the attempt and concentrated moving 200 sacks of registered mail to the empty passenger cabins on D Deck.

- Back up on the bridge, Smith gave the order to uncover the lifeboats, assigning Chief Officer Wilde the responsibility. Wilde immediately delegated the work to Second Officer Lightoller. Lightoller went to Lifeboat 4 on the port side and began removing the canvas cover while waiting for some crewmen to show up. He proceeded to each boat as additional crewmen arrived, giving instructions with hand signals because of the noise from the escaping steam coming from the funnels. Shortly, First Officer Murdoch proceeded to the port side and started to gather crewmen to uncover the lifeboats along that side of the ship.

- Harold Bride reported about this time that,

  > "The Carpathia answered our signal, and we told her our position, and said we were sinking by the head . . . in five minutes the operator returned and told us Carpathia was putting about and heading for us."

- **12:10 A.M.:** Captain Rostron ordered *Carpathia* turned northwest at full-speed. All off duty firemen, trimmers, and stokers were ordered to their workstations to help feed the boiler fires. Before long, *Carpathia* would be steaming in excess of 17 knots, almost 20 percent faster than she had ever steamed before.

  Rostron ordered four extra lookouts posted on the bow and had every officer report to the bridge. There he posted the officers with orders to look for icebergs. Rostron had all unnecessary equipment and the ship's heating system turned off so that every once of steam could be fed into the engines.

  As *Carpathia* steamed north toward the ice field, the temperature began to drop. With the heat turned off, many of the passengers inquired about the cold, but they were told that the lack of heat was just a temporary problem. For some passengers this was the first indication they had that something unusual was taking place.

  Meanwhile, Rostron ordered that all of *Carpathia's* lifeboats be readied for launching, at which time he told his officers that the reason for this was *Titanic* had struck an iceberg and was sinking.

  Rostron then issued a whole series of orders:

Every crewman was to report to duty at his normal duty station, and each was to be fed and served all the hot coffee he wanted to help keep him awake and warm;

Crewmembers from the steward's department were to gather up all of the blankets, towels and extra crew's clothing to hand out to survivors and to prepare all the public areas with beds;

The cooks were to prepare hot coffee and food for survivors;

All Third Class passengers were to be placed into one section of the Third Class area so that there would be room for *Titanic's* survivors;

All empty cabins and all officers cabins, including Rostron's, were to be readied. All cabins with passengers but with empty beds were to be identified so that the empties could be utilized;

There were three ship's doctors on board *Carpathia*, an Englishman, Italian, and Hungarian. Each was told to prepare for the arrival of survivors, one doctor each for the First, Second and Third class passengers;

After the lifeboats were readied, every gangway door was opened and all stewards, pursers, and extra crewmen were to remain by them to help people onto the ship. At each gangway, the crew slung a chair which could be lowered so that survivors could sit in it while being lifted onto the ship;

The crew readied canvas bags and cargo nets to be used to haul children aboard;

The crew readied ladders for survivors to climb on and hung powerful lights over the sides;

Oil buckets were lined up at the forward toilets. If the seas were rough, oil would be poured into the toilets and dumped into the sea to help calm it.

■ As steam was diverted from the cabin heat to the engines, even more passengers complained about the drop in temperature. They also noticed the increased speed and that the ship seemed to be pounding through the water. Some even noticed they were steaming in a new direction. Stewards were placed in every corridor to answer questions without giving out too much information, and they asked all of the passengers to remain in their cabins and keep the corridors clear.

■ While Rostron was preparing his ship, wireless operator Cottam sat at his Marconi station monitoring messages. He had a steward available who passed every message to Rostron on the bridge.

- **12:50 A.M.:** Cottam copied a message from *Titanic* to *Olympic*, (which was more than 500 miles away): *"I require immediate assistance."*

- **1:10 A.M.:** Another message to *Olympic*: *"We are in collision with berg. Sinking head down. Come as soon as possible. Get your boats ready."*

- **1:25 A.M.:** *"We are putting the women off in small boats."*

- **1:35 A.M.:** *"Engine room getting flooded."*

- **1:45 A.M.:** *"Engine room full up to the boilers."* This was the last message Cottam would hear directly from *Titanic*.

- Meanwhile, *Carpathia* churned through the crystal clear and cold night air. All officers and lookouts were now straining to see the ever-increasing number of icebergs looming up out of the dark. *Carpathia* dodged and weaved through them, many larger than the ship herself. Care had to be taken. Colliding with an iceberg would not do the more than 1,000 passengers and crew on *Carpathia* or the survivors from *Titanic* any good.

  Carpathia was making 17.5 knots. At this speed, she would reach *Titanic's* reported position around 4:00 a.m. For Captain Arthur Henry Rostron, the ship *Carpathia*, and her crew, it was now *Carpathia* to the rescue.

  But time was quickly running out for most of the 2,208 souls on *Titanic*.

CHAPTER 12

NOT ENOUGH LIFEBOATS

MIDNIGHT–2:20 A.M., APRIL 15, 1912

After Captain Smith ordered the engines stopped for the last time in order to prevent the boilers from exploding as they came into contact with the water, the boiler steam was vented through the escape valves in the funnels. The resulting noise was so loud that it prevented any sort of conversation on the deck, and served to awaken those passengers and crew still asleep.

According to Second Officer Lightoller,

> *"The ship had been running under a big head of steam, therefore the instant the engines were stopped the steam started roaring off at all eight exhausts, kicking up a row that would have dwarfed the row of a thousand railway engines thundering through a culvert."*

There was not a public address system or a warning bell to notify the passengers. Once Smith ordered the uncovering of the lifeboats, officers and crew were sent throughout the passenger areas, knocking on each door until someone answered. In many cases, the crew forced the doors open.

▪ In the First Class areas, the order was to put on warm clothing and a life belt and report to the Boat Deck. Second Class passengers were told to report to the dining saloon. Third Class passengers faired poorly in the warning process. Mostly the stewards just used their pass key and threw open the cabin doors, pulled the life belts off the top shelf where they were stored, dumped them on the floor, and told everyone to get up and put them on. Those who did not understand English were left to their own devices to figure out what the stewards were telling them to do. And of course, conversation throughout the ship was extremely difficult for a time because of the noise generated by the escaping steam.

Since most of the crew were in some sort of dormitory or multi-person rooms, the crew chain-of-command was used to awaken them. As they were encountered, all deck hands and Able Bodied Seamen were ordered to the Boat Deck to help with the launching of the lifeboats. The saga of the lifeboats was about to begin.

LOADING THE LIFEBOATS

Shortly after the collision, Colonel Archibald Gracie decided to go up to the Boat Deck, but he did not see anything or anyone. Everything seemed to be quiet and in order. Returning to his cabin, he ran into his friend James Clinch Smith, who showed him a piece of ice he had picked up off the forward edge of A Deck. Gracie returned to his cabin and dressed in his warmest clothes in the belief that he might spend some of his evening out on the deck.

▪ In cabin C91, 19-year-old First Class passenger Margaret Graham heard her governess, Miss Elizabeth Shutes, ask an officer in the corridor if there was any danger. The officer replied, *"No, I think we can keep out of the water a bit longer."* Margaret was trying to eat a chicken sandwich, but her hand started shaking so hard the chicken kept falling out of her sandwich.

▪ For the first half hour after the collision, or until about 12:10 a.m., most of the normal shipboard activities continued. The lookouts were replaced at midnight, and the Dining Room stewards continued setting tables for breakfast.

▪ Down in the Third Class areas, people generally remained in or near their cabins awaiting further orders. Without someone to tell them where they should go, they remained where they were.

▪ Meanwhile, up on the Boat Deck and in various public rooms, First and Second Class passengers were wandering around, talking, swapping stories or asking questions. They were largely unconcerned, and most at this time did not believe the ship would actually sink.

▪ On the Boat Deck, according to Lightoller,

> *"All the Seamen came tumbling up on the boat deck in response to the order 'All hands on deck.'"*

- Down at the First Class Purser's Office on C Deck, many of the passengers lined up to retrieve their valuables. According to Second Officer Lightoller,

> *"The passengers by this time were beginning to flock up on the boat deck, with anxious faces, the appalling din [from the escaping steam] only adding to their anxiety in a situation already terrifying enough in all conscience."*

- Major Arthur Peuchen of the Royal Canadian Army was in his cabin, C104, when the collision occurred. He was already awake and dressed, so he went up the Grand Staircase to the Boat Deck. After watching some of the lifeboats being uncovered, he went back to his cabin and dressed in his warmest clothing. He then left his cabin and locked it behind him. On the desk was a tin box containing over $300,000 in negotiable securities.

- **12:20 A.M.:** Some 40 minutes had passed since striking the iceberg. The lifeboats were uncovered and the officers were back on the bridge awaiting further orders from Captain Smith. Lightoller asked Chief Officer Wilde if the lifeboats should be swung out. Wilde replied with a single word: *"No."*

- **12:25 A.M.:** Forty-five minutes after *Titanic* struck the ice, Captain Smith finally gave the orders to swing out the lifeboats and begin loading the passengers. Remarkably, few of the passengers were yet aware that *Titanic* was sinking. Second Officer Lightoller reported,

> *"...having got the boats swung out I made for the Captain, and happened to meet him near by on the boat deck. 'Hadn't we better get the women and children into the boats, sir?' He heard me and nodded a reply. One of my reasons for suggesting getting the boats afloat was, that I could see a steamer's steaming lights a couple of miles away on our port bow. If I could get the women and children into the boats, they would be perfectly safe in that smooth sea until this ship picked them up. . . . My idea was that I would lower the boats with a few people in each and when safely in the water fill them up from the gangway doors on the lower decks, and transfer them to the other ship."*

To accomplish this, Lightoller later reported, he told

> *"the Bosun's Mate to take six hands and open the port lower-deck gangway door, which was abreast of No. 2 hatch. He took his men and proceeded to carry out the order, but neither he or the men were ever seen again."*

- Lightoller and several of the passengers and crew reported seeing the lights of another ship north of *Titanic's* position a couple of miles away. Lightholler was an experienced seaman, and on such a clear night it is doubtful he was mistaken. These lights, if they actually existed, could have come from a ship close enough to help save almost everyone on *Titanic.*

- Up in the First and Second Class areas, the pending disaster was already having its effect on some of the passengers and crew. Many of them took to the open and available liquor cabinets in order to prepare themselves for whatever lay ahead.

- **12:25 A.M.:** Colonel Gracie was wandering through the corridors on C Deck looking for blankets that could be given to the people who would soon be leaving in the lifeboats when he encountered squash racquet instructor Fred Wright on the stairway. Remembering that he had an appointment the next morning with Wright, Gracie jokingly asked him, *"Hadn't we better cancel that appointment for tomorrow morning?"* Wright agreed, but he did not tell Gracie that the water was already to the ceiling of the Squash Racquet Court down on G Deck.

- **12:30 A.M.:** A few of the passengers were beginning to mingle around the lifeboats up on the Boat Deck, but the noise of the escaping steam and the freezing cold was too much for most of them, so they remained indoors in the First Class Entrance or the gymnasium. Among the group in the gymnasium were Colonel and Mrs. Astor. He was sitting with his wife, using his penknife to slice open a life belt to show Madeleine Astor what was inside. Shortly thereafter, the Astor's moved down to A Deck to wait for Lifeboat 4 to be lowered.

- On A Deck, one deck below the Boat Deck and directly under Lifeboat 4 on the port side forward, a small group of some very rich and influential passengers had been rounded up by their stewards and were waiting for the boat to be prepared for lowering. Having them wait on A Deck kept the passengers out of the cold because this was the deck that had been glassed in to keep the spray out. This was one of the last-minute design changes Ismay had ordered.
    Waiting in this group were the Astor's, Widener's, Ryerson's, Thayer's, and several other family groups along with their maids, valets, and other servants. Here these captains of industry, millionaires all, waited patiently for the lifeboat to be lowered from the Boat Deck above. None of them were dressed warmly because they were the first to be aroused from their cabins. Most of them sent their maids and valets back to their cabins to gather up warmer clothing and blankets. All had on

their life belts, and later the women would be seen wearing some of their finest fur coats with the men in their warmest jackets.

Officer Lightoller ordered Lifeboat 4 swung out and lowered to A Deck, but once it was there, it was found that the newly installed screened and glass windows could not be opened without a special tool. There was not anyone available to go search for a crewman who had the tool, so Lightoller told the passengers to wait and he would be back. They waited.

- Deep down in the hull, water in the forward five compartments was rising at the rate of one and one-half feet per minute. The bow of *Titanic* was starting to dip. Only people walking down a stairway facing forward noticed it, an odd sensation as the stairs tilted forward. There was beginning to be a slight list to the port as well, although most people did not notice it yet.

Down in the Third Class common areas, many of the Irish Catholic passengers gathered together to pray and await their fate. Several Third Class passengers had already found their way through the maze of corridors and had arrived on the Boat Deck. Most of the others were still waiting for someone to come and tell them where they should go.

- In the bow of the ship, Third Class steward John Hart was checking the passenger cabins to make sure everyone was out of them and sending the passengers aft down "Scotland Road," and then up to the Boat Deck through the Second Class areas. When he finished checking the cabins, he went up "Scotland Road" past the open door to the Second Class staircase. None of the Third Class passengers had gone up the staircase. They did not know whether they were allowed to do so. Hart figured he would have to lead them out from the Third Class areas.

- For First or Second Class male passengers, much of the determination as to whether they got into a lifeboat or not was based upon which side of the ship they happened to be. First Officer Murdoch generally oversaw the launching of the starboard side lifeboats. If there were not any women or children around when they were ready to launch, he allowed any male into the lifeboat who was close by, including crewmen. However, on the port side, Second Officer Lightoller carried out his orders to the letter: no men were allowed onto the boats except whatever crew was needed to man them. Even if the lifeboats were not full and there were men standing by, they were not allowed to enter the lifeboats. Seaman Joseph Scarrott said,

> "The usual order was given, 'Women and children first.' That order was carried out without any class distinction whatever. In some cases we had to force women into the boats as they would not leave their husbands."

- In this era, children were considered children until the age of five, at which time they became 'boys' and 'girls.' At the age of 15 they were considered adults. When the order came to load "women and children first" it was assumed to include all females of any age and male children under the age of five. Boys between the age of five and fifteen were not expected to be included in the group.

- **12:40 A.M.:** The horrible sound of escaping steam finally came to a sudden stop when the steam in all the boilers except Boiler Room 1 was finally bled off. The steam in Boiler Room 1 was being maintained in order to power the generators to keep the lights on. Now that there was not any noise from the escaping steam, the ship's orchestra, led by Wallace Hartley, set up in the forward First Class Entrance and played music while the passengers mingled about. Later, the orchestra would move to the starboard side of the Boat Deck outside the gymnasium.

12:45 A.M.: LIFEBOAT 7

One hour and five minutes after striking the iceberg, Lifeboat 7 was lowered on the starboard side of the Boat Deck across from the entrance to the gymnasium. It was the first boat in the water after the collision. This lifeboat was designed to hold 65 persons but was launched with exactly 28 (12 male and 12 female First Class and one male Second Class passenger, plus three crewmen). Included in this group were the newlyweds Mr. and Mrs. Dickinson Bishop, Miss Margaret Hays and her little Pomeranian dog, James R. McGough, the French aviator Pierre Maréchal, Alfred Nourney, the "Baron von Drachstedt," and two of the lookouts, Archie Jewell and George Hogg. Also among the passengers was Catherine Crosby, who was escorted to the lifeboat by her husband Edward. Men were not allowed on during the loading process, so Mr. Crosby kissed his wife good-bye and stepped back. Men were later allowed to board, but Crosby was nowhere to be found, and he did not survive.

- Loading and launching Lifeboat 7 did not seem to be very complicated. There also were not many people to put into the lifeboat because at this point few thought the ship would sink. Other than Captain Smith, Ismay, Andrews, Murdoch, and Lightoller, none of the other officers knew of the danger. It does not appear that they were told until it was too late—or they realized it themselves.

Lifeboat 7 and most of the remaining lifeboats were lowered so that the top of the lifeboat was even with the gunwale of the Boat Deck. Mrs. Dickinson H. Bishop later reported,

"About five minutes later the boats were lowered and we were pushed in. . . . My husband was pushed in with me and we were lowered with twenty-eight people in the boat. . . . Somewhat later five people were put into our boat from another one. . . . We had no compass or light."

Lifeboat 7 was ordered to remain around the forward gangway door, which it did for several minutes until the crewmen rowed it down the length of the ship and about 200 yards away from the starboard side. It was rowed even further away later to avoid the anticipated suction as the ship sank. The twenty-eight people in lifeboat 7 would spend the next 90 minutes in a front row seat, watching *Titanic* sink before their eyes.

■ **12:45 A.M.:** On the Docking Bridge above the Poop Deck, quartermaster George Rowe had spent the last hour wondering what was going on and trying to keep from freezing. Since he had seen the "sailing ship" (iceberg) pass the starboard side, he had seen little and heard less because of the escaping steam. Suddenly, he noticed a lifeboat full of people being rowed along the side of the ship. Rowe called the bridge to report to Fourth Officer Boxhall that there was a lifeboat in the water! Boxhall told Rowe to report to the bridge and bring a load of signal rockets with him.

■ A few minutes later Boxhall fired the first rocket. Each rocket shot up to about 800 feet, where it exploded with a loud bang and scattered 12 white stars. Shortly before he fired the first rocket, Boxhall thought he saw the lights of another ship in the distance and with his binoculars could even see her masthead lights. The rockets were fired to attract the attention of the ship that Boxhall and several other officers and crewmen could see in the distance to the north off the port bow. According to Second Officer Lightoller,

"We were firing rocket distress signals, which explode with a loud report a couple hundred feet in the air. Every minute or two one of these went up, bursting overhead with a cascade of stars."

Lightoller was mistaken on the timing. Quartermaster Rowe was firing a rocket about every five minutes or so, eight rockets in all.

■ Both Boxhall and Rowe watched as the other ship approached so close they could see both the red and green marker lights without their binoculars. If they could see both lights, it meant the ship was approaching them and it would have to be less than five miles away to be able see the lights without binoculars.

Other members of the crew, including Captain Smith, also saw the ship. It was just a few degrees off the port bow, and Smith estimated it was but five miles away. Soon just the red port light could be seen, which meant the ship had turned to starboard. Because the other ship was apparently so close, Boxhall tried to raise it with the Morse lamp, but there was no response.

Before long only the white stern lamp of the other ship was visible. This meant that it was actually moving away from *Titanic*. Given that *Titanic* was dead in the water and drifting with the current, the other ship appeared to have approached *Titanic* and then, inexplicably, turned around and steamed off.

- **12:45 A.M.:** While Boxhall, Rowe, and Captain Smith were watching a ship that seemed to be moving toward them, back on the Boat Deck Second Officer Lightoller also thought he saw a ship, stationary, off the port bow (in the same direction the others had seen the moving ship). This stationary ship is the one Lightoller kept telling the crews of the lifeboats to row toward.

The identity of this ship, if it ever existed, is one of the mysteries of the tragedy. If it did exist, it could not have been *Californian*, which was much further away, stopped dead, and surrounded by the ice field.

- **12:45 A.M.:** Down in Boiler Room 5, the crew had already shut down the dampers so they would not explode if the water reached them. The ship's pumps were pumping the water out of the room almost as fast as it came in, and additional hoses had been strung through the watertight doors, which were partially opened to allow easier passage between the compartments.

Leading Fireman Fred Barrett was working in Boiler Room 5 after having been driven from Boiler Room 6. He had pulled the grating off a portion of the floor to make some adjustments to the pump valves below. The room was full of steam and smoke and visibility was severely limited. Several crewmen were working in it, and engineer Jonathan Shepard ran across the deck and fell into the opening where the grating had been removed. The fall snapped his leg. Barrett and several others moved Shepard into a corner and continued their work.

- **12:45 A.M.:** Shortly after the crew moved Shepard, the entire bulkhead between Boiler Rooms 6 and 5 collapsed. Boiler Room 6 was filled to the ceiling with water, and Boiler Room 5 was also instantly filled, drowning everyone in the room except for Barrett, who was able to once again climb up the escape ladder ahead of the rushing icy water. He did not have time to close the watertight door to Boiler Room 4 that was partially opened to allow the passage of hoses for the pumps.

The bulkhead that collapsed is the one next to the coal fire that had smoldered for two weeks. The bulkhead probably collapsed because the fire that had smoldered for days had weakened it. The collapse hastened the sinking of *Titanic*. The bow had been slowly dipping since striking the iceberg, but the collapse of the bulkhead dropped the front of the liner several feet, a sudden jolt that was felt by almost everyone on board.

■ **12:50 A.M.:** Chief Baker Charles Joughin returned to his cabin to obtain liquid refreshment and ran into Dr. William O'Loughlin, who had the same idea.

■ **12:50 A.M.:** Seaman John Poingdestre had been working on the Boat Deck but decided to return to his cabin on E Deck to pick up his boots. Before he started back up to the Boat Deck, the entire wooden wall between his cabin and the Third Class area next to it crashed in, followed by a solid wall of water. Poingdestre had to struggle for several minutes to get out of the water and up to the next deck above.

Meanwhile, Mr. and Mrs. Lucian Smith and Mrs. and Mrs. Henry Sleeper Harper were chatting away in the gymnasium, watching some of the other passengers work the mechanical equipment.

12:55 A.M.: LIFEBOAT 5

Lifeboat 5 was the second lifeboat launched, and it too was from the starboard side. Although the lifeboat was capable of holding 65 passengers, there were between 35 and 41 people on board. (The actual number of passengers on most of the lifeboats is open to dispute. Once launched, several boats traded passengers or picked people out of the water. Also, some people died on the boats, and there was no official tabulation of the number of passengers, by boat, who climbed aboard *Carpathia*. In the dark and the haste to load the lifeboats, no one bothered to count the people or to take their names. Names and numbers come from survivor recollections, which are often suspect.)

There were 13 male, 14 female, and one child First Class passengers, and two female and about six male crewmembers. Among the passengers were Mr. and Mrs. Richard Beckwith and their married daughter Helen Newsom, Mrs. Washington Dodge and her son Washington Jr., Dr. Henry Frauenthal, his wife Clara, and his brother Isaac, and Mrs. Charles Stengel. Miss Helene Ostby left her father behind, and Mrs. Anna S. Warren and Mrs. Stengel left their husbands. Also on board was Edward Calderhead, who had just helped dump fellow passenger Margaret Brown into Lifeboat 6 on the port side before crossing to the opposite side of the ship to get into Lifeboat 5. Among the crewmembers were Quartermaster Alfred Olliver and Third Officer Pitman, who were ordered into the lifeboat by Murdoch to assist with the other lifeboats being lowered into the water.

▪ Bruce Ismay decided to help load this lifeboat, and just before it was lowered he called out, *"Are there any more women before this boat goes?"* Although there was no answer, a woman walked up and Ismay said, *"Come along; jump in."* She replied, *"I am only a stewardess."* Ismay responded, *"Never mind–you are a woman; take your place."*

Ismay was still hanging around the lifeboat and as it was being slowly lowered toward the water yelled out, *"Lower away! Lower away!"* at which time Fourth Officer Boxhall, who was in charge of getting the lifeboat launched, and may not have known who Ismay was, angrily shot back, *"If you'll get the hell out of the way I'll be able to do something! You want me to lower away quickly? You'll have me drown the whole lot of them!"* Disheartened and embarrassed, Ismay quickly left the area.

▪ Standing on the deck watching Lifeboat 5 being lowered were Dr. Henry W. Frauenthal and his brother Isaac. Dr. Frauenthal's wife Clara was in the lifeboat and he decided to join her, so the two brothers jumped in when the lifeboat was about four feet below the deck. The good doctor landed on top of Mrs. Annie May Stengel and dislocated two of her ribs, knocking her unconscious. This proved to be a double blow for Mrs. Stengel because she had said good-bye to her husband Charles on the deck, probably not expecting to see him again. However, Mr. Stengel somehow managed to get onto Lifeboat 1 and was reunited with his wife on *Carpathia*.

Mrs. Warren's husband Frank had actually entered the boat with her, but stepped out to help assist other women and was not able to rejoin his wife. He was lost.

Mrs. Washington Dodge and her son Washington Jr. said good-bye to Mr. Dodge, who stood back while the lifeboat was launched. During the night Mrs. Dodge and her son were transferred to Lifeboat 7. In the morning there would be another joyous reunion when Mr. Dodge was found on *Carpathia*. He survived by securing a seat in Lifeboat 13.

▪ Third Officer Pitman was ordered into the lifeboat to arrange for it to row around to pick up swimmers. Instead the crew rowed out about 200 yards from *Titanic*–and waited. Later, when Pitman wanted to row back to pick up people floating in the icy water, the women in the boat objected. Steward H. S. Etches later reported,

> *"After it sank, Mr. Pitman then said to pull back to the scene of the wreck. The ladies started calling out 'Appeal to the officer not to go back. Why should we lose all of our lives in a useless attempt to save others from the ship.' . . . . We did not go back."*

■ **12:50 A.M.:** Down in the Third Class areas, Steward John Hart and a couple of other crewmen gathered up small groups of people. Hart led a group of about 30 women and children along a circuitous route through the Second Class and First Class areas and up several decks before arriving, finally, on the Boat Deck.

12:55 A.M.: LIFEBOAT 6

Lifeboat 6, the first one launched from the port side, was lowered into the water with between 24 and 28 people (16 female and one male First Class passengers, two First Class female servants, one Third Class male passenger, and at least four crew members, including two women.) Some of the more dramatic events of the night occurred on Lifeboat 6.

Among the passengers were Margaret "Molly" Brown, Helen Churchill Candee, and Madame Berthe de Villiers. Its crew included lookout Frederick Fleet (who had first spotted the iceberg) and Quartermaster Robert Hichens, who was placed in command. Hichens had been at the ship's wheel when *Titanic* struck the iceberg.

■ Mrs. James Baxter left her 24-year old son Queeg behind. He managed to get his girlfriend, Bertha Mayné, into the lifeboat. Mrs. Tyrell Cavendish exchanged a long, lingering kiss with her husband before he placed her into the lifeboat and stepped back. Mrs. Edgar Meyer, Mrs. Martin Rothschild, and Mrs. William Spencer, would also lose their husbands. Recently married Mrs. Lucien Smith would lose her husband, too, and become an 18-year old widow. Marjorie and Madeleine Newell left their father on the deck.

Molly Brown had assisted some of the other women into the lifeboat and was walking away from it to round up more. As the lifeboat began to descend, two of her friends, Edward Calderhead and James McGough, picked her up and dumped her over the railing. Molly fell four feet into the bottom of the lifeboat.

■ There were just two crewmen on the lifeboat as it was being lowered. Some of the women passengers started calling up to the deck to send down more men to help with the rowing. This was a serious situation. Virtually none of the passengers and few of the crew on any of the lifeboats knew how to row one. And only about a half dozen people on *Titanic* knew rescue was close at hand. Most of the women on the lifeboats had a valid concern—they were almost totally helpless without someone to row the lifeboat or at least to show them how to do it—in the dark.

Since there were not any trained crewmen left in the area, Second Officer Lightoller was trying to decide what to do when Major Arthur Peuchen called out, *"If you like, I will go."* Lightoller replied, *"Are you a* seaman?" and Peuchen responded, "*I am a yachtsman.*" Lightoller then replied, "*If you are sailor enough to get out on that fall . . . you can go down.*"

Peuchen climbed out eight feet on the boat davit to the fall line then sixty feet down to the lifeboat. Just prior to making his descent, Peuchen had been speaking with Charles Hays, who said, "*Peuchen, this ship is good for eight hours yet. I have just been getting this from one of the best old seamen, Mr. Crosby.*" This was an interesting comment because a few minutes before, Edward Crosby had been in his cabin telling his wife, "*You'll lie there and drown! This ship is badly damaged!*" By the time Crosby had seen Hays, Crosby had gotten his wife and daughter onto Lifeboat 7. Now he was helping women enter Lifeboat 6. Neither Hays nor Crosby would survive.

- Both Major Peuchen and Mrs. Candee reported seeing about 100 stokers and firemen come up from below decks. They were met by one of the officers who ordered them all back down below. They complied, just like soldiers following the orders of their officers. As she was entering the lifeboat, Mrs. Candee slipped on an oar and fell into the lifeboat, breaking her ankle.

- Several passengers told of a stowaway in the lifeboat: an Italian boy (and the term *Italian* was used derisively). However, it seems that in an attempt to find more seamen for the boat, Lightoller had grabbed the first male he found and tossed him into the lifeboat. This person turned out to be a Third Class passenger with a broken arm, but the passengers thought he was a stowaway.

- With only four men on the lifeboat—Hichens manning the tiller, Fleet and Peuchen trying to row and the Third Class passenger with the broken arm not able to do much of anything—it was impossible for two men to make any headway by themselves. Hichens refused to help row. Wishing to make some headway, Molly Brown and one of the Newell sisters grabbed oars and helped row the boat away from the side of the ship.

Every survivor in Lifeboat 6 complained about the conduct of Quartermaster Hichens. Several times one of the ship's officers tried to call the lifeboat back, but Hichens refused. Major Peuchen later remembered his reply this way: "*No, we are not going back to the boat: it is our lives now, not theirs.*" Peuchen also claimed that Hichens said, "*There was no use going back—that there were only a lot of stiffs there.*" Mrs. Candee reported that, "*Hichens was cowardly and almost crazed with fear all the time.*"

Molly Brown reported that when she asked him to help row the lifeboat, Hichens said no, that it was not his duty to do so. Sometime during the night Lifeboat 6 picked up a half frozen stoker from another lifeboat. Hichens protested when some of the women wrapped him up in blankets and furs to keep him warm. Hichens moved to prevent it, but Mrs. Helen Candee reported that Molly Brown told him that if he did, *"he [Hichens] would be thrown overboard."* Mrs. Candee also stated, *"It would not be necessary to toss him [Hichens] in, for if she had moved in his direction, he would have tumbled into the sea, so paralyzed was he with fright."*

And so Lifeboat 6 with its load of women serving as part of its rowing crew moved out into the night with room for another forty people. Despite the protests of the women, Hitchens refused to go back for more.

1:00 A.M.: LIFEBOAT 3

Lifeboat 3 was another 65-passenger lifeboat on the starboard side, and it was lowered with between 38 and 40 people in it. There were ten First Class males, eight First Class females and one First Class child passenger, one First Class male and five First Class female servants and at least thirteen crewmen (ten firemen, one pantryman and two seamen.) This lifeboat was under the command of Able Bodied Seaman George A. Moore.

Lifeboat 3 included Mrs. James Cardeza, her son Thomas, her maid Anna Ward, and Thomas' manservant Gustave Lesueur. Also on board were Mr. and Mrs. Henry Sleeper Harper, their dragoman Hammad Hassab (and Mr. Harper's Pekinese dog Sun Yat Sen,) Mr. and Mrs. Frederick Spedden, their child Robert, Mrs. Spedden's maid Helen Wilson, and the child's nurse Elizabeth Burns. Mrs. Thornton Davidson, the daughter of Mr. and Mrs. Charles Hays was also on board, and while Mrs. Charles Hays would leave her husband behind, Mrs. Davidson would lose both her husband and father. Being a starboard side lifeboat, all the male passengers got in after the available women had been loaded.

- Standing on the Boat Deck helping load the passengers into Lifeboat 3 were Thornton Davidson, Charles Hays, Charles Case, and Washington A. Roebling. There was still room in the lifeboat when it began to be lowered, so First Officer Murdoch offered to let men board it. Although several men, mostly crewmen, got into the lifeboat, Davidson, Hays, Case, and Roebling remained behind and moved off to help wherever they could. Mrs. Hays later reported seeing the four of them standing together when the lifeboat slowly rowed away from the ship. All four men were lost.

- Henry Sleeper Harper and his wife were returning from a long vacation and research trip in Egypt. For whatever reason, maybe for his own amusement, Harper hired Hamad Hassab, a dragoman (an Egyptian interpreter) to accompany him to New York. In 1902, Harper had been on another ship that collided with an iceberg and sank without any loss of life. This was his second such event, so he did not hesitate to get into the lifeboat when the opportunity arose. Harper, his wife, his dragoman and his pet dog all survived.

All ten of the firemen congregated at the bow of the lifeboat. Seaman Moore manned the tiller. None of the firemen knew how to row a lifeboat, and shortly two of the four oars were lost in the water. Lifeboat 3 drifted all night. Whenever someone suggested they return to pick up people out of the water the idea was immediately rejected by the crewmen, who were afraid the lifeboat would be sucked under when *Titanic* sank. Throughout the night the crewmen kept lighting matches and holding them up, but after the ship sank they could not see any other lifeboats. When *Carpathia's* lights were spotted in the morning, someone lit a newspaper and later, Mrs. Davidson's straw hat, to attract attention.

When the sun began peeking over the horizon and the immense ice field could be seen, six-year-old Douglas Spedden called out, *"Oh, Muddie, look at the beautiful North Pole with no Santa Claus on it!"*

1:10 A.M.: LIFEBOAT 8

Lifeboat 8 on the port side was launched at 1:10 a.m., ninety minutes after *Titanic* struck the iceberg. In keeping with Lightoller's directives, no male passengers were allowed to board. There were seventeen First Class women passengers and six First Class servants, plus four crewmen on board—27 people in a lifeboat with a capacity of 65. Able Bodied Seaman Thomas Jones was in charge of this lifeboat.

No less than six of the women left their husbands behind and two more left their fathers. Seventeen-year-old Mrs. Victor Penasco lost her husband, whom she married when she was 15. Also losing husbands that night were Mrs. Alexander Holverson, Mrs. Frederick Kenyon, and Mrs. Thomas Pears. Also losing a husband and father were Mrs. Emil Taussig and daughter Ruth, and Mrs. George Wick and her daughter Mary.

▪ Among the other people in Lifeboat 8 were Mrs. Noel Lucy Dyer-Edwards, the Countess of Rothes, her maid Roberta Maioni, and her cousin Miss Gladys Cherry. Also on board was Mrs. William Bucknell and her maid Albina Bazzani (Mr. Bucknell was the founder of Bucknell University in Pennsylvania, but he was not on the ship), Miss Ellen Bird, maid to Mrs. Isador Straus, and Miss Sarah Daniels, maid to Mrs. Hudson J. C. Allison.

▪ Standing together on the deck as the lifeboat was being loaded was Macy's Department Store owner Isador Straus and his wife Ida, their maid Miss Ellen Bird, and Colonel Gracie. When Mrs. Straus was asked to enter the lifeboat, she replied, *"No! I will not be separated from my husband. As we have lived, so will we die. Together."* When it was suggested that because of his advanced age no one would object to his entering the lifeboat with his wife, Mr. Straus replied, *"No. I do not wish any distinction in my favor which is not granted to others."* The Strauses ordered their maid Ellen Bird to enter the lifeboat. The gallant couple walked slowly down to A Deck and sat down on some deck chairs to watch the activity going on around them. Sometime later they were seen going back to their cabin, and that is probably where they died. Second Officer Lightoller later reported speaking with them that night,

> *". . . on the deck I passed Mr. and Mrs. Straus leaning up against the deck house, chatting quite cheerily. I stopped and asked Mrs. Straus 'Can I take you along to the boats?' She replied 'I think I'll stay here for the moment . . . and they went down together.*

> *"I found another couple sitting on a fan casing, I asked the girl, 'Won't you let me put you in one of the boats?' She replied with a frank smile, 'Not on your life. We started together, and if need be, we'll finish together."*

- Steward John Hart arrived with his group of thirty Third Class women and children in tow. Several of them were escorted into the lifeboat, but they immediately jumped out and went inside where it was warm. Dismayed, Hart went back down to the Third Class areas to bring up another group.

- None of the women in Lifeboat 8 had anything much good to say (by now a common refrain) about the four male crewmen on their lifeboat. None of the crew could row, and the two bedroom stewards on board did not even know enough to put the oars into an oarlock before rowing. It was up to Mrs. J. Stuart White to show them how to do so.

  Eventually, the women took over the oars, partly to get away from the anticipated suction of the sinking ship, but also because the crewmen were under orders to row towards a light that could be seen in the distance. Upon reaching what was believed to be a ship, they were to discharge the passengers and return for more. The rowing also helped keep the women warm. At some point the Countess of Rothes took over the tiller, and her cousin, Miss Gladys Cherry, rowed all night. By the time *Titanic* sank, they were so far away they did not even see it happen. They never did find the ship whose lights they thought they saw.

1:10 A.M.: EMERGENCY LIFEBOAT 1

Emergency Lifeboat 1 was the small 40-person lifeboat on the starboard side next to the bridge wing. There were exactly twelve people on this boat: four First Class male and one First Class female passenger, one First Class servant and seven crewmen. This was the lifeboat in which Sir Cosmo Duff Gordon, and Lady Lucy Duff Gordon and her maid escaped. Lookout George Symons was in charge.

■ First Officer Murdoch needed to get this lifeboat launched for a couple of reasons. It was closest to the bow and the bow was sinking ever lower. In a short time the water would cover the forward Well Deck (C Deck) and the lifeboat needed to be launched so that the davits could be freed up to attach Collapsible C, which was sitting on the deck, and later Collapsible A, which was on the roof of the officer's quarters. Thus, the davits had to be used for three lifeboats. Murdoch loaded five crewmen into it with orders to drop into the water and pick up anyone who jumped in or climbed down the falls.

As the lifeboat was being lowered, the Duff Gordon's walked up. Sir Cosmo asked Murdoch, *"May we get in that boat?"* Murdoch replied, *"With the greatest pleasure,"* and helped Lady Duff Gordon and her maid Miss Laura Francatelli get into the lifeboat. Sir Cosmo and two other male passengers who were standing by were also allowed to board. Amazingly, there were no other passengers anywhere to be seen, so two additional crewmen were allowed to enter. Lifeboat 1 was then lowered away.

■ Instead of waiting around the side of the ship to pick up additional people as ordered, the crew rowed away from the ship and pulled up about 200 yards from *Titanic's* side. There the lifeboat and its passengers waited while everyone watched the activity on the ship. No one recommended they go back to pick anyone up: none of the crew wanted to assume responsibility for it, fearing the lifeboat would be swamped. Lookout Symons, who was in charge, said nothing. They waited and watched for the next hour and ten minutes as *Titanic* slipped beneath the sea, taking 1,500 souls with her.

Sometime after *Titanic* sank, crewmen R. W. Pusey heard Lady Duff Gordon tell her maid Miss Francatelli, *"You have lost your beautiful nightdress,"* and Pusey replied, *"Never mind, you have saved your lives; but we have lost our kit."* Because of this comment, Sir Cosmo offered to replace the kits (personal effects) of all the crewmen on Lifeboat 1, which he did when they reached New York.

Unfortunately, this act of kindness caused one of the biggest post-sinking scandals. It was later asserted that Sir Cosmo was paying off the crew with a bribe to *not* go back to pick up any more people in order to save his wife and himself. Although not true, once the newspapers printed this story, the Duff Gordon's spent the rest of their lives defending themselves against it. The Duff Gordon's were also the only surviving passengers to have to testify about their behavior during the court hearings in England.

■ **1:10 A.M.:** Back on the Boat Deck, Second Officer Lightoller later reported,

> "I met the Purser, Assistant Purser, and the Senior and Junior Surgeons. . . .
> There was only time to pass a few words, then they all shook hands and said
> 'Goodbye.'"

■ **1:15 A.M.:** To prevent a rush on the lifeboats, some of the single Third Class male passengers had been held in their section of the ship. Third Class Steward John Hart was now trying to gather up another group of passengers down on E Deck. They were mostly married women, and Hart was under orders to bring out only women and children. The women would not leave without their husbands, so Hart gathered a few of them who would leave and several single women, about 25 in all, and started back for the Boat Deck.

Meanwhile, the single Third Class passengers were released and they set out for the Boat Deck. Nobody showed them how to get there, however. Many of them climbed up on the Well Deck crane, crawled along the crane's boom, and dropped down on A Deck. From there they made their way up to the Boat Deck.

1:20 A.M.: LIFEBOAT 10

Lifeboat 10, the forward most of the four lifeboats located on the port side in the aft section of the Boat Deck was lowered. By this time, one hour and forty minutes after *Titanic* had struck the iceberg, virtually everyone was aware the ship was in grave peril. Finding people to get into the lifeboats was becoming much easier. Passengers in the lifeboats already launched would later say that the tops of the propellers could be seen as the bow continued to sink. Water was pouring into the forward Well Deck, where it had free access to flow throughout the forward part of the ship. Lifeboat 10 left with around 55 people on board, ten short of its capacity. Every surviving passenger remembered that, at this time anyway, there was still no panic on board the ship.

■ At the time Lifeboat 10 was launched, there were no male passengers on board because of Second Officer Lightoller's restrictions. So some 41 women and seven children were on board with all three classes about equally represented. There were also seven crewmen, commanded by Able Bodied Seaman Frank Evans. He was later transferred to Lifeboat 14, at which time Able Bodied Seaman Edward J. Buley was placed in charge.

Among the passengers were Mrs. Mark Fortune and her three daughters, but left behind was her husband and a son. Most of the remaining passengers left behind a husband or father.

- Lifeboat 10 was Chief Baker Charles Joughin's assigned lifeboat, but he was so busy helping other passengers he was not able to get into it before the lifeboat was launched. Seaman Frank Evans reported that Joughin,

> *"was getting the children and chucking them into the boat. Mr. Murdoch and the baker made the women jump across into the boat about two feet and a half. . . . He threw them [the children] on to the women and he was catching children by their dresses and chucking them in."*

Later Evans reported,

> *"One woman in a black dress slipped and fell. She seemed nervous and did not like to jump at first. When she did jump she did not go far enough, but fell between the ship and the boat. She was pulled in by some men on the deck below, went up to the Boat Deck again, took another jump, and landed safely in the boat."*

- As lifeboat 10 was being lowered past A Deck, Third Class passenger Mr. N. Krekorian (referred to in different reports as an "Armenian" or as a "crazed Italian") jumped into it. Some passengers later thought he was hiding under the seats before the lifeboat was launched, but he jumped in and he survived.

When the lifeboat reached the water, its weight and the total lack of any wave action prevented the crew from releasing the falls. Normally there would be enough slack in the falls as the lifeboat crested a wave to allow the releases to work. Consequently, the boat remained tied to the falls until someone found a knife to cut them.

Finally, Lifeboat 10 was rowed away about 200 yards and the survivors waited. Later it was tied up to three other lifeboats under the direction of Officer Lowe. Because this lifeboat was essentially full, there was not any attempt to pick up survivors.

1:20 A.M.: LIFEBOAT 9

Lifeboat 9 was lowered from the starboard side of the ship with between 48 and 56 people in it. This left room for another ten or so. Word was passed that no men were allowed until all the women in the area were loaded. Madame Leontine Aubert, the mistress of Benjamin

Guggenheim, was on this lifeboat along with Miss Marion Wright. Boatswain's Mate Albert Haines was in charge. In all, there were a few First Class and Third Class, but most were Second Class passengers. One elderly lady waiting on the deck was ordered to board and several of the crewmen tried to assist her, but she caused quite a commotion and broke away. She was last seen going back inside the ship.

After all the women that could be found were loaded, Murdoch allowed male passengers in the vicinity to board. Gambler George Bradley (George Brayton) entered the lifeboat, as did at least nine other male passengers. Finally, Murdoch ordered any of the crewmen standing around to get in and about 15 of them did. Even then, the lifeboat was lowered with room available for more.

- By this time *Titanic* had developed a noticeable list to starboard due to the water entering on that side. The lifeboats hanging on their falls were swinging away from the ship, and it was becoming difficult for the passengers to navigate the gap between the lifeboat and the hull. Murdoch stood with one foot in the lifeboat and one on the deck rail to help assist the women into the lifeboats.

- Novelist Jacques Futrelle escorted his wife May Futrelle to the side of the lifeboat. When she objected to leaving, he told her, *"For God's sake, go! It's your last chance! Go!"* Mrs. Futrelle was still standing on the deck when one of the officers forced her into the lifeboat. Like so many wives that night, she would never see her husband again.

- After the lifeboat was lowered into the water, it took a while until someone could find a knife to cut the lashings for the oars. Once free, Lifeboat 9 was rowed out about 100 yards. No attempt was made to go back to pick up others, but for the next hour or so the crew rowed toward the light of a ship they believed they could see hovering about in the distance.

1:20 A.M.: LIFEBOAT 11

Lifeboat 11 was the third one launched at 1:20 a.m. Everyone realized that those lifeboats still remaining would have to be loaded as fully as possible. All of the lifeboats launched so far had rowed off, and none were coming back to pick up additional people. Starboard side Lifeboat 11, with a capacity of 65 people, was launched with 70 people and a good mix of second and third class passengers and crew. Quartermaster Sidney Humphreys was in charge.

Lifeboats 11 and 13 were loaded at almost the same time from A Deck, and a human chain made up of stewards was created to pass women and children into the lifeboats. One of these children was six-year-old Nina Harper, whose father Reverend Harper wrapped her up in a blanket and handed her off to her aunt, Miss Jessie Leitch, as she was entering the lifeboat. Reverend Harper remained behind and was lost.

■   Mrs. Nellie Becker and her three children were all on the deck together. During the confusion Mrs. Becker, her four-year old daughter and one-year old son were loaded into the lifeboat, but twelve-year old daughter Ruth was left behind on the deck. Mrs. Becker was beside herself with grief all night, and it was not until she was on *Carpathia* that she found Ruth, who had managed to get onto Lifeboat 13.

■   Eight-year-old Marshall Drew remembered his lifeboat experience this way:

> *"The lowering of the lifeboat seventy feet into the sea was perilous. Davits, ropes, nothing worked properly so that first one end of the lifeboat was tilted up and then far down. I think it was the only time I was scared."*

■   One of the more tragic events in this night full of tragedy was the saga of the Allison family: First Class passenger Hudson Allison, his wife Bessie, their two-year-old daughter Helen, and one-year-old son Hudson Trevor. Also part of the Allison group was a maid, Sarah Daniels, Trevor's nurse Mrs. Alice Cleaver, cook Mildred Brown, and chauffeur George Swane.

Shortly after *Titanic* struck the iceberg, Alice Cleaver, who was sharing a room with the Allison children, wrapped baby Trevor up in a blanket and took him up to the Boat Deck without telling anyone where she was going. Mildred Brown joined her and they managed to get into Lifeboat 11. During the ensuing confusion Mr. and Mrs. Allison and the servants looked all over the ship for Alice and Trevor. At some point Sarah Daniels also got off the ship. By the time the Allison's finally figured out that Trevor was either safe with Alice or lost, there were not any lifeboats left. They were last seen sitting on A Deck behind the windows with their daughter. Little Helen was the only child from First or Second Class lost that night. Mr. Allison's body was later found, and he was buried in Canada. Young Trevor died when he was 18 and is buried next to his father. Mrs. Allison was one of only four First Class women passengers who did not survive.

Alice Cleaver was initially hailed as a heroine for saving Trevor, but the families of Hudson and Bess would always condemn her for leaving the rest of the family to die on the ship.

■   Another bizarre incident occurred on this lifeboat. Eighteen-year old Leah Aks was standing near Madeleine Astor on A Deck with her

10-month old son Philip "Filly" Aks. Mrs. Astor gave Leah a shawl in which to wrap the baby.

While Lifeboat 11 was being loaded, someone thought Leah was trying to rush the line and she was held back. Then, someone else grabbed the baby out of her arms and tossed him into the lifeboat. Passenger Elizabeth Nye caught baby Philip much like a football and held onto him all night. No one knew who the baby belonged to, and Leah could not get on the lifeboat. Fortunately, Leah managed to get into Lifeboat 13 and was saved.

Once on board *Carpathia*, Elizabeth Nye refused to give up the baby to Leah because she did not know for sure she was the mother. Eventually, Captain Rostron settled the dispute when Leah identified a birthmark on the child, and so Filly was returned to his mother.

Because this lifeboat was seriously overcrowded, many of the passengers had to stand all night. There was a considerable amount of squabbling and complaining among the women about this. Many of them would later register complaints about the crewmen who were smoking in front of them.

Obviously, the survivors in Lifeboat 11 did not attempt to pick up anyone else. It was enough work for the crewmen just to row the lifeboat away from the ship before it sank.

1:25 A.M.: LIFEBOAT 13

Just a few minutes after Lifeboat 11 was launched, Lifeboat 13 on the starboard side was lowered with between 60 and 64 people on board. There was only one First Class passenger, Dr. Washington Dodge, and he would meet up with the rest of his family on *Carpathia*. Also aboard was Miss Ruth Becker, who had gotten separated from her mother and brothers in Lifeboat 11.

Another Second Class passenger was Lawrence Beesley, who had wanted to find a good vantage point when *Titanic* arrived in New York so he could see her massive size in a single view. He would get his wish, though not in New York. Instead, his chance arrived a few hundred yards off her starboard side in the middle of the North Atlantic. Beesley would one day write one of the best accounts of the sinking of the ship.

▪ Among the Third Class passengers was Mr. Eugene Daly, who had played "Erin's Lament" on his Irish pipes as *Titanic* steamed away from the coast of Ireland. (There is some confusion about which lifeboat Daly was on; various accounts place him on Lifeboat 13, 15, and Collapsible B). Other Third Class passengers included Johan Svensson, a fourteen-year old boy traveling alone who was denied boarding on two lifeboats prior to getting onto Lifeboat 13, and Leah Aks, whose baby had been taken away from her and tossed into Lifeboat 11.

- There were about 30 Third Class passengers and 25 crewmen in Lifeboat 13. Most of the Third Class passengers were those brought up from below by Steward Hart on his first trip. They apparently decided it was better to be in the lifeboat than warm inside the ship. Leading Fireman Frederick Barrett, who had escaped from flooding in both Boiler Rooms 5 and 6, made it to A Deck and managed to get into Lifeboat 13, where he was placed in charge of it. Barrett had been soaked by freezing water twice in the past 90 minutes, and once he was in the open lifeboat, he was so cold he could not continue in command, so someone else took over. One of the women wrapped Barrett up in a piece of canvas to keep him from freezing to death.

- After placing his family into Lifeboat 5, Dr. Washington Dodge assisted other passengers near Lifeboat 13. His steward was also helping load the lifeboat and told Dr. Dodge, *"You had better get in here then."* The steward got behind the doctor and pushed him into the boat and then followed him in as it was being lowered toward the water.

- As the lifeboat neared the sea, several people saw a huge discharge of water shooting out of the side of the ship directly below them. The water was from the huge pumps pumping saltwater out of the ship. If the lifeboat was lowered into the discharge, it would have been immediately swamped.

  The passengers called up to the deck to stop lowering the lifeboat. The oars were used to push it further away from the side of the ship while the lifeboat was lowered into the water. While this was happening, Lifeboat 13 drifted backward from the splash caused by the discharge, so the falls could not be released. If this was not enough of a problem, Lifeboat 13 had drifted directly underneath Lifeboat 15, which was now being lowered right on top of it. Once again the passengers had to call out to the deck to stop lowering Lifeboat 15 until the falls on Lifeboat 13 were finally cut with a knife. Once the falls were sliced, Lifeboat 13 was rowed away from the doomed liner.

- **1:25 A.M.:** Quartermaster Rowe fired his eighth and last distress rocket.

- **1:25 A.M.:** Earlier, Benjamin Guggenheim and his servant Victor Giglio had returned to their cabins, where they shed their warm clothing and lifebelts for their best evening clothes. By this time they were sitting comfortably in the First Class Smoking Room, drinks in hand. Bruce Ismay stopped by and inquired why Guggenheim was not trying to get into a lifeboat. Guggenheim replied: *"We've dressed up in our best and are prepared to go down like gentlemen."* Later, Guggenheim told a steward to *"tell my wife I've done my best in doing my duty."*

1:30 A.M.: LIFEBOAT 15

Lifeboat 15 was the last regular lifeboat launched from the starboard side off A Deck. It contained one First Class male passenger, about 40 Third Class passengers (almost an equal number of male and female passengers and about six children) and about 25 crewmen and one female crewmember. By this time *Titanic* had acquired a slight list to port as it rocked from side to side with the changing weight of the water in the hull and movement of the passengers on the decks. This meant that, for a time, it was easier to load the passengers from A Deck.

▪ On Lifeboat 15 were all of the women and children Steward John Hart had brought up in his second group of Third Class passengers, plus the remaining few from his first trip into the ship. In all, Hart was directly responsible for saving 58 Third Class passengers. This was almost one-third of the Third Class passengers saved. Hart was on his way down for a third group when Murdoch ordered him to get into Lifeboat 15. Murdoch's order saved Hart's life. He was one of many heroes that night.

▪ Few of the survivors on this lifeboat left any recollections about the launch. Fireman Frank Dymond was in charge, and his testimony centered on how quiet the passengers on the decks were as they watched the last boat on that side of the ship lowered away. Because the boat was full, the crew rowed away from the ship about 500 yards and waited while *Titanic* sank.

▪ **1:30 A.M.:** Second Officer Lightoller reported,

> "The Chief Officer [Wilde] came over and asked did I know where the firearms were?. . . .[I]nto the First Officer's cabin we went . . . where I hauled them out still in all their pristine newness and grease."

1:30 A.M.: LIFEBOAT 12

Lifeboat 12 was launched at this late time with between 30 and 40 people aboard. Once again there were no male passengers on the lifeboat. Lightoller launched it half full; when there were no women in the vicinity he sent it away instead of allowing any men to board. Most of the people came from Second Class, with only about five Third Class passengers and two crewmen on the lifeboat. Able Bodied Seaman John Poingdestre was in charge of Lifeboat 12.

As the lifeboat was being lowered, one Third Class male jumped in from A Deck. Seaman Fredrick Clench, the other crewman on the lifeboat, said he saw the man jump in and then disappear under the seats where he hid until the lifeboat was rowed away. Shortly, Lifeboat 12 joined up with Lifeboats 14 and 4, and some of those passengers were transferred to Lifeboat 12. With only two crewmembers on board, there was no attempt to pick up people in the water.

1:30 A.M.: LIFEBOAT 14

Lifeboat 14 was launched from the port side with about sixty people on board and commanded by Fifth Officer Lowe, who was ordered into the lifeboat by Second Officer Lightoller. Most of the passengers were women from Second Class, although there were several from First Class and Third Class.

▪   First Class passenger Mrs. Alexander Compton and her daughter Sara were in this lifeboat, but they left Sara's brother Alexander Jr. behind. Most of the other women passengers left a male family member on the ship. Passenger Edith Brown remembered,

> "My father never said anything . . . he put my mother and me into a lifeboat. . . then he walked away . . ."

▪   While loading this lifeboat, Officer Lowe fired his revolver into the water alongside the ship. This was the first lifeboat loaded where passengers were beginning to realize they might be left behind to die a terrible death. Lowe later reported on the issue:

> "As we were coming down past the open decks, I saw a lot of Latin people all along the ship's rails. They were glaring more or less like wild beasts, ready to spring. That is why I yelled out to 'look out.' and let go, bang! right along the ship's side."

This and other statements by Lowe and other survivors demonstrate the prejudice of the day toward anyone who was not obviously English or American.

1:35 A.M.: LIFEBOAT 16

Somewhere between 50 and 56 people were in Lifeboat 16 when it was launched from the port side by Second Officer Lightoller. It, too, shoved off bearing Lightoller's trademark—not a single male passenger. Most of the crew were women from the Stewards Department.
The majority of the passengers were Third Class women and children, although "Winnie" Troutt from Second Class did end up on this boat. Most of the women left their husbands on the deck. Master-at-Arms Joseph Bailey was in charge, and he had to climb down

the falls to get into the lifeboat. There were only four male crewmembers on board.

■   One of the stewardesses was Violet Jessop, who was now living through her second ship disaster. Miss Jessop had been on *Olympic* when it was involved in the collision with HMS *Hawke*. Now she would survive the sinking of *Titanic* and would continue to work for White Star Line. Four years later in September 1916, Jessop would be working as a nurse on *Titanic's* third sister ship *Britannic*, when that ship was sunk by a mine in the Aegean Sea. Violet would go down in history with the dubious (and rather remarkable) honor of serving on all three of the *Olympic*-class ships when they met with disaster.

■   Crewman John Priest, a fireman who escapted on Lifeboat 15, was also on all three ships and survived. During World War I, Priest would serve on two merchant ships that were also sunk, which meant that four ships he had served on sank from under him and another had been seriously damaged. He had to retire because the word was out that he was unlucky, and no one would serve on the same ship with him.

Lifeboat 16 later tied up to Lifeboat 6 to transfer passengers to help balance the loads. Although there was some room on the boat, no attempt was made to go back and pick up anyone else.

1:40 A.M.: LIFEBOAT COLLAPSIBLE C

It was now exactly two hours since the ship struck the iceberg. The last of the boats were being prepared for launching. It was now time for Collapsible C to be launched from the same davits that Lifeboat 1 had been attached. This was also the last boat to be launched on the starboard side. The list to port was now enough that, as it was being lowered, the lifeboat had to be pushed away from the side of the ship to keep from rubbing its canvas sides against the rivet heads.

With one notable exception, all the passengers were from the Third Class areas (about 40 in all), and all women except for a couple of men and about six crewmen. The one exception was James Bruce Ismay, President of the White Star Line.

■   The lifeboat was only partially full when Quartermaster George Rowe arrived and a call was made for more women and children. When none were found, the mass of men waiting nearby started to move toward the lifeboat, so Chief Purser Herbert McElroy fired his pistol into the air twice to hold them back. It worked. Shortly, a few more women came up from below deck and First Officer Murdoch ordered the lifeboat lowered so that Collapsible A on the roof of the officer's quarters could be prepared. By this time the group of men had moved off, and as the lifeboat was lowered two male passengers, William Carter and Bruce Ismay, stepped into it.

- After having helped with Lifeboat 5, Ismay went down the Boat Deck toward the bow to help load Collapsible C that had been attached to the davits. As it was starting to be lowered, he stepped into it and took a seat. Most of the people on the lifeboat observed this, although few knew who he was. Chief Officer Wilde, First Officer Murdoch, and Chief Purser McElroy also observed Ismay get into the lifeboat. Since none of them survived, it can only be imagined what they thought when they saw the owner of the company, the person who had decided that more lifeboats would not be needed, take a seat in one of the few available boats while they knew they were doomed to die when the ship sank.

- The crew of Collapsible C thought they saw a light in the distance and rowed all night in an effort to reach it. By daylight the lifeboat was more than five miles from where *Titanic* sank. Five men thought to be stowaways were found under the seats of the lifeboat. In reality, the five were Chinese sailors traveling Third Class to New York to meet up with another ship. None of them spoke English, but they had been at sea long enough to know when it was time to take to the lifeboats. They also knew that being Chinese, and so would not have been voluntarily allowed into a lifeboat. Instead, they managed to slip into one while it was dark and hide until daylight.

1:45 A.M.: EMERGENCY LIFEBOAT 2

Emergency Lifeboat 2 on the port side forward, with a capacity of about 40, was launched with between 19 and 25 people in it. There were four crewmen on this lifeboat including Fourth Officer Boxhall, who was ordered into it by Lightoller. The rest of the people were evenly divided among First and Third Class passengers, all women and children except for one Third Class male who got on with his family.

- Prior to the official loading of the boat, a whole group of crewmen, estimated to be about 25 or more, had already gotten into it. Second Officer Lightoller, carrying a pistol in his hand saw them and shouted, *"Get out of there, you damned cowards! I'd like to see every one of you overboard!"* Everyone scrambled out of the boat, and the women were loaded in their place. Lightoller and Boxhall oversaw the loading and launching of the boat. Lightoller was in a hurry because he wanted to get Collapsible D hooked up to the davits and launched before it was too late to do so. By now the water had climbed over the top of the bow and was approaching the front of B Deck, and the ship was down sharply by the bow (more than 60 feet) and had developed a substantial list to port.

■ Murdoch ordered Boxhall into the lifeboat, and Boxhall brought along a box of small green rockets. There was also a small lantern on board, the only lifeboat to have one. Boxhall and the remaining seaman, Frank Osman, had to do the rowing, so they enlisted First Class passenger Mrs. Walter Douglas to man the tiller, which she did all night. Murdoch had ordered Boxhall to row around to the starboard side to pick up people in the water, but by the time they got around the ship, suction from water flowing into the open portholes prevented them from getting close enough to pick anyone up.

■ Boxhall attached the lighted lantern to the end of a pole and had one of the women passengers hold it up high so it could be seen. Throughout the night Boxhall also fired off his little rockets, and it was these rockets that the crew of *Carpathia* saw and guided upon as they neared the wreckage a few hours later.

1:55 A.M.: LIFEBOAT 4

The last regular lifeboat to be launched was Lifeboat 4. This is the lifeboat that was originally going to be the first one launched almost 90 minutes earlier. It was forgotten by the crew after it was discovered that the passengers could not be loaded from A Deck because of the glass-and-screened windows that no one had the correct tool to open.

For more than thirty minutes the Astor's, Carter's, Ryerson's, Thayer's, and Widener's, along with their servants, had waited on A Deck for someone to come back with the tool needed to open the windows. Around 1:00 a.m., Steward George Dodd appeared and sent them all up to the Boat Deck via the small crew stairway. Dodd figured that since all the other lifeboats were being loaded from the Boat Deck, Lifeboat 4 would be raised back up so the passengers could load from there.

And so the wealthy waited while all around them the other lifeboats were loaded and launched. They watched the rockets being fired and listened to the orchestra play. Lifeboat 4, meanwhile, sat empty below them, next to A Deck.

After Lifeboat 2 had been launched, Lightoller came back to number 4 and discovered that not only had it not been launched, but that the passengers were on the Boat Deck and the lifeboat was on A Deck. Lightoller promptly ordered the passengers back down to A Deck because by now someone had found the tool needed to crank open the windows. The ship was listing seriously to port, and Lifeboat 4 had swung too far away from the ship for safe access. Grappling hooks and wire were used to secure the lifeboat to the side of the ship.

A small ladder was found, and with Lightoller straddling the gap with one foot on the ship and one in the lifeboat, the women and children climbed the ladder, crouched to get through the window and stepped into the lifeboat outside. They were stepping from the bright lights of the ship into almost total freezing darkness.

- The first person to climb aboard this lifeboat was Madeleine Astor. Colonel Astor helped her up the steps and then asked Lightoller if he could join her because she was pregnant, or as Astor put it, *"in a delicate condition."* Lightoller, a stickler for protocol, refused. Astor would not be let aboard until all the women were loaded. The richest man on the ship calmly stepped back and helped the other women through the window.

- The Ryerson family came next. When Arthur Ryerson noticed that his wife's maid did not have a lifebelt, he took his off and put it on her. Mrs. Ryerson led her two daughters and son to the window, but Lightoller told her, *"That boy can't go!"* Arthur Ryerson replied, *"Of course that boy goes with his mother—he is only thirteen."* Lightoller let him pass, but announced to all who were near, *"No more boys!"*

- Mrs. William E. Carter, together with her son and daughter, were escorted into the lifeboat by Mr. Carter. Once aboard, Mr. Carter quickly moved to the starboard side of the ship and stepped into Collapsible C with Bruce Ismay. The Carters enjoyed a grand reunion on *Carpathia*, a rare occurrence.

- Mrs. Ida Hippach and her daughter Jean were also in Lifeboat 4. Eight years earlier Mrs. Hippach had lost two sons in the infamous fire that had destroyed Chicago's Iroquois Theater. She was still in mourning. Ida and her daughter had been in Europe trying to put the past behind them. About two years after *Titanic* sank, Ida's third son would be killed in an automobile accident.

- Mrs. John Thayer and Mrs. George Widener both kissed their husbands and sons goodbye and boarded the lifeboat. After the rest of the available women passengers were loaded, Lifeboat 4 was lowered the few remaining feet to the water, which was now only about one deck below. Before the lifeboat was lowered, all of the husbands and sons were offered seats: Astor, the Ryerson's, and the Widener's. Millionaires all, not a single one opted to climb in. When it was discovered that there were not any sailors in the lifeboat, Quartermaster Walter Perkis and Seaman William McCarthy were ordered to slide down the falls and assist in the boat.

- As the lifeboat was rowed away, the passengers could see John Jacob Astor, the two Thayer's (father John and son Jack), the two Widener men (father George and son Harry), and Arthur Ryerson standing together in a group, waving at their families in the lifeboat and all deep in their own thoughts. Colonel Astor eventually went down to the dog kennels and let the dogs out. Madeleine Astor would later say that as the ship started to go under, she could see Colonel Astor's Airdale dog "Kitty" running around on the Boat Deck.

- Quartermaster Perkis had orders to row to the aft gangway hatch to pick up people. En route he saw two crewmen slide down the falls of Lifeboat 16. One was able to get into the lifeboat but the other fell into the water and was fished out and pulled into Lifeboat 4.

Within the next few minutes, six more men were pulled from the water but one of them, Steward Sidney Siebert, died from exposure on the lifeboat. Another, Seaman William Lyons, died on *Carpathia*. In all, Lifeboat 4, capable of holding 65, rowed away with only some 40 people in it.

- **2:00 A.M.:** Colonel Archibald Butt, Francis Millet, Clarence Moore, and Arthur Ryerson retired to the First Class Smoking Room on A Deck aft, sat at their usual table, and played one last hand of cards while they waited for the end. About 2:10 a.m., Archibald Gracie watched them finish their game, shake hands, and leave, none to be seen again.

2:05 A.M.: LIFEBOAT COLLAPSIBLE D

It was now two hours and twenty-five minutes since *Titanic* struck the iceberg and time was visibly running out. The bow was well down under water and the ship was slipping away. Collapsible D was attached to the davits where Lifeboat 2 had been. This was the last lifeboat that had any reasonable chance of being launched. Collapsibles A and B were still tied down on top of the officer's quarters and, without a crane to lift them, there was not a viable way to launch them other than floating them off the roof as the ship sank from under them.

The good news was that there was room for 49 people in Collapsible D. The bad news was that there were more than 1,500 people still on *Titanic*. Even then, Collapsible D was launched with only about 40 people in it. In order to keep people from storming the lifeboat, a human chain was formed by the crewmen on deck, and they allowed only women and children through.

First Class passenger Frederick Hoyt saw his wife into the lifeboat and then jumped into the water near where he thought it might pass. As the lifeboat was rowed by, Hoyt was hauled into it, where he sat shivering in the cold for the rest of the night.

Theater owner Henry Harris escorted his wife to the edge of the human chain, and when told he could not go any further, he kissed her and said, *"Yes, I know. I will stay."*

- Two small boys were brought to the edge of the chain by their father and passed through to the lifeboat. Some of the women there wrapped them up to keep them warm. The father told the people in the lifeboat that his name was "Mr. Hoffman" traveling to New York. He then stepped back. Nobody knew it at the time, of course, but the boys were Edmond and Michel Navratil. The father, Michel Navratil, had kidnapped his children from his estranged wife in France.

Since Hoffman (Navratil) did not survive, for some time no one knew the real identity of the two small boys. The newspapers picked up the story and published a photograph of them, which was reprinted in newspapers throughout Europe. Eventually their mother, still in France, saw the photograph and made her way to New York, where she was reunited with her kidnapped and lost children. Little Michel Navratil lived to be 91-years old. He died in January 2001, the last male survivor of *Titanic* to pass on.

- Colonel Archibald Gracie showed up with two of the women he had been "protecting," Mrs. John M. Brown and Miss Edith Evans. Colonel Gracie was stopped at the line but the two women got through just as the lifeboat was being lowered away. Gallantry was not confined to the men that night. Miss Evans told Mrs. Brown, *"You go first. You have children waiting at home."* She helped Mrs. Brown over the rail. When she got aboard Mrs. Brown discovered there was not enough room for Edith Evans to join her. Edith remained behind and died with some of the men who had befriended her. She was one of but four First Class women who did not survive.

- Down on A Deck, First Class passengers Hugh Woolner and Bjornstrom-Steffanson had been helping people into lifeboats for two hours and now the deck was deserted. They walked forward through the door to the open Promenade Deck and decided it was time to take their chances in the water, which was already over the tops of their shoes anyway. They got onto the railing to prepare to dive in when, just a few feet below them, they saw Collapsible D descending toward the water. They decided to make a jump for it, and Steffanson jumped into the bow of the lifeboat, landing on his head. Woolner followed, but missed and ended up half in and half out, hanging over the side. He was pulled in just as the lifeboat hit the water.

Quartermaster Arthur Bright was in charge of Collapsible D. Once it was in the water, everyone rowed or paddled to get as far away from *Titanic* as possible. By now, water was up to the bridge and the stern had completely lifted free of the sea, exposing the giant propellers. They did not want to be sucked under when the ship went down.

■   **2:05 A.M.:** Captain Smith went into the wireless room and told Marconi operators Phillips and Bride that their work was done and to save themselves. Both would remain on duty for another 12 minutes while Phillips sent another message. On his way back to the bridge, Smith told several crewmen, *"It's every man for himself."*

■   **2:10 A.M.:** A steward saw Thomas Andrews in the First Class Smoking Room, alone. His arms were folded across his chest, and his lifebelt was lying next to him on a table. One can only wonder what was running through the mind of the builder of *Titanic*, the ship of dreams, as he starred at Norman Wilkinson's painting "Plymouth Harbor." He was not seen again.

■   **2:10 A.M.:** Wallace Hartley and the three remaining members of the orchestra, now wearing jackets and lifebelts, began to play their final tune. Hartley had always said that his favorite piece of music was *"Nearer, My God, to Thee,"* and that he wanted it played at his funeral. Hartley probably called out to play this favorite song of his even though it was not on the "approved list" of pre-numbered pieces. All of the musicians knew it anyway.

Survivors disagreed about which piece of music the orchestra played last. Three different testimonials survive: *"Nearer, My God, to Thee,"* *"Autumn,"* and *"Songe d'Automne."* And it might have been a different tune altogether. The "last" song heard by a survivor depended on how far he or she was from the ship when they heard it. They had no way of knowing whether another song was played thereafter—or not. In any case, with the water rushing up the Boat Deck, Hartley and the orchestra played their final selection. At this late date we know one thing for certain: will never know for sure what song it was.

2:15 A.M.: LIFEBOAT COLLAPSIBLE B

The only two lifeboats left were Collapsible B on the port side roof of the officer's quarters, and Collapsible A on the starboard side roof. *Titanic* was sinking rapidly now, and those nearby worked frantically to unlash the boats and move them off the roof.

After the lashings were cut, several dozen men pushed Collapsible B off the roof, but it landed on the Boat Deck upside down. Although they tried to right it, the lifeboat weighed too much and there was not enough time. As the bridge slid under the water, a wave pushed the lifeboat over the railing into the sea. It was still upside down. The wave also washed Second Officer Lightoller, Sixth Officer Moody, and dozens of others into the frigid Atlantic water.

- As they were struggling in the freezing water, people tried desperately to climb onto the bottom of the upside-down lifeboat. A few had made it when the giant forward funnel fell over. Although it missed the lifeboat, it crushed dozens of people beneath it. The wave from that impact washed everyone off the lifeboat and pushed it about twenty yards away.

Lightoller reported what happened to him after he fell into the sea:

> *"I was driven back against the blower, which is a large thing which faces forward to the wind and which then goes down to the stoke hole: but there is a grating there and it was against this grating that I was sucked by the water, and held there under water. There was a terrific blast of air and water and I was blown out clear. . . . Colonel Gracie, I believe, was sucked down in identically the same manner. . . caused by the water rushing down below as the ship was going down."*

- After being sucked into the blower holes—twice each—both Lightoller and Gracie, freezing and exhausted, managed to get on top of Collapsible B. Also on the overturned lifeboat was young Jack Thayer, First Class passenger Algernon Barkworth wearing an enormous fur coat that kept him afloat and alive, wireless operator Harold Bride, and about thirty other men. There were no women because everyone on the lifeboat had to get on it by their own devices, and everyone had to climb out of the freezing water.

- The story of Collapsible B is one of the more dramatic of a very dramatic night. The water temperature was 28 degrees, and the air temperature was 31 degrees. The men on the upside-down lifeboat all climbed out of the water, which meant they were soaked. They huddled together throughout the night. At first, about three dozen people were able to get onto the lifeboat, but it was soon seriously overcrowded and newcomers had to be pushed away. While many of the men in the center section of the lifeboat were standing, those on the bow and stern were kneeling and using wooden planks to try to paddle away from both the sinking ship and the mass of humanity trying to climb onto their lifeboat.

> *"Hold on to what you have, old boy. One more would sink us all,"* someone on the lifeboat shouted to one of the swimmers in the water. *"That's all right, boys; keep cool. Good luck, God bless you,"* replied the unidentified swimmer as he swam away to die.

- Chief Baker Charles Joughin (who would experience one of the most remarkable exits from *Titanic*) managed to get on top of Collapsible B after holding onto its side and treading water for well over ninety minutes. Joughin did not freeze as most of the other people in the water did. His size provided a lot of body fat, and prior to entering the water he had consumed most of a bottle of Scotch, which kept him warm.

- Although the sea had been flat calm all night, a slight swell developed as morning approached. Collapsible B rolled with it, each time letting a little more air escape from under the sides of the lifeboat. As the air escaped, the lifeboat sank lower. All of the men on the lifeboat were standing, huddled together, trying to conserve body heat. To keep the lifeboat from sinking or having everyone dumped off, the indomitable Lightoller kept counting cadence, *"Lean to the left, lean to the right,"* as the lifeboat rolled with the swells. Several men on the lifeboat died during the night and they were allowed to slide off to make more room for the others. One of the dead was probably John Phillips, the Marconi operator. At least several survivors said they saw him there, but he was not among the final survivors.

- **2:15 A.M.:** The wave that swept over the bridge probably also claimed the life of Captain Edward J. Smith. Although many stories have circulated about people who supposedly saw Smith in the water (one has him swimming up to a lifeboat with a baby in his arms), the bridge is the last place Lightoller saw him, and his is the last credible sighting. In all likelihood, Smith was standing on the port side bridge wing when the wave crashed over it. Standing next to him was his longtime friend John Jacob Astor.

- **2:15 A.M.:** The forward funnel had stabilizing wires attached to various parts of the deck. Some of the wires were attached to the far side of the forward expansion joint. As the front of the ship filled with water, the joint expanded and the resulting tension snapped the stabilizing wires. The forward funnel—the same one that nearly swamped Collapsible B and pushed it away from the ship—tumbled toward the sea. It fell toward the port side, crushing the port side bridge wing and killing everyone under it. John Astor was one of them. His body was later found crushed beyond recognition and covered with soot. The funnel may have also killed Captain Smith.

- Marconi operator Harold Bride found himself *under* the overturned lifeboat with only his head above the freezing water. As more people climbed onto the bottom of the lifeboat, it kept sinking lower, and at some point Bride swam out from under it and tried to get on, but was prevented from doing so by the people already on the lifeboat. He then swam around to the other side and found someone who knew him and was let climb aboard. Harold Bride later stated,

"I was just lending a hand when a large wave came awash of the deck. The wave carried the boat off. I had hold of an oar-lock and went off with it. The next I knew I was in the boat . . . and the boat was upside down, and I was under it. . . . I was under water. How I got out from under the boat I don't know. There were men all around me—hundreds of them. The sea was dotted with them, all depending on their lifebelts."

2:15 A.M.: Collapsible Lifeboat A

The last lifeboat, Collapsible A, had also been pushed off the top of the officer's quarters. It landed upright on the Boat Deck. Several crewmen tried to attach it to the falls of Lifeboat 1, but the ship was sinking too fast. Finally, a few people managed to jump into it while the rest were washed away by the same wave that floated Collapsible B off the port side deck. Most survivors were surprised to see that this lifeboat survived at all. It was tangled up in all the loose ropes and cables lying around the deck. Somehow it floated free and several more people managed to climb into it.

The boat was floating when a couple of crewmen cut the falls away to keep it from being pulled under as the ship sank. It was filling up with people who were climbing out of the water when the forward funnel fell over. The resulting wave washed everyone out of the lifeboat and filled it with water. The canvas sides were also down, so it had little buoyancy. However, several men did get back on board, and they helped several others, including one woman, into the lifeboat. Mrs. Stanton (Rosa) Abbott, who lost her two sons when the ship went down, was the lucky woman. During the night a dozen of the men died from exposure and most of their bodies were dumped overboard to improve buoyancy. Three corpses were left in the lifeboat. Perhaps its occupants did not have the strength to pitch them overboard.

■ **2:15 A.M.:** As the stern rose ever higher, every item inside *Titanic*—furniture, dishes, beds, lamps, boilers, coal, engines, and people—began sliding toward the bow of the ship in one continuous cacophony of noise, one continuous roar.

In his excellent book *A Night to Remember*, Walter Lord provides a fascinating description that cannot be improved upon:

> There has never been a mixture like it—29 boilers . . . the jeweled copy of the Rubáiyát . . . 800 cases of shelled walnuts . . . 15,000 bottles of ale and stout . . . huge anchor chains (each link weighed 175 pounds) . . . 30 cases of golf clubs and tennis rackets for Spalding . . . Eleanor Widener's trousseau . . . tons of coal . . . Major Peuchen's tin box . . . 30,000 fresh eggs . . . dozens of potted palms . . . 5 grand

pianos . . . a little mantel clock in B-38 . . . the massive silver duck press . . . And still it grew—tumbling trellises, ivy pots and wicker chairs in the Café Parisien . . . shuffleboard sticks . . . the 50-phone switchboard . . . two reciprocating engines and the revolutionary low-pressure turbine . . . 8 dozen tennis balls for R.F. Downey & Co., a cask of china for Tiffany's, a case of gloves for Marshall Field . . . the remarkable ice-making machine on G deck . . . Billy Carter's new English automobile . . . the Ryerson's 16 trunks, beautifully packed by Victorine.

■ **2:15 A.M.:** As the stern rose higher, the three huge propellers towered above everyone in the water. The after-decks crawled with people trying to avoid the inevitable, trying to delay death for a few more moments. On the aft Well Deck, Father Thomas R. Byles had about a hundred people gathered around him. He was hearing confessions until the end. He had to hold onto a piece of machinery to keep from falling off the tilting deck.

■ **2:17 A.M.:** Marconi operator Jack Phillips sent his last transmission and then walked out of the wireless office to the port side and stepped into the water that rushed up the Boat Deck and into the cabin.

■ **2:18 A.M.:** The engineers, who had remained in the very bottom of the ship while struggling to maintain power for the lights and thus sacrificed themselves, finally lost the battle that could not have ever been fully won. The lights flickered once and then went out forever. The entire engineering crew, all 35 of those gallant men, went down with the ship.

■ **2:20 A.M.:** By this time the ship was almost vertical in the water. That portion behind the after-expansion joint suddenly split down to the keel. The stern settled back as the forward three-fourths of the ship broke away except at the keel. Within a few moments the bulk of *Titanic* would begin her descent toward the bottom of the sea more than two miles away. The remaining funnels broke off as they came in contact with the water.

> *"When the Titanic upended to sink,"* reported young Marshall Drew, *"all was blacked out until the tons of machinery crashed to the bow. . . . As this happened the hundreds and hundreds of people were thrown into the sea. I shall never forget the screams of these people as they perished in water said to be 28 degrees."*

As reported by storekeeper Frank M. Prentiss,

> "I hung on by the rail and then let myself drop into the sea. The distance to the water was quite 75 feet, and I thought I was never going to get there. When I did come into contact with the water, it was like a great knife cutting into me. My limbs and body ached for days afterwards."

- The after part of the ship, which appeared to have broken off from the rest, was still attached at the keel, and as the forward part of the ship sank, it pulled the after-portion, almost 200 feet of the ship, upright into a vertical position. It remained there for a few seconds, stationary, as bulkheads collapsed and she lost her buoyancy. And then the stern portion began its final slide into the sea.

- Chief Baker Joughin stood on top of the railing at the very back of the ship (where the fictional Rose and Jack stood in the film *Titanic*). Joughin, using the flagstaff as a support, reported that the ship went down much as an elevator does. A big bubble of trapped air burst to the surface, and as the stern went under, Joughin simply stepped off it into the water. He did not even get his hair wet.

- **2:20 A.M.:** Five minutes after the last lifeboat floated off the ship and two hours and forty minutes after striking the iceberg, RMS *Titanic*, the world's largest and most luxurious ship, disappeared beneath the surface of the frigid North Atlantic Ocean.

CHAPTER 13

RESCUE

2:20 A.M.–4:00 P.M., APRIL 15, 1912

While the lifeboats were being loaded and the various dramas played out on *Titanic*, Captain Arthur H. Rostron and the crew of *Carpathia* were speeding northwest at more than 17 knots to try and rescue the survivors. The speed was well beyond her rating and much faster than she had ever traveled before.

The journey took hours, and there was nothing for most of the crew to do but wait—and hope. 1:00 a.m. came and passed, as did 2:00, 3:00, and 4:00 a.m., and still *Carpathia* steamed on. The air and water temperature were below freezing and time was of the essence. Rostron clung to the vain hope that *Carpathia* would arrive at *Titanic's* location before she sank.

IN THE LIFEBOATS

At 2:18 a.m., April 15, 1912, *Titanic's* lights flickered once before falling dark forever. Two minutes later, *Titanic's* stern disappeared under the surface of the ocean. Only 680 passengers and crew had been put aboard the lifeboats, and another fourteen picked up out of the water, seven of whom would later die. Dozens more climbed aboard the overturned Collapsible C; 18 would survive. In and on the twenty lifeboats were some 712 people. More than 1,500 others were struggling and screaming and dying in the freezing water—or had been trapped inside the ship and were already deep beneath the dark Atlantic waters.

The only light came from the stars, a match, or an occasional flare. It had taken 90 minutes to launch the lifeboats, and most of them were now scattered across miles of sea. Daylight would reveal the full extent of this dispersal; some were more than five miles away when the sun rose above the horizon. Dawn would also reveal the lifeboats were what they

CARPATHIA'S WIRELESS OPERATOR HAROLD T. COTTAM HAD HIS WIRELESS SET RUNNING AFTER ITS PLANNED SHUTDOWN. HIS QUICK ACTIONS BROUGHT RELIEF TO THE SURVIVORS IN THE LIFEBOATS. *(National Archives)*

CAPTAIN ARTHUR H. ROSTRON OF THE CARPATHIA. ROSTRON IS ONE OF THE TRUE HEROES OF THE TITANIC DISASTER. QUICK AND DECISIVE ACTION BROUGHT HIS SHIP TO THE WRECK SITE TWO HOURS AFER TITANIC SANK. HE RESCUED ALL OF THE SURVIVORS. *(National Archives)*

THE CUNARD LINER CARPATHIA *(National Archives)*

were—tiny objects surrounded by dozens of mountainous icebergs, including one that looked like a huge rock with black and red paint smudged along its side.

■ When *Titanic's* stern slid beneath the water an amazing thing happened: nothing. The giant suction everyone believed would pull even the lifeboats under never materialized. There was a small ripple but little else to disturb the surface of the calm sea. The slight gulp did not even create a wave. Because the fires in the boilers had been put out earlier, none of them exploded when submerged in the icy water.

■ There were, however, 1,500 people thrashing around in the 28-degree water. Their screams for help were loud at first, as might be expected with so many in such a small area clinging to the faint hope of salvation. Within just a few minutes they began to grow fainter. Within about twenty minutes there was silence.

Young Eva Hart remembered the moment with a simple, chilling statement: *"[T]wenty boats and a quiet sea."* She later recalled,

> *"[A]nd finally the ghastly noise of the people thrashing about and screaming and drowning, that finally ceased. I remember saying to my mother once, 'How dreadful that noise was' and I'll always remember her reply 'yes, but think back about the silence that followed it.' . . .But all of a sudden the ship wasn't there, the lights weren't there and the cries weren't there. . . "*

Twelve-year-old Ruth Becker was on Lifeboat 13. She knew her mother and siblings were on another lifeboat so she was not overly concerned about them. Years later she wrote:

> *"It [the lifeboat] was filled to standing room with men and women in every conceivable condition of dress and undress. It was bitter cold—a curious, deadening, bitter cold. And then with all of this, there fell on the ear the most terrible noises that human beings ever listened to—the cries of hundreds of people struggling in the icy cold water, crying for help with a cry that we knew could not be answered."*

■ Also on Lifeboat 13 was Leah Aks. Ruth Becker recalled . . .

> *"Standing on one side of me was a little German lady. She was crying and I asked her why. She told me—through an interpreter standing near—that her little six-weeks-old baby had been taken away from her . . . and put into another boat. The baby was wrapped so heavily in blankets that she was afraid it would be taken for baggage and thrown in the ocean."*

- One would imagine a lifeboat would be permanently equipped with emergency equipment, food, water, a compass, lights, and oars. One would be wrong. Most of them had only oars, and inexperienced crewmen lost many of them. Only one lifeboat had a lantern. Before the lifeboats were loaded, some were supplied with loaves of bread brought up from the storeroom by the bakers. It was bad enough that the survivors had to watch the world's largest ship sink before their eyes, but until a rescue ship arrived, they were stranded in the middle of the North Atlantic with absolutely nothing except the clothes they were wearing and the lifeboat in which they were sitting.

- Few if any of the survivors knew a rescue ship was steaming toward them. The only lifeboat in which anyone knew for certain help was close at hand was overturned Collapsible B, which supported both Lightoller and Marconi operator Bride. The people in the other lifeboats could only wait through the night, hoping that daylight would bring rescue.

- Once he had sorted things out on Lifeboat 14, Fifth Officer Lowe started rounding up some of the other lifeboats. He figured he could move some of the passengers around and have an empty lifeboat with which he could pick up swimmers. Lowe gathered up Lifeboats 10, 12, and 4, and along with 14, tied them all together. He then transferred 55 passengers in his lifeboat to the other four and accepted some experienced oarsmen to help him row. He asked for volunteers to go back to the wreck and later reported,

> "It was at this time that I found the Italian. He came aft and had a shawl over his head, and I suppose he had skirts. Anyhow, I pulled the shawl off his face and saw he was a man. He was in a great hurry to get into the other boat and I got hold of him and pitched him in [to the other boat] . . . he was not worth being handled better."

Edith Brown later related that Lowe told the passenger, "I've a good mind to shoot you, you might have capsized the boat."

- Seaman Joseph Scarrott recalled that they. . .

> "divided the passengers of our boat amongst the other four. . . . [W]e rowed away amongst the wreckage as we heard cries for help coming from that direction. When we got to it the sight we saw was awful. We were amongst hundreds of dead bodies floating in lifebelts."

■ Transferring passengers was enough to drive Lowe crazy: it was 2:30 in the morning, pitch black, freezing, and the passengers were hopping from lifeboat to lifeboat in the middle of the ocean. Lowe lost his patience and began swearing, shouting to one of the hesitant women, *"Jump, damn you, jump!"* His language did not endear him to many of the ladies, and several later complained about it. Some launched a rumor that he was drunk. Lowe enjoyed that one because, as anyone that knew Lowe also knew he was a lifelong teetotaler.

Eventually he got everyone moved around and at 3:00 a.m. set off to look for survivors in the mass of wreckage and humanity that was all that was left of *Titanic*.

Lowe and his crew could hear some people making feeble calls for help out of the darkness, but locating them proved to be almost impossible. In all, only four people were plucked from the sea, including First Class passenger William Hoyt, who shortly died from the cold. While transferring the passengers and looking for survivors, Lowe came upon a floating door with the body of a small person on it that, by all appearances, was already dead. It turned out to be Japanese passenger Masabumi Hosono, who had tied himself to the floating piece of wood. When he didn't answer when called, Lowe said, *"What's the use? He's dead, likely, and if he isn't there's others better worth saving than a Jap!"* After he moved, indicating he was still alive, Hosono was hauled into the lifeboat and a couple of the women rubbed him down and warmed him up. A short time later Hosono stood up, stretched his arms, stamped his feet, and within a few minutes regained most of his strength. When one of the crewmen became too tired to continue rowing, Hosono pushed him aside and rowed the rest of the night. Later, a chagrined Lowe changed his tune: *"I'm ashamed of what I said about the little blighter. I'd save the likes o' him six times over if I got the chance."* Unfortunately, when he arrived home in Japan, Hosono was ostracized for the rest of his life for having survived the disaster.

Lowe's effort was a heroic but largely fruitless attempt to find more survivors, but at least he went back and tried. He was the only one who made the effort. However, he was only able to recover four people, one of whom later died.

■ Lifeboat 1 held 12 people. Fireman Charles Hendrickson told the others, *"It's up to us to go back and pick up anyone in the water."* No one said a word in reply. When Hendrickson said it again, Sir Cosmo Duff Gordon said he did not think they should try it because the lifeboat would be swamped, so the dozen people in Lifeboat 1 drifted around a couple hundred yards from hundreds of people, many of whom could have been saved.

Fourth Officer Boxhall asked the women in Lifeboat 2 if they should go back, but not a single woman was in favor of the idea. His lifeboat, too, drifted aimlessly in the night. In every one of the lifeboats a similar act was played out. Someone would suggest going back, but the suggestion was refused and nothing was done.

■ There were eighteen lifeboats capable of picking up survivors and only 14 people were hauled out of the water: Collapsible D picked up one passenger (Mr. Hoyt, whose wife was on that lifeboat); Lifeboat 4 picked up eight who just happened to be in the right place at the right time; Lowe picked up four in Lifeboat 14, and one more was picked up by Lifeboat 13.

■ It was now after 3:00 a.m. and the sea was quiet. Almost all of those in the water were dead, many already frozen stiff by the below-freezing temperature of the water. The adrenaline generated during the past few hours while *Titanic* was sinking began to take its toll on the survivors in the lifeboats. Most were in shock, and few fully realized just how many family members and friends were lost forever. It had not really occurred to them yet, and most survivors comforted themselves by believing that their families and friends were on other lifeboats.

■ Because the lifeboats were scattered for miles over the ocean and only one was equipped with a lantern, it was impossible to see the other boats. Fourth Officer Boxhall began firing off his little green flares, hoping that survivors in some of the other lifeboats would see them and row his way. Although he did not know that *Carpathia* was en route, firing the rockets would help guide that ship toward them.

■ Several other lifeboats joined up over time: Lifeboats 6 and 16 tied up and transferred a stoker to 6 to help with rowing. Other lifeboats met up and transferred passengers. Mrs. Washington Dodge was in Lifeboat 5 and kept pleading with everyone to go back to pick up some of the people in the water. They refused, and Mrs. Dodge decided she did not want anything more to do with them, so when Lifeboat 7 rowed by, she switched boats.

■ Throughout the night the survivors coped as best they could under the circumstances. Everyone was lost in their own thoughts, waiting for whatever the immediate future might bring.
Surrounding all of the lifeboats was a sea full of debris. Everything that could float off the decks did so as *Titanic* went down—cork, wooden doors and deck chairs, paneling, furniture, chunks of timber, lifebelts, and bodies. There were also icebergs in the area and in the quiet night, water could be heard splashing against them. Some of the lifeboats even bumped into icebergs in the dark.

- With the exception of the engineering crew, the men who drowned in Boiler Rooms 6 and 5 when they flooded and the staff of the à la carte restaurant who had been locked into their cabins below decks, most of the 1,500 people who died were probably on one of the open decks when the ship sank, and their corpses were now floating around the lifeboats. It was probably good it was so dark because the survivors could not see them. The current would quickly pick them up and within a few hours the bodies would be drifting away in all directions, many pushed up against the icebergs, which would hold them there for days.

- Second Officer Lightoller recalled the sensation of being in the 28 degree water *"was that of a thousand knives being driven into the body."* Few of the people in the water lived more than 10 minutes, and most had gone into shock within moments of coming in contact with it. The one notable exception was Chief Baker Joughin, who had enough alcohol in his system to keep him alive for well over 90 minutes while he hung onto the side of Collapsible B waiting for someone to fall off so he could take his place.
  Since only Collapsible A and Collapsible B were close enough for any of the swimmers to reasonably get to, that is where they headed. Neither was a good choice, with Collapsible B floating upside down and Collapsible A almost swamped. The best and strongest swimmers had the best chance of making it, but in the cold, even they did not last long.

- The survivors in all the lifeboats except Collapsibles B and A were reasonably well off for the short term, and those standing on top of B at least had an officer who took control and had knowledge that help was soon at hand. The twenty-odd men and one woman standing on Collapsible A, which was awash with ice water up to everyone's knees, had nothing to sustain them. Mrs. Abbott, the only woman on the boat, had actually been on the poop deck when the stern went under, and what little suction there was pulled her and her two sons down. She somehow managed to get to the surface and onto Collapsible A, but she spent the night pondering the terrible fate of her sons. Passenger Edvard Lindell managed to get onto the lifeboat and someone tried to pull his wife on board, but she slipped away and was lost. When Lindell was told what had happened, it was already too late because he had already frozen to death.

- As reality set in and shock wore off, some of the women hailed each passing lifeboat calling for their husbands or sons or friends. In Lifeboat 6, Madame de Villiers kept calling for her son. She was imagining things because fortunately for her, her son had not even been on the ship.

- It did not take long for the cold night air and wet clothes to affect many of the survivors. Mrs. Charlotte Collyer was so cold and numb she fell over, catching her hair in an oarlock, which resulted in a good portion of it being pulled out by the roots. Most of the firemen, stokers, and trimmers who had been on duty down in the boiler rooms were only wearing sleeveless shirts and short pants, and these men suffered terribly from the icy night air. Other people in the various boats tried to help keep them warm as best they could, often giving some of their own clothing to help others.

A crewman even gave Mrs. Washington Dodge the stockings off his feet, explaining, "*I assure you, ma'am, they are perfectly clean. I just put them on this morning.*" Proper decorum had to be maintained.

■ Many of the women helped with the rowing or manning of the tiller, partly because they were needed and partly because it helped keep them warm. On Lifeboat 8, however, Mrs. J. Stuart White appointed herself as the keeper of the light. She had a cane with a little built-in light, and she waved it about all night, helping no one and confusing most. She became so animated that one of the crewmen threatened to toss the cane into the sea.

■ As the night wore on, as if there wasn't enough to concern themselves, the survivors on most of the lifeboats broke out in petty squabbles. Some complained about the men who smoked, Mrs. Washington Dodge complained about the people who would not go back to look for survivors, and in Lifeboat 11 *Titanic's* masseuse, Maud Slocombe, threatened to toss a woman overboard who kept setting off an alarm clock!

■ Over in Lifeboat 6, Major Peuchen and Quartermaster Hichens quarreled all night—Peuchen wanting to give orders and Hichens not wanting to take them. Things got so out of hand that Molly Brown finally had to step in and threaten to toss Hichens into the water if he did not shut up. He did, wrapping himself in the lifeboat's sail where he spent the rest of the night sulking.

■ Passenger Millvina Dean later told of,

> "*another woman whose husband was left behind was only concerned that she'd lost her feather bed . . . she didn't say anything about her husband, just that her feather bed had gone.*"

■ Another survivor remembered,

> "*We sang as we rowed, all of us. . . and we were still singing when we saw the lights of the Carpathia. Then we stopped singing, and prayed.*"

- Throughout the night, Boxhall in Lifeboat 2 kept firing his little green flares and at 2:30 a.m., ten minutes after *Titanic* slipped beneath the waves, one of these flares was seen far in the distance by the crew of *Carpathia*, speeding toward the spot where *Titanic* had gone down.

RESCUE

Around 3:00 a.m., Captain Rostron on *Carpathia* ordered the firing of rockets every 15 minutes to let the survivors know that help was on its way.

- **3:30 A.M.:** Someone on a lifeboat noticed a rocket fired by *Carpathia* and yelled out. On several of the other lifeboats people also saw it—a flash of light on the horizon followed by a distant boom. Some thought it was lightning; Hichens thought it was a falling star. It was enough, though, to those who saw it hope that help was on its way. Before long many could see salvation—a large steamer coming up, firing rockets and showing several rows of bright lights along the side.

- **3:35 A.M.:** *Carpathia* was at the location *Titanic* should have been had the coordinates Boxhall worked out not been off by several miles. If afloat, *Titanic* should have been seen, but all the crew saw were the outlines of numerous icebergs. Off in the distance, a small green light could be seen low in the water, so Rostron had the ship change course and slow down. He had the engine room alerted for a quick stop.

- By now survivors in all of the lifeboats had seen the steamer. In Lifeboat 3, someone put a match to a newspaper and then to Mrs. Davidson's straw hat. Boxhall in Lifeboat 2 burned his last flare, and Mrs. White in Lifeboat 8 waved her cane with the light in it.

- **4:00 A.M.:** Rostron ordered the engines stopped. There was a lifeboat only 300 yards ahead showing a small green light, and Rostron did not want to run it down. He ordered "dead slow ahead" to move up to the lifeboat and blew the ship's whistle to let the people know they had been seen. Rostron wanted to bring the lifeboat up on *Carpathia's* port side, but an iceberg was in the way, so the ship turned and the lifeboat approached on the starboard side.

- **4:10 A.M.:** The women on Lifeboat 2 started climbing up the side of *Carpathia* with the assistance of crewmen on the ship and Fourth Officer Boxhall in the lifeboat. Later, Boxhall was asked by Rostron to report to the bridge and when he arrived, soaked and shivering, Boxhall told Rostron that *Titanic* had sunk at 2:20 a.m., less than two hours before.

COLLAPSIBLE D WITH 40 PEOPLE AND PARTIALLY FLOODED IS BEING TOWED BY LIFEBOAT 14 AS IT DRAWS NEAR CARPATHIA. *(National Archives)*

LIFEBOAT 6 WITH AROUND 28 PEOPLE, INCLUDING MOLLY BROWN AND ROBERT HICHENS (STANDING AT THE TILLER) APPROACHES CARPATHIA. *(National Archives)*

By now, most of the passengers on *Carpathia* knew what was going on and they poured out of their cabins and lined the decks of the ship, searching in the dark for more lifeboats. Because of the dark and the fear of running down unseen lifeboats, *Carpathia* remained stationary and the lifeboats had to be rowed to the ship until it became light enough to see. Only then did *Carpathia* slowly move through the ice, going from lifeboat to lifeboat, picking up the half frozen and mournful survivors.

One by one, the sad little fleet of lifeboats, all that remained of the world's largest and most luxurious ocean liner, slowly drew closer to *Carpathia*, their survivors cheered by the prospect of rescue.

- Those who could not climb up the ladders were hauled up in slings and chairs while the children were brought up in ash bags. Everyone was met on the deck and taken below, where they were warmed up and given food and something hot to drink. Young Ruth Becker reported she was so cold she could not move. She was put into a sling and tied in because she could not hold on.

- The first light of dawn began a beautiful new day. Many commented on how the icebergs, some a hundred feet high, looked pink and yellow in the morning sun. Seaman Joseph Scarrott later remembered,

  > ". . . the day was just beginning to dawn. We then saw we were surrounded with icebergs and field ice. Some of the fields of ice were from sixteen to twenty miles long."

- When Young Marshall Drew awoke in the lifeboat . . .

  > "it was broad daylight as we approached the Carpathia. Looking around over the gunwale it seemed to me like the Arctic. Icebergs of huge size ringed the horizon for 360 degrees..."

- After Fifth Officer Lowe in Lifeboat 14 had made his attempt to save people in the water, he spent the next hour rowing from lifeboat to lifeboat checking on their condition. He left a little group of lifeboats (4, 10, and 12) tied together for mutual support.

- Once *Carpathia* was in sight, Lowe hoisted the sail on Lifeboat 14 and set off to reach the rescue ship. When asked how he knew enough to set a sail, he replied: "Not all sailors are boatmen, and not all boatmen are sailors." Shortly Lowe came up on Collapsible D, which was low in the water and did not have enough crew to row. Lowe tied a rope to the collapsible and pulled it along.

At about that point Lowe spotted the swamped Collapsible A more than a mile off, looking as if it would sink at any moment. More than half the thirty people who had been on it during the night had frozen to death standing in knee-deep water. Lowe sailed over to Collapsible A and transferred the dozen remaining survivors, including Mrs. Rosa Abbott, and one body, to Lifeboat 14. He then removed the sea plugs so the lifeboat would sink. Left on board were the bodies of three men.

▪ Over on Collapsible B, Second Officer Lightoller was still calling *"lean to the left, lean to the right"* every time a wave rocked the little lifeboat, trying to keep what little air was left under it from out escaping under the sides. Shortly after the sky was bright enough to see, Lightoller saw Lowe's little group of boats and began blowing his whistle.

▪ About the time Lowe was hitching up to Collapsible D and the little flotilla he had left behind was making its way toward *Carpathia*, Quartermaster Perkis in Lifeboat 4 and Seaman Clinch in Lifeboat 12 heard an officer's whistle blowing in the distance. Scanning the horizon, they noticed, off in the dark to the west about one-half mile away, what looked to be a group of men standing atop one of the funnels that had broken off *Titanic*.

Perkis and Clinch immediately untied from the other two lifeboats and rowed toward them. As they drew near, they realized the survivors were standing on an overturned lifeboat. It was Lightholler's Collapsible B. The boat was barely above water, and most of the men were almost knee deep in it. When Lifeboat 4 rowed alongside, its wake nearly washed everyone off. Lightoller supervised the transfer, one by one, of all the people on his lifeboat into Lifeboats 12 and 4. Young Jack Thayer crawled into Lifeboat 12, so cold and stiff he did not even notice his mother huddled in Lifeboat 4. Lifeboat 12 was now seriously overloaded, so Lightoller took command of it and slowly steered it toward *Carpathia*.

▪ The small fleet of small boats started to converge upon *Carpathia*, some rowing toward it until daylight when *Carpathia* was able to steam toward them. At 4:45 a.m. Lifeboat 13 tied up, and forty-five minutes later Lifeboat 7 pulled alongside. One of the very few happy reunions took place at this point when Dr. Washington Dodge climbed off Lifeboat 7 and met his wife and son, who had been on Lifeboat 13.

▪ **6:00 A.M.:** Lifeboat 3 pulled alongside *Carpathia*. Miss Elizabeth Shutes recalled that she was so weak that she had to be lifted up by a sling. One of the passengers on *Carpathia* was Louis Ogden. He was watching the activities from the deck, to his amazement, he watched his old friend Henry Sleeper Harper climb aboard with his wife, dog, and dragoman Hammad Hassab.

- **6:15 A.M.:** Collapsible C pulled up next to *Carpathia* and the first person off the boat was Bruce Ismay. When asked if he wanted to go below deck for something hot to eat or drink, he replied,

> *"No, I do not want anything at all . . . If you will leave me alone, I'll be much happier here. No, wait, if you can get me in some room where I can be quiet, I wish you would."*

- With that, Dr. Frank McGhee, *Carpathia's* senior doctor, led Ismay to his own stateroom, where Ismay sequestered himself for the rest of the trip.

  Ismay's self-imposed isolation did not win him any favors in the world of public opinion. It was bad enough he had taken a precious seat in a lifeboat, but now it appeared he wanted special privilege. He would be pilloried for his actions, and from that day forward, J. Bruce Ismay was a ruined man.

- William Carter also climbed off Collapsible C. He knew he had put his family on a lifeboat, but did not know which one. Carter, at least, would stand on the deck and watch each approaching boat with interest.

- **7:00 A.M.:** Fifth Officer Lowe brought Lifeboat 14, still towing Collapsible D, alongside and off-loaded his passengers. He carefully put the sail and mast away so the boat could be used again, if necessary.

- Lifeboat 4 eventually pulled up and William Carter saw his wife and daughter but not his ten-year-old son. Carter shouted down to the boat, *"Where's my boy?"* Little William Jr. looked up and replied, *"Here I am, Father."* He had been wearing a girl's hat and his father did not recognize him.

  The Thayers, mother and son, found each other on *Carpathia,* but they would not find Mr. Thayer amongst the survivors.

- A breeze came up around 7:00 a.m. and the water became choppy. By 8:15 a.m., every boat except Lifeboat 12 had unloaded. This particular (and unique) lifeboat was seriously overloaded: 74 people were jammed in a small boat designed to hold 65. Slowly Rostron moved *Carpathia* closer to it and at 8:30 a.m. Lifeboat 12 tied up to *Carpathia* and began unloading its weary passengers. All of the lifeboats were now accounted for and by 8:45 a.m. it was all over. The last person to board *Carpathia* was Second Officer Lightoller.

Passenger Ruth Becker later commented:

> *"That was the saddest time of all. So many of the women who had been put into lifeboats by their husbands—and told they would meet each other later—realized that they would never see each other again."*

- With all 20 of *Titanic's* lifeboats accounted for, 18 having come up with passengers and Collapsible B sunk and Collapsible A cast adrift with three bodies on it, Rostron knew he had all the survivors he would find. *Carpathia* made several swings through the area where Rostron thought *Titanic* had gone down, but not a single living person was to be seen. In fact, there wasn't much of anything. A few deck chairs, bits of paper and other flotsam, and a single body, marked the last known location of the greatest ocean liner the world had ever known. Everything else that had escaped *Titanic's* plunge to the bottom was now drifting off with the currents.

- Rostron counted heads and found he had 708 survivors and one body from *Titanic*. The corpse was that of Edvard Lindell, who had been brought along from Collapsible A. Within a few hours three of the survivors—all men plucked from the water—would die. Only 705 survivors would make the trip to New York.

- Rostron had to make an immediate but easy decision about where to go with his survivors. He did not have enough supplies on his ship to continue east, so he ordered *Carpathia* to turn about and make for New York City. Before doing so, he ordered thirteen of *Titanic's* lifeboats (all except Lifeboats 4, 14, 15, and the four collapsibles) winched up and stowed. Rostron may have been thinking that he might need them later, or that there might be some sentimental reason for keeping them. Possibly he was thinking of the survivors, who according to the insurance rules of the time would only be able to collectively receive the value of anything recovered from the wreck.

- Before *Carpathia* left the scene, *Mount Temple*, answering *Titanic's* distress message, arrived on the scene. Rostron asked the captain of *Mount Temple* to continue the search.
   Carpathia steamed south and then west around the ice field. It would take four hours and 56 miles before she got out of the field to begin the sad trip home. One more ship came up before *Carpathia* left the scene. The ship snooped around a bit, checked with both *Carpathia* and *Mount Temple*, then headed for Boston. The ship was *Californian*, which had taken several hours to navigate through the ice once the sun had come up.

- **4:00 P.M.:** Rostron had the engines on *Carpathia* stopped and a brief religious service was held in the main lounge. When that was completed, Father Roger B. T. Anderson oversaw the sea burial of four bodies: Edvard Lindell and the three unknown survivors who died after rescue. It was so cold and windy that most of the passengers remained inside. When the burial was over, Rostron restarted the engines and *Carpathia* slowly steamed to New York.

CHAPTER 14

A Sad Awakening

On April 15 at 1:20 a.m. local time at *The New York Times* office in New York City, a wireless message was received from the Cape Race, Newfoundland, land station. "*At 10:25 o'clock tonight,*" it began . . .

"THE WHITE STAR LINE STEAMSHIP TITANIC CALLED 'CQD' TO THE MARCONI STATION HERE, AND REPORTED HAVING STRUCK AN ICEBERG. THE STEAMER SAID THAT IMMEDIATE ASSISTANCE WAS REQUIRED."

Further inquiry by the editors of the newspaper showed that several other ships including *Virginian*, *Baltic*, and *Olympic* had received the message and were steaming toward *Titanic*. Shortly before passing out of wireless range, *Virginian* reported that she had received a message that had suddenly been cut off.

The New York Times early morning edition ran the headline:

NEW LINER TITANIC HITS AN ICEBERG; SINKING BY THE BOW AT MIDNIGHT; WOMEN PUT OFF IN LIFEBOATS; LAST WIRELESS AT 12:27 A.M. BLURRED.

■ Throughout the morning of Monday April 15, all sorts of messages were being received in New York. The offices of the International Mercantile Marine were inundated with visitors and phone calls. Around noon a message was received from Cape Race that reported the kind of news that made everyone breathe a deep sigh of relief:

"ALL TITANIC PASSENGERS SAFE, VIRGINIAN TOWING THE LINER INTO HALIFAX"

■ International Mercantile Marine New York Manager and White Star Line Vice President P. A. S. Franklin accepted this great news and

arranged to have an express train readied to take family members to
Halifax and then bring them and *Titanic's* passengers back to New York.

White Star Line sent telegrams to many of the families:

> "ALL TITANIC'S PASSENGER'S SAFE, LINER BEING TOWED
> TO HALIFAX"

- Later in the day *The New York Times* reported in its afternoon city
edition that *Titanic* had foundered with great loss of life. This headline
was printed without confirmation but based upon several credible
assumptions. The editors had no idea just how right they were.

- Around 2:00 p.m. another message from an unknown source in
"mid-ocean" reported that *Carpathia* and *Parisian* were making for New
York with all passengers safely transferred, with *Parisian* towing *Titanic.*
Since the ships were coming to New York, the express train en route to
Halifax was ordered back to New York.

- The most powerful radio receiver/transmitter on the eastern
seaboard was located on top of Wanamaker's Department Store in New
York City. At 4:30 p.m. on Monday, twenty-one-year old David Sarnoff
went on duty at the Marconi wireless station on Wanamaker's. At 4:35
p.m. he received a faint signal from *Olympic*, almost unreadable because
of jamming by other stations. The message made Sarnoff's blood run
cold: *Titanic* had foundered at 12:47 a.m. New York time, and only some
675 people—the only known survivors—were headed to New York on the
Carpathia.
    The news stunned the world. This was the first firm report that there
had been a great loss of life. Sarnoff remained at his station for most of
the next two days. He went on to become one of the biggest and well
known names in radio and early television.

- Once the last of the survivors had been brought aboard *Carpathia*,
Rostron and Ismay met in Dr. McGhee's quarters. Ismay gave the captain
a message to send to P. A. S. Franklin in New York, via Cape Race:

> "DEEPLY REGRET ADVISE YOU TITANIC SANK THIS MORNING
> AFTER COLLISION WITH ICEBERG, RESULTING IN SERIOUS
> LOSS OF LIFE. FULL PARTICULARS LATER. BRUCE ISMAY."

Rostron passed the message to wireless operator Harold Cottam, but
told him not to send it right away. Ismay, meanwhile, believing the first
message had been sent, drafted another message and had it wired
immediately to Franklin:

"Very important you should hold Cedric daylight
for Titanic's crew. Answer. YAMSI."

- Ismay, under a poorly disguised name, was trying to have the White Star Line ship *Cedric* held up in New York for an extra day so that the surviving crew could be put on it immediately and sent home to Britain. The message caused considerable confusion at the IMM office in New York because it was sent and received before the earlier message detailing *Titanic's* sinking.

- By late Monday afternoon the word was out that *Titanic* had gone down with a heavy loss of life. On *Carpathia*, Harold Cottam was handed a complete listing of all of the survivors and told to send the list to Cape Race and anyone else who might receive it. On top of Wanamaker's Department Store, David Sarnoff was trying to copy down the list but there was so much static and other traffic breaking in that it was difficult to get the names right. In addition, Cottam had been working for over 24 hours and was extremely fatigued, and his transmissions were slow and garbled.

- Second Office Lightoller rounded up Harold Bride, who by this time had recovered somewhat from his ordeal. Though his feet were bandaged because of frostbite and he was as exhausted as anyone, Bride offered to spell Cottam. For the rest of the trip Cottam and Bride took turns processing messages and transmitting names.
  The pair (with Rostron's approval), made an early decision that they would not acknowledge any incoming messages received from newspapers or private individuals because there was just too much for them to do. With 700 names to transmit and outgoing messages from the survivors, it was more than they could handle and they did not have time to attend to incoming messages. They even refused to acknowledge a message from President William Howard Taft, who inquired about his friend Archibald Butt.

- With everyone screaming for information and with none forthcoming, President Taft ordered the U.S. Navy warship *Chester* to steam out to meet the *Carpathia*. *Chester*, with a better wireless set than *Carpathia*, was supposed to find out what was going on and then relay that information. When she arrived near *Carpathia*, Rostron essentially ignored her. No one was going to know anything until *Carpathia* docked in New York. Eventually, Taft ordered all wireless stations on the eastern seaboard to cease transmission except *Carpathia*, *Chester*, and David Sarnoff's station on top of Wanamaker's Department Store in New York City.

- By Wednesday April 17, the names of most of the survivors were finally known in New York. By this time they had been sent and resent several times. Many of *Carpathia's* messages were received and forwarded on by *Olympic* to England and by *Chester* to New York, so by now everyone had an idea of the scope of the disaster. *Carpathia* was expected to arrive in New York City on Thursday, April 18, about 10:00 p.m.

- While on board *Carpathia*, the survivors organized a committee and collected $15,000 to be given to *Carpathia's* crew on their next trip to New York City as thanks for coming to the rescue. The committee also obtained a silver loving cup that would be given to Rostron on a later trip.

  Cunard Line, owner of *Carpathia*, refused to allow the crew to accept the money, and instead turned it over to charity for the survivors. White Star Line later tried to pay Cunard for the expenses incurred in rescuing the survivors and bringing them back to New York. Cunard refused this as well, stating that this was a humanitarian gesture. Cunard, however, paid all the crewmen on *Carpathia* an extra month's pay for their efforts. Meanwhile, since they were no longer employed on *Titanic*, White Star Line stopped paying the surviving crewmembers the moment *Titanic* sank, and never offered them anything for their ordeal.

- April 18 was a cold, wet, and miserable day, but people started to line up at the Cunard pier at 6:00 p.m. Normal customs regulations were suspended and *Carpathia's* passengers would not have to clear through the Immigration Office on Ellis Island. The press and public were barred from the Cunard pier, and only immediate family members were allowed onto it. Hundreds of New York City policemen were called out to control the crowd. By 9:00 p.m. there were more than 40,000 people milling about in the streets around the pier waiting for *Carpathia's* arrival.

- Shortly after 9:00 p.m. *Carpathia* appeared out of the dark and drizzle, surrounded by a flotilla of boats of all sizes and shapes. Some were loaded with family members but most were full of reporters who were having a collective coronary as they fell over one another trying to get some information from the survivors.

  There had been a court injunction ordering reporters to stay away from *Carpathia*, but some managed to bribe their way onto the pilot boat. Once *Carpathia* slowed to allow the pilot to board, several of the newsmen tried to get on the ship but were forced back by the crew. One did manage to get aboard, but he was prevented from talking to the survivors.

  Carpathia managed to outrun the small boats and as the ship passed by the Statue of Liberty, a hard rain started coming down accompanied by lightning and thunder. Over on the Battery, more than 10,000 people waited in silence while *Carpathia* passed quietly by.

- The Cunard pier was in the Hudson River at the foot of Fourteenth Street. Some 30,000 people waited there for *Carpathia's* arrival. Instead of pulling into the Cunard pier, however, *Carpathia* steamed past it to the White Star Line pier at the foot of Nineteenth and Twentieth Streets. There she stopped long enough to unload *Titanic's* thirteen lifeboats, all that remained of what a few days before had been the world's largest and most luxurious ship.

    Finally, at 9:30 p.m. tugs pushed *Carpathia* into the Cunard pier and the First Class and Second Class passengers were allowed to get off to meet the friends and family who had come to greet them.

- Most of these passengers had made arrangements to get home, some even by private train. Mrs. Charles Hays, whose husband had been the president of the Grand Trunk Railroad, boarded a private train to take her and her daughter home to Montreal. Mrs. John Thayer and her son Jack, and Mrs. George Widener each had their own trains to take them back to Philadelphia. Mrs. Thayer had lost her husband and Mrs. Widener both her husband and son.

- Many others took waiting cars to one of the many hotel rooms that had been reserved by White Star Line. Ruth Becker later recalled,

    > *"Mother went shopping . . . and bought us clothes to wear. . . . The hotel made us honorary guests and would take nothing for food and lodging. . . . When we boarded the train to Indiana, Mother took me aside and said, 'Ruth, don't you dare tell anybody that we are survivors of the Titanic disaster.' But, when we got on the train, we were showered with cookies and gifts for my little brother and sister from the passengers."*

- By 10:30 p.m. all the First and Second Class passengers, family and friends were gone from the pier, as was most of the throng of people. Gone too were all the reporters; none were willing to wait around for the next group of *Titanic* survivors. At 11:00 p.m. the Third Class passengers were allowed off. Most of the 173 passengers were absolutely destitute with no money or belongings, and few had any place to go. White Star Line and several private relief organizations, including the American Red Cross, put the survivors up in the local armory and several hotels, and then helped them arrange transportation to their final destination.

- Except for one individual, the very last group to depart was *Titanic's* crew. *Cedric* had been allowed to leave port, so the crew was placed on the Red Star Line ship *Lapland*. There they remained until they were allowed to go home. Most of the crew was in as bad a shape as the Third Class survivors. They, too, had lost everything and their pay ended the moment *Titanic* slipped beneath the sea.

■   At noon on Saturday, April 20, thirty-six hours after *Carpathia* arrived in New York, and just fifteen minutes before it was to resume its much-delayed trip to the Mediterranean, the last *Titanic* survivor departed *Carpathia*. He was Harold Bride, *Titanic's* lone surviving Marconi operator. Bride worked the entire time after *Carpathia* docked, catching up on all the messages that had not been sent. Carried ashore on the shoulders of two of *Carpathia's* officers, he was taken to a hospital to recover from his frostbitten feet and extreme fatigue.

THE ICEBERG WITH RED AND BLACK PAINT ON ITS SIDE. IT IS OVER 100 FEET HIGH AND 90% OF IT IS UNDER WATER. PHOTOGRAPHED ON APRIL 15 BY A PAGGENGER ON CARPATHIA AS THE LIFEBOATS WERE BEING RECOVERED. *(National Archives)*

CHAPTER 15

RECOVERY OPERATIONS

Late in the afternoon of Monday April 15, while the news about potential survivors from *Titanic* became more depressing with each passing hour, White Star Line chartered the cable ship *Mackay-Bennett* out of Halifax to return to the area where *Titanic* sank and recover as many of the bodies as possible. The undertaking firm of John Snow and Company was hired to oversee the arrangements.

- With proper supplies on board including tons of ice, tools, 100 coffins and volunteer crewmen who was being paid double, *Mackay-Bennett* steamed out of Halifax at noon on Wednesday April 17, the day before *Carpathia* docked in New York.

- Once word was out that *Titanic* had sunk, most of the other ships crossing the Atlantic steamed many miles out of the way to avoid the wreckage in order to avoid distressing their own passengers. A ship named *Bremen*, however, steamed right through the wreckage and the crew spotted more than 100 corpses.

One of *Bremen's* passengers, Mrs. Johanna Stunke, later told reporters:

> *"We saw the body of one woman dressed only in her night dress, and clasping a baby to her breast. Close by was the body of another woman with her arms tightly clasped around a shaggy dog. . . . We saw the bodies of three men in a group, all clinging to a chair. Floating by just beyond them were the bodies of a dozen men, all wearing lifebelts and clinging desperately together."*

- At 8:00 p.m. on Saturday April 20, *Mackay-Bennett* arrived on the scene and the recovery operation began the next morning. Fifty-one bodies were recovered the first day. Any valuables found with the corpses removed and a complete description of each body was recorded. By this time the bodies had been in the water for almost one week, and many had deteriorated beyond the point of easy recognition.

- That night twenty-four of the bodies, almost all of them crewmen and none identifiable, were placed in canvas bags and weighted down with iron grates. The rest were embalmed for their return to Halifax. Engineer Frederick Hamilton described in his diary that night a brief memorial service:

> "For nearly an hour the words 'For as much as it hath pleased . . . we commit this body to the deep' are repeated and at each interval there comes, splash! As the weighted body plunges into the sea, there to sink to a depth of about two miles. Splash, splash, splash."

- The fourth body brought on board was an unidentified child about two years old. He was the only child recovered, and he is buried today in Halifax.

- What was left of John Jacob Astor—the richest man on *Titanic*—was also found that day, smashed to a pulp and covered with soot, which is how we know he was killed when the forward funnel broke loose and fell over the port side bridge wing into the sea. Astor was identified by his monogrammed clothing, watch, and diamond cufflinks.

- As the bodies were identified—many by the clothing they wore or items in their pockets—their names were sent back to shore via wireless. The rest would await identification in Halifax.

- While the *Mackay-Bennett* was engaged in her grisly work, a steady stream of reports was received from ships all over the North Atlantic that were finding bodies and wreckage. The current had scattered the floating debris over hundreds of square miles. Virtually anything that could float off *Titanic* did, and crews would continue seeing the flotsam for weeks. Although numerous ships reported finding bodies, not a single one stopped to recover them.

- On April 21 the captain of *Mackey-Bennett* wired for help, and on the following day *Minia* left Halifax with more coffins and supplies. By the end of April 23 there were 80 bodies on *Mackay-Bennett*. The next day 87 more were found. *Minia* arrived on April 26.

- After *Minia* arrived, *Mackay-Bennett* departed for Halifax. The crew had recovered 306 bodies and had returned 116 of them to the sea—"*splash, splash, splash*" 116 times. Of the remaining, 100 were in coffins and the rest were placed in canvas bags. Class structure was maintained. The remains of crewmembers were stored on the open deck and iced down; they were neither embalmed nor prepared in any way. Remains of Second and Third Class passengers were placed in canvas bags and for the most part remained unidentified. Remains of First Class passengers were embalmed and placed in coffins; most of them were identified.

- *Minia* was only able to recover 15 bodies, including First Class passenger Charles M. Hays, before bad weather set in. Most of the remaining corpses drifted into the Gulf Stream and were lost forever.

- Upon the return of the *Mackay-Bennett* to Halifax, the 190 bodies were unloaded at the coaling wharf. Sailors and police managed to keep the curious away except for one photographer who took some photos but had his camera confiscated for his efforts.

- In Halifax, a curling rink was set up as a morgue and the rest of the bodies were embalmed. They were arranged in cubicles so family or friends could come in to try to identify them. The bodies were kept for two weeks and death certificates prepared. The cause of death on each was the same: "Accidental Drowning, SS Titanic, at sea." Technically speaking, "accidental drowning" was not correct, because most of the victims who died in the water froze to death.

Those not taken away for burial by family members were buried at one of three cemeteries in Halifax based upon either their known or assumed religion. There were some mistakes. "Mr. Hoffman," the real Michel Navratil, was not claimed by his wife and although Catholic, is buried in the Jewish cemetery.

- Much of the town turned out for the burial of the unidentified small boy and hundreds wanted to take responsibility for his burial. In the end, the crew of the *Mackay-Bennett* asked for and was given the honor. They paid for a marker for the child with an inscription that reads as follows:

**Erected to the Memory of an Unknown Child
Whose Remains Were Recovered after the Disaster
to the Titanic, April 15, 1912.**

- Another recovery ship, *Montmagny*, found four more bodies over the next few weeks, and on May 14 *Algerine* found one more.

Two months after *Titanic* buried its bow in the bottom of the North Atlantic, *Oceanic*, en route to New York in mid-June, came upon Collapsible A. The lifeboat was still floating at sea with the three bodies left behind by Officer Lowe when he rescued the survivors from it. In the bottom of the lifeboat was Mrs. Edvard Lindell's wedding ring. She died trying to climb into the lifeboat with her husband, but he was so weak he could not help her. He died shortly thereafter, and his body was recovered by Lowe and taken onto *Carpathia*, where he was buried at sea.

Oceanic picked up the bodies and the lifeboat and took them back to New York. The remains were eventually buried at Halifax.

- In all, 328 bodies were recovered, 119 of which were buried at sea. Of the 209 returned to Halifax, family members removed 59 and the remaining 150 were buried in Halifax. Of these, 128 were never identified. They are buried under numbered headstones with room left for a name if one is ever matched to the remains.

CHAPTER 16

LORD OF THE CALIFORNIAN

When wireless operator Cyril Evans on the Leyland Line steamship *Californian* shut down his wireless at 11:35 p.m. on April 14, he went to bed without rewinding the detector, a mechanical device that allowed incoming messages to be received. Evans figured he would rewind it in the morning, standard operating procedure for the times; otherwise, it would chatter all night. Five minutes after Evans shut down his wireless system *Titanic* struck the iceberg. Twenty-five minutes later at 12:05 a.m., Marconi operator Jack Phillips on *Titanic* sent his first CQD message calling for assistance. By this time Cyril Evans was fast asleep.

The story of what did or did not transpire on board the *Californian* during the next few hours is one of the great mysteries of the *Titanic* tragedy. The story highlights some of the more obvious problems found at sea during that age, including unmanned wireless systems, distress rockets improperly used or ignored, subordinates unwilling to take a risk, a ship's captain who may have ignored the warnings and who may have been unwilling or unable to act on them. Ironically, when the events of that night are put into proper relief and context, given the society and laws of the time Captain Stanley Lord and *Californian's* crew probably did not do anything wrong.

- **10:20 P.M.:** Captain Lord ordered the engines stopped and let *Californian* drift to a stop just short of a large ice field. A field of icebergs surrounded his ship. Lord was a responsible and experienced seaman. In the pitch black and dead-calm night, Lord was not about to move his ship through what was essentially a minefield for ships. He checked and logged the position of *Californian* as 42° 5' N, 50° 7' W. His ship was now pointed northeast after his hard turn to starboard to miss the ice field.

- **10:30 P.M.:** Lord saw what looked like a steamer coming up from the east, but *Californian's* Third Officer Charles V. Groves thought it was just a star.

- **10:45 P.M.:** Lord pointed out the light to his chief engineer, which now appeared to be a steamer coming up from the south and the east.

- **10:55 P.M.:** Lord asked Cyril Evans if he knew of any other ships in the vicinity. When Evans replied that *Titanic* was the only such reported ship, Lord told him that the ship he had seen wasn't *Titanic*, but a ship close to the size of the much smaller *Californian*. Lord did, however, instruct Evans to contact *Titanic* and warn her about the heavy ice. Evans' message is the one that irritated Jack Phillips, who wired back, *"Keep out! Shut up! You're jamming my signal. I'm working Cape Race."* Rebuffed, Evans did not try to contact *Titanic* again.

- **11:30 P.M.:** The other ship was much larger and closer now, and Lord could see the starboard green marker light indicating it was moving west toward the ice. He estimated that the ship was only five miles away. Lord asked Groves to watch the ship and left the bridge. Groves also thought the ship was about the same size as *Californian*. It also looked as if it had masts: in other words, a sailing vessel, possibly steam powered.

- **11:35 P.M.:** Evans shut down the wireless and went to bed.

- **11:40 P.M.:** *Titanic* struck the iceberg.

- **12:00 A.M.:** Lord decided to retire and told his replacement, Second Officer Herbert Stone, to notify him if the other ship directly off *Californian's* starboard side moved any closer to their position. The entire starboard side of the ship, including the green marker light, was visible from *Californian's* deck.

- Although not underway, *Californian's* bow was now swinging with the current, and the ship was facing almost due east. This put the other ship due south of *Californian*, off the starboard side and apparently still moving. *Titanic*, at this time, was stopped and facing northeast, which means it was bow on, facing *Californian*.
    Instead of retiring to his stateroom, Lord rested on a settee in the navigation room just off *Californian's* bridge. This way, he was close and available if needed.

- **12:05 A.M.:** Jack Phillips on *Titanic* sent out the first CQD call for assistance.

- **12:10 A.M.:** Fireman Ernest Gill, on *Californian's* deck after his eight to midnight watch below, thought he saw the lights of a large steamer off the starboard side and about 10 miles away. Gill went down to his bunk and told his mate that the ship was going full speed. At this time *Titanic* was not moving and was preparing the lifeboats for loading.

- **12:15 A.M.:** Now off duty, Groves decided to stop by the wireless room to listen in on some of the messages. He wore the headphones for a while, heard nothing, and left. Groves was unaware of the fact that Evans had not rewound the detector. During the fifteen minutes between 12:15 and 12:30 a.m., Jack Phillips on *Titanic* sent a total of 10 distress messages.

- **12.30 A.M.:** Gill went back up on the deck for a cigarette. About fifteen minutes later he saw a white rocket off the starboard side, about ten miles away. Thinking it was a shooting star, he waited and watched for awhile. About 10 minutes later he saw another one, this time a rocket for sure. Later Gill reported, *"It was not my business to notify the bridge. . . . I turned in immediately after."* He did not report hearing a rocket explode or any escaping steam.

  Second Officer Stone reported to the bridge and he also saw the steamer. Lord told him to watch its actions, so Stone kept an eye on it and noticed, eventually, that her red port side light was showing, which meant she was also facing east—the direction from which she had come. If true, the ship had turned around.

- **12.35 A.M.:** Lord checked with the bridge to see if the other ship had moved. Stone reported that she had not and that several attempts to reach her via Morse (light) lamp had failed.

- **12:45 A.M.:** Stone reported a flash in the sky directly over the other ship. He, too, thought it was a shooting star. A few minutes later he saw another flash. These were the same flashes Gill had seen. Over the next fifteen minutes Stone saw three more flashes. It appeared to Stone that there was a ship of some type between *Californian* and the ship firing the rockets far off in the distance.

- **1:15 A.M.:** Stone notified Captain Lord of the signal rockets he had seen. Asked if they were private signals, Stone told Lord he did not know, only that they were white. Lord ordered Stone to keep signaling with Morse lamp and *"when you get an answer let me know."* Stone continued to signal and Lord returned to his settee.

- **1:50 A.M.:** By now Stone had seen eight rockets, the last one about 1:25 a.m. *Californian* was now facing almost west-southwest having turned by drift more than 90 degrees and was now facing directly toward the other ship. The other ship was stationary, was to the southwest and

CAPTAIN STANLEY LORD OF THE CALIFORNIAN. ALTHOUGH HE HAD NOTHING TO DO WITH TITANIC'S STRIKING AN ICEBERG AND SINKING WITH 1,500 PEOPLE, HE WAS CONSIDERED THE VILLIAN AND BLAMED FOR THE HUGE LOSS OF LIFE BECAUSE HE DIDN'T COME TO TITANIC'S AID. GIVEN THE CIRCUMSTANCES, THERE IS LITTLE HE COULD HAVE DONE TO HELP THE FOUNDERING SHIP. (*Washington Evening Star*)

TWO VIEWS OF THE LELAND LINER CALIFORNIAN, THE SHIP THAT MIGHT HAVE COME TO THE AID OF TITANIC BUT WAS TRAPPED IN THE ICE IN THE DARK. (*National Archives*)

was still with its port side red light showing, which meant it was facing either northeast or east.

- **2:00 A.M.:** From the deck of *Californian*, it appeared to Stone the other ship had begun steaming away to the southwest. The red light disappeared and soon all that was visible was the white stern light. (Could it be that the ship he was watching actually was sinking, and the light was *Titanic's* stern light just before the power failed?)

Stone sent Apprentice James Gibson to tell Lord that the other ship was leaving. Gibson later reported that he woke Lord, told him the ship was leaving and told him of the eight rockets. Lord asked, "*Are you sure there were no colors in them?*" Gibson replied that they were white rockets, and returned to the bridge. Lord went back to sleep. Stone did not go to see Lord because he could not leave the bridge.

Lord would later relate that he did not remember the conversation although he did remember Gibson coming in to wake him up. From this time on, all was quiet on *Californian's* deck.

- **4:30 A.M.:** The officer of the watch, Chief Officer G. V. Stewart, woke Lord. This was his normal wake-up call, and it was still dark outside.

- **5:15 A.M.:** It was starting to get light now, and Stewart saw a four-masted sailing ship off to the southwest. Concerned that it might be in trouble, he told Lord that Stone said he had seen the ship fire rockets during the night. Deciding it was finally safe to navigate west through the ice field, Lord had Cyril Evans awakened to check with the ship to find out if she needed any help.

- **5:20 A.M.:** Evans rewound the detector, turned on his set, and sent a request for someone to wireless back that his transmitter was working. He immediately received a message from *Virginian* reporting that *Titanic* had sunk during the night along with its position at the time of the sinking. The message was given to Lord who calculated that *Californian* was about 19 miles north of where *Titanic* had gone down. Lord ordered his ship to steam west through the ice field and then south toward the reported area of the sinking. Once through the ice, *Californian* steamed south at full speed, or 13.5 knots.

- **7:30 A.M.:** *Californian* passed *Mount Temple*, which was stopped in the area that *Titanic* had reportedly struck the iceberg. There was no wreckage of any kind. *Californian* continued south, passed another ship that did not have a wireless set, and sighted *Carpathia* on the east, or far side of the ice field. After confirming *Carpathia* was picking up survivors (the last lifeboat was picked up at 8:45 a.m.), Lord passed back through the ice field and pulled alongside at 9:00 a.m., just as *Carpathia* was about to begin her trip to New York. After looking for survivors for a few hours and finding none, Lord ordered *Californian* underway for Boston.

▪   Given these facts, it does not appear as though Captain Lord or his crew had done anything wrong. At least, that is what Lord would always say. And he might be right. There were three major things that transpired that his detractors have steadfastly used against him. Lord, however, had an answer for each.

1) **The wireless system was shut down for the night.** This is correct, and it's also not an issue. Only a very few ships, large ones such as *Titanic* and *Olympic,* had more than one wireless operator. There were no U.S. or international laws that required more, especially since the purpose of the wireless was a commercial venture primarily used by the passengers. With only one operator, there were going to be times when the wireless system was not working and most operators shut down from 11:00 p.m. until 6:00 a.m. The fact that Evans went to sleep or that he did not rewind the detector does not have any bearing on this issue. He was following the accepted procedures of the time.

2) **Neither Lord nor any other officer responded to the rockets fired by** *Titanic.* This is also true, but Lord offered a reasonable rebuttal. Many ships in 1912 were not equipped with wireless and the usual method of communications between them at night, as had been the case for well over 100 years, was by the use of rockets—especially white rockets. In fact, the British Board of Trade regulations in effect at the time stipulated that whaling vessels, which often worked in fleets, were to use white rockets to communicate. Intra-company communications (such as from one White Star Line ship to another White Star Line ship) were also supposed to use white rockets to communicate. There were no Board of Trade regulations that rockets were to be used as distress signals. Also, *Californian* was in a known whaling area and had seen several whaling vessels the day before. The white rockets could very well have been whaling ships communicating with each other.

3) **Lord slept through the night while** *Titanic* **sank a few miles away.** His ship was stopped by an ice field, he had a competent set of officers on watch and the only other ship in the vicinity also appeared to be stopped by the ice field. It was all rather routine, and it was an appropriate time for Lord to retire. There appeared to be nothing happening that was out of the ordinary. Even the rockets were a fairly ordinary event during

that time period, and they never signified a need for a call to action.

■   Many books and articles have been written about whether Lord was incompetent or in any way responsible for the great loss of life by not coming to the aid of *Titanic*. Two issues in particular have interested historians and Titanic enthusiasts:

1) *How far apart were the two ships?* Estimates vary from five to 25 miles. Whether they could see one other, or how well they could see one another, is unclear. Because of the curvature of the earth, the officers on the bridge of *Californian* would only have been able to see an object the size of *Titanic* about eight miles distant. Based upon the reported logged position of *Californian* and Officer Boxhall's reported position after *Titanic* struck the iceberg, the two ships were almost 20 miles apart with a great deal of ice between them. Some of this ice was more than 100 feet tall. There is also evidence that *Titanic* was almost six miles further away from *Californian* because Boxhall's reported position was almost surely wrong. At 25 or more miles distant, the two ships would not have been able to see one another—although flares fired from *Titanic* would have been visible from *Californian's* bridge.

2) There has always been speculation that another ship was actually between *Californian* and *Titanic*, and that this may be the ship the officers on both vessels saw that night. There is some evidence that the Norwegian sealing ship *Sampson*, which was slightly smaller than *Californian*, was in the area and it did not have a wireless set. *Sampson* was also a three-masted sailing ship with a steam engine, which closely matches the description of what both Second Officer Lightoller on *Titanic* and Third Officer Groves on *Californian* believed they saw.

On *Titanic*, both Lightoller and Boxhall later reported seeing a four-masted sailing ship move toward them about five miles away (they could see both the red port and green starboard running lights), before the ship turned to port and reversed course.

There are enough similarities between what the crew of the two ships saw to credibly believe that another ship, perhaps the *Sampson*, was between them that night. This claim is substantially bolstered by a confidential report to the Norwegian government filed by *Sampson's* First Officer which stated, among other things, that the *Sampson* was close enough to *Titanic* to see her lights and distress rockets. However, this report was not released until 1962.

If *Sampson* was close enough to see the rockets of a ship to the south and the lights of a ship to the north, she almost certainly was between *Titanic* and *Californian*. However, she too failed to act on behalf of *Titanic*. Why? There was a good reason: *Sampson* was illegally hunting seals and already had a good catch. The captain of the ship was concerned that he would get caught, and believed the rockets were being fired to signal his position to another ship trying to apprehend him. And so *Sampson* left the area, weaving in and out of the ice until morning, when Lord saw her nearby, heading east.

It is unlikely anyone will ever solve the riddle about *Californian* and whether she was in a position to help the passengers on *Titanic*. Even in daylight it took Lord more than two hours to navigate through the ice to get reach *Carpathia's* location. Whether the same trip could have been made in the dead of night in time to save anyone is doubtful.

▪ Another question frequently asked is whether Stanley Lord should have been accused of criminal neglect or gross negligence. Given everything we know, probably not. Perhaps he should have been more concerned about what was going on with the rockets, but white rockets were not unusual in his day and age. To accuse him of knowingly failing to go to the aid of *Titanic* is simply not fair. Did Lord experience a lapse in judgment? Maybe. Could the crew of *Californian* have done anything to save some of the people on *Titanic*? We will never know. One thing seems clear: Lord should not have been made the scapegoat for the disaster and vilified by the press and public.

▪ *Titanic's* loss was a mammoth disaster, however, and disasters of this magnitude require more than one scapegoat. J. Bruce Ismay was not about to shoulder the entire blame for the loss. Someone had to share it with him, and Captain Smith was gone. He could not blame the White Star line's senior dead officer—so the blame fell upon Stanley Lord, who happened to be in the wrong place at the wrong time. And so history has recorded the *Californian's* unlucky skipper as the scapegoat for the huge loss of life on *Titanic*.

"There had been no discrimination against third class passengers in the saving of life."

CHAPTER 17

AFTERMATH

Early on the afternoon of April 11, 1912, RMS *Titanic* departed Queenstown, Ireland, bound for New York City with 2,208 people on board. Four days later, 705 of them were survivors on the Cunard Steamer *Carpathia.* The remaining 1,503 had died, either by drowning or freezing to death in the North Atlantic.

■   Following is a breakdown of the losses by class and gender:

	MEN SAVED	MEN LOST	WOMEN SAVED	WOMEN LOST	CHILDREN SAVED	CHILDREN LOST
FIRST	59	118	136	4	6	1
SECOND	14	150	78	13	28	0
THIRD	59	387	83	87	31	63
CREW	193	677	19	2		
TOTAL	325	1332	316	106	65	64

THE AMERICAN HEARINGS

Although news of the disaster was known fairly quickly in both the United States and England, it was two days before confirmation of the extent of the loss was received by White Star Line, and then communicated to the rest of the world. *Carpathia's* Harold Cottam did not transmit Ismay's early morning April 15th message to P. A. S. Franklin until 10:00 a.m. on the 15th, but Franklin did not receive it until the afternoon of the 17th.

■   It did not take long for the United States Senate to respond to the tragedy. Early on the morning of Wednesday, April 17, Senator William

Alden Smith of Michigan, having guessed the extent of the disaster, got President William Howard Taft to appoint him as the head of a Senate committee to study the loss.

Smith worked fast. He selected his committee immediately and had it in New York City in time to meet *Carpathia* when she arrived on Thursday night. Armed with enough official paperwork to hold all the crewmen as well as the ship's officers and Bruce Ismay in New York, Smith set to work to find out what happened to *Titanic*. The American inquiry began the day after *Carpathia* arrived in New York; Bruce Ismay was called as the first witness.

Smith was trying to find out what happened, but he was more interested in *why* it happened so he could determine how to prevent such a terrible thing from happening again. Smith was also very concerned about who was going to pay damages to the survivors and the families of the lost, which underscored another agenda driving the Senator. His archenemy was J. P. Morgan. If Smith could establish negligence on the part of White Star Line, he would win the right for the survivors and families to sue Morgan for damages.

- In 1898, a law called the Harter Act was passed that allowed individual passengers to sue for damages if it could be established that a steamship company knew of any negligence before an incident but had not acted to address the negligence. Otherwise, under international law, if negligence could not be established the passengers could only claim a portion of the material that had been salvaged from the wreck. The only value left of from *Titanic* were the 13 lifeboats Captain Rostron had brought with him to New York.

The Harter Act only applied to American-owned ships, which is why the whole relationship between the International Mercantile Marine, White Star Line, and *Titanic* was important. Although manned with a British crew and built in Ireland, *Titanic* was owned by an American company and was en route to an American port.

- The Senate hearings lasted a total of 17 days (things happened quickly in those days), beginning in New York City on April 17 and ending in Washington D.C. on May 25. The testimony totaled 1,145 pages. A total of 82 witnesses were called, including 53 British subjects and 29 American residents. In addition to Ismay, the surviving ship's officers, the two Marconi operators Cottam and Bride, and 29 crewmembers were called. The detained crewmembers were actually prevented from returning to England when the rest of the crew departed on *Lapland* on Saturday, April 20. They did not get to leave for home until their testimony was completed a few days later.

Smith and his committee, in spite of a total lack of knowledge of things related to ships and the sea, managed to conduct a fairly comprehensive investigation. Many newspapers and even his peers called Smith a moron because of his lack of knowledge, but in the end the committee identified several things that went wrong and needed changing. The committee did not agree, however, that anyone at the International Mercantile Marine, White Star Line, or Bruce Ismay could be held at fault for the disaster, which had been the focus of the investigation.

■   William Alden Smith presented his findings to the entire United States Senate on May 28. He called for three resolutions:

> 1) To present a medal to Captain Rostron from President Taft on behalf of the people of the United States;
> 2) To examine and re-evaluate all maritime legislation;
> 3) To investigate the laws and regulations concerning construction and operation of all ocean going ships.

■   The outcome of the American inquiry resulted in great praise for Rostron and his crew on *Carpathia* while Captain Lord of the *Californian* was thoroughly condemned. More importantly, however, laws were passed to override the British Board of Trade's lifeboat requirements so that all ships using an American port would have to meet the following requirements: carry enough lifeboats to hold all passengers and crews; be equipped with survival material for all people on board a lifeboat; insure all lifeboats are adequately manned with trained crews; the holding of a lifeboat drill for each person on each voyage. Some of the British newspapers complained about the restrictions, but there was no avoiding the reality that if a ship intended to enter an American port, it now had to abide by American laws. These requirements had to be satisfied prior to the future departure of any ship for any port in the U.S. In other words, there was not a grace period.

Additionally, all ships that carried passengers would have to be equipped with a wireless system, the crew who manned them could not favor the transmission of one company over another, ship traffic would take precedence over passenger traffic and the wireless would have to be manned 24 hours per day.

THE BRITISH HEARINGS

The British government had its own set of hearings. While the American hearings were designed more to determine *who* was at fault, the British hearings were geared more too *why* and *how* the disaster happened. The British inquiry was called the Mersey Commission because John Charles Bingham, Lord Mersey, headed it.

- When *Lapland* arrived in England, the remaining *Titanic* crew was immediately detained and each member interviewed before being allowed to leave. Although most were interviewed and released the day they arrived in England, many had to wait overnight before they were allowed to leave.

  The Mersey Commission hearings started on April 30 and ended on July 30. Dozens of people were questioned and the 25,600 questions filled 960 pages of text. *Olympic* was used to simulate tests, and huge models of *Titanic* were built as props. Other than Bruce Ismay, only two civilians were called to testify: Sir Cosmo and Lady Duff Gordon. They were asked to explain their actions that night in not going back to pick up people with their lifeboat (which was only one-quarter full), and whether they had paid off the crew of the lifeboat not to go back.

- The Mersey Commission found:

  > "The collision . . . was due to excessive speed . . . that a proper watch was not kept . . . that the ship[']s boats were properly lowered but insufficiently manned; that the Leyland liner Californian might have reached Titanic if she had attempted to do so . . . and that there had been no discrimination against third class passengers in the saving of life."

- The majority of the 679 crew members lost were from Southampton, so when the remaining 160 Southampton survivors arrived there in two groups over two days, more than 50,000 people met them at the train station. Hundreds of families and entire city blocks had lost their principle wage earner. There were more than 500 widows and 1,500 orphaned children in Southampton alone. In an era when very few women worked outside the home, losses on this level were crushing to the economy and people of Southhampton. Local charities would be aiding families who were now destitute for years to come.

COMPENSATION

Because of the Merchant Shipping Act of 1894, White Star Line was held liable for all freight losses, or about $600,000. Almost all of it was covered by insurance.

- Claims by Americans for loss of life and property were in the millions of dollars, with the smallest claim filed on behalf of the United States Postal Service for $41.00. Mrs. Charlotte Cardeza filed the largest property claim for her lost luggage to the value of $177,352.74. Mrs. Henry B. Harris filed the largest claim for loss of life for $1 million (or in excess of $18 million in 2002 dollars.)

Because American law limited compensation for losses to the value of the salvage value of the ship (the thirteen lifeboats), the owners of *Titanic* filed suit in American courts to limit the liability to American law. The only other requirement, by law, was to compensate the families of passengers who *did not survive* for the cost of the tickets they had purchased. Survivors would not be paid anything because they survived and finished their trip in New York!

- The sum of the liability under American law was $97,772 and the claims filed were worth $16,804,112. Because British law allowed claimants to gain more in a lawsuit, eventually most of the lawsuits were transferred to Britain.

- In 1916, four years after the disaster, the courts finally settled all the lawsuits for a total of $663,000, which was divided among all the claimants.

HEROES AND VILLIANS

Every man and woman who stepped back and gave a seat to someone else was a hero in this story, although probably none of them would have considered themselves in that light. By the standards of the early 20th century, that is what people did—women and children first. It is doubtful that today's society would react the same way.

There were other heroes too—the engineering staff, all of whom remained at their job deep inside the ship to the very end to keep the lights burning, the Marconi operators who worked up to three minutes before the ship went down, and Officer Harold G. Lowe, who bravely guided his lifeboat back to look for survivors when so many other refused.

- One of the true heroes of this story is Captain Arthur H. Rostron of *Carpathia*. He was honored as such by both the American and British governments and by the public as a whole. Medals, loving cups, and all sorts of gadgets would be handed to him, and for the rest of his life he would be known as Rostron of *Carpathia*.

- In addition to Officer Lowe, Third Class steward John E. Hart should also be classified as heroic. Hart, it will be recalled, led some 58 Third Class women and children from their cabins deep inside the ship up to the Boat Deck so they could get into lifeboats.

- Villains also haunt this story—the White Star Line and Bruce Ismay for not adding enough lifeboats; the British Board of Trade for not requiring enough lifeboats; International Mercantile Marine; White Star

Line, Bruce Ismay, and Captain Smith for not reporting the fire in the coalbunker; Harland & Wolff for not building a ship of this magnitude with adequate waterproof bulkheads or a double hull.

- J. Bruce Ismay returned to England—as a hero. The British public thought he had been treated badly by the American press (one newspaper called him 'J. Brute Ismay') and public, and looked upon him as something of a victim. The British public was more kind. Ismay was not a ruined man, however he did give up his IMM and White Star Line jobs. He remained in business life until he retired in 1934, and he died in 1937.

- The real villain in the *Titanic* disaster, according to both the American and British governments, and to the newspapers and the citizens of both countries, was Captain Stanley Lord of *Californian*. His vessel was the lone ship that everyone believed was close enough to save most of the victims—and yet Lord had not so much as raised a finger to help. The fact that he had nothing to do with the poor string of decisions made that caused *Titanic* to crash into an iceberg in the first place did not seem to make a difference to the press and public.

- Perhaps the true villain was simply complacency. The Gilded Age was in full swing, the Victorian Era had passed, and 1912 represented the climax of the industrial revolution. Man could build anything now, so the thought went, and neither man nor nature could destroy it. The largest and most luxurious ship ever built did not need enough lifeboats to accommodate every person on board because this ship could not sink. The lifeboats were needed only to save people on other ships who were in danger. Wireless operators worked for the passengers first and the ship second. They weren't needed for the safe navigation of the ship.

The *Titanic* disaster marked the end of an era. Suddenly people were not so sure anymore. Maybe Nature could control man, and maybe man did not have all the answers. Things seemed to be out of control, out of balance. And within two years, the entire world would be at war.

THE FUTURE

Even before *Carpathia* reached New York, it suddenly occurred to everyone that there was, in fact, room on the world's passenger liners to carry enough lifeboats for everyone on board. When *Olympic* steamed out of Southampton for her next trip to New York, she was carrying 64 of them.

- Within a year, *Olympic* would go back to Harland and Wolff's Belfast shipyard for a complete upgrade. In addition to a double bottom *Olympic* had a double hull and watertight bulkheads installed that went all the way to the main, or C Deck. A ship-wide signaling system was also installed.

- *Titanic's* other sister ship, the still under-construction *Gigantic*, underwent similar upgrades. Her name was eventually changed to *Britannic*. She was launched under that name in April 1914.

- In the United States, a new North Atlantic Ice Patrol was established to track all icebergs and field ice in the Atlantic. Ships were now required to steam around ice instead of trying to navigate through it.

- In May 1940, Sir Winston Churchill put out a call for every available boat, yacht, and skiff on the south coast of England to make their way to the coast of France to extract the tens of thousands of British and French soldiers trapped by Hitler's army around Dunkirk. Hundreds of ships answered the call. One in particular was *Sundowner*, a 58-foot private boat crewed by three men.

  She had never carried more than 21 people, but her owner and crew decided to throw away the rule book and do everything they could to save their soldiers and their country at a time of great peril. She made the dangerous trip and returned to England to unload the 130 British soldiers who had been crammed into every nook and cranny. This time, no one would accuse 66-year-old retired Second Officer Charles Herbert Lightoller of not filling a boat to capacity.

- Colonel Archibald Gracie's health failed because of his immersion in the frigid water and he did not survive even one year. He wrote a small book titled *The Truth About the Titanic* in late 1912 and died shortly thereafter.

- Sir Cosmo Duff Gordon was never convicted of having done anything wrong and his government exonerated him. Not being one to squabble with the newspapers, he never answered any of the questions asked of him. His trip on *Titanic* was a mixture of bad luck and even worse taste. He died in 1931.

  Lady Lucile Duff Gordon died in 1935, defending her husband's actions to the very end. Her fashion business died along with the millions who perished in the trenches during World War I.

- Lawrence Beesley also wrote a book in 1912 titled *The Loss of the S. S. Titanic: Its Story and Its Lessons*. He lived until 1967.

- Helen Churchill Candee would become a well-known author and world traveler. She lived to be 90 years old.

- "Winnie" Troutt beat out Mrs. Candee. She died in 1984 at the age of 100.

- None of the surviving *Titanic* officers was ever given command of a ship. Lightoller retired in the mid-1920s and died in 1952. Fifth Officer Lowe died in 1944 after having served in the Royal Navy during World War I. Third Officer Pitman remained at sea for many years and died in 1961.
Fourth Officer Boxhall defended until his death the position he had worked out for *Titanic* the night she sank—not that being off a few miles would have made much difference. When he died in 1963, his ashes were scattered over the spot where he had plotted *Titanic's* final position.

- Seventeen-year-old Jack Thayer would go on to serve as an artillery officer in World War I, and became financial vice president of the University of Pennsylvania. The teenager was one of the few people who reported that the ship great liner had split in two before sinking (something most people refused to believe). After his only son, Edward C. Thayer, was killed during World War II, the tormented father climbed into his car, drove to a parking spot adjacent to the trolley loop on the south side of Parkside Avenue in Philadelphia, and slit his wrists and throat. He was 50.

- Many people would forever call J. Bruce Ismay a coward, although some of the British public were dismayed by the way he was treated in the United States Senate hearings. Within a year he resigned as Chairman of the White Star Line. This was followed shortly thereafter by his resignation from the International Mercantile Marine. Although some of the public felt there was a moral obligation to go down with his ship, to do so would have just added another name to the casualty list. Ismay died in 1937.

- Stanley Lord, Captain of *Californian,* spent the rest of his life defending his actions that night. He lost his job with the Leyland Line and ended up accepting smaller commands for the remainder of his professional life. His career effectively ended that cold April night in 1912. The debut of the movie *A Night To Remember* in 1958 brought Lord out of retirement because a key part of the movie laid blame on him for the huge loss of life. He died in 1962, and to this day his family is still trying to clear his name.

- Arthur H. Rostron, in contrast, had done the right thing that night, a decision that made his career and secured his slot in the pantheon of naval history's heroes. Eventually he was given command of *Mauretania* and remained with her until 1926, when he was made Commodore of the Cunard Line and retired in 1931. Rostron died in 1940.

■   A good number of the women survivors, many whom lived into the 1970s and beyond, discovered they could not talk candidly about their experiences without crying. Many refused to talk about *Titanic* at all. Some passengers never told their families they were on *Titanic*, and took that information with them to the grave.

■   In Cherbourg, France, the White Star Line passenger tender *Traffic* which had carried passengers to and from *Titanic* for her maiden voyage, was scuttled in 1940 before German troops occupied the port. Raised and used by the German Navy, she was sunk by the Royal Navy in 1941.

■   *Nomadic*, the other Cherbourg tender, was made into a floating restaurant on the River Seine in Paris near the Eiffel Tower. She was still in use in this capacity in late 1990s.

■   Harland and Wolff no longer builds new passenger ships, though the company is a major builder of heavy lift cranes, cargo ships, bridges and other steel structures. The Queen's Island shipyard, the birthplace of *Olympic*, *Titanic*, and *Britannic*, was a victim of age and economy. The place was demolished in 2001.

■   *Olympic* had a distinguished career before being scrapped in 1937. During World War I she rammed and sank U-103, a German U-boat that had fired a torpedo at her. In May 1934, in a heavy fog, *Olympic* ran over and sunk the Nantucket Lightship off New York City, killing all 11 people on board.

■   *Britannic*, originally to be named *Gigantic* but renamed before she was launched, was put to sea in April 1914—two years after *Titanic* sank. Immediately pressed into wartime service, *Britannic* became a hospital ship. In September 1916, she struck a mine in the Aegean Sea and sank in less than an hour. This time, however, there were plenty of lifeboats and warm water. Only 38 people were lost, most during the initial explosion. Although *Britannic* had a double bottom, double hull, and watertight bulkheads up to the main deck, she struck the mine at the very moment the watertight doors were opened to allow for a crew change. Like *Titanic*, she did not stand a chance.

■   Sufficient lifeboats were not always going to be the answer to avoiding heavy loss of life at sea. A German U-boat torpedoed the giant passenger liner *Lusitania* in the waters off Queenstown, Ireland, in 1915. She sank in 18 minutes and took with her more than 1,200 people.

Although there were ample lifeboats, there was not time to launch them. *Lusitania* rolled over on her starboard side and crushed most of the lifeboats located there. Lifeboats on the port side could not be launched because that side was high and out of the water at an angle that prevented their launch—a common occurrence when a ship capsizes.

- Ironically, neither *Carpathia*, the rescue ship of *Titanic* survivors, nor *Californian*, Lord's ice-bound command, survived for long. A German U-boat torpedoed and sank *Californian* in 1917 off Cape Metapan, Greece. Another U-boat torpedoed and sank *Carpathia* in 1918. Five of her crewmen died when *Carpathia* was torpedoed. In 2001 her remains were found 120 miles off Cork, Ireland.

- In 1926 Oceanic Steam Navigation Company and White Star Line was sold to the Royal Mail Steamship Co. Then in 1934 Royal Mail Steamship, due to financial difficulties, filed for bankruptcy and was purchased by the Cunard Steamship Company (Cunard Lines), forming Cunard-White Star Ltd.

In 1947 Cunard purchased the remainder of RMS-White Star stock and in 1949 took over all White Star operations. Cunard-White Star retained the name until 1960 when the White Star Line name was dropped forever.

"...the ship is its own memorial. Leave it there."

CHAPTER 18

RESURRECTION

Soon after the disaster, several families of the wealthy dead considered pooling their funds to locate and raise *Titanic* from her watery grave. After studying the idea, however, the engineering company they contracted with told them the technology did not exist to either find or salvage the great ship.

■ The idea of finding *Titanic* refused to fade. Many people believed they might be able to salvage *Titanic*, primarily because of the presumed value of the cargo and personal items waiting to be recovered. None of the schemes reached fruition, mostly because technology had not yet developed to meet their desires.

Several attempts were made between 1956 and 1978 to locate funding to finance an expedition to locate the wreck, but in the end nothing came of them. An insurmountable yet fundamental problem confronted the dreamers: no one really knew the final resting place of *Titanic*. Was Officer Boxhall's position fix correct, or was Captain Rostron's? Perhaps they were both wrong. Did the hull drift as it sank? Even a slight error in calculation would place the wreck miles from her true resting place. That, plus the immense depth of the north Atlantic would make finding her tantamount to locating a very slender needle in a field of haystacks.

■ In 1978, *National Geographic* magazine and Walt Disney Productions explored the possibility of doing a movie about the disaster. They intended to use a submersible to film the wreck. The idea was dropped because, once again, no one knew were it was located or even how to go about finding it in an efficient manner.

■ In 1980, Texas oil millionaire Jack Grimm and Florida filmmaker Mike Harris joined together to find the wreck. This for-profit expedition intended to film *Titanic* and sell the photographs. Grimm already had a reputation for leading exotic searches for Bigfoot, the Loch Ness Monster, and Noah's Ark. Fighting terrible weather, Grimm and his group managed to get a sonar reading of the ocean bottom in the area where Boxhall had reported the sinking. Nothing was found.

- In 1981 the United States Office of Naval Research funded a joint expedition developed by the Scripps Institute of Oceanography and the Wood's Hole Oceanographic Institution. This expedition searched the area looking for the wreck, but once again came up empty handed. *Titanic* was not yet ready to be found.

- Three days after the Scripps/Woods Hole expedition left the area, Jack Grimm arrived and started his second expedition to find the wreck. To his utter dismay, rough weather once again ruined his effort. Determined to succeed, Grimm made his third futile attempt in 1983. He had spent millions of dollars and found absolutely nothing. The fruitless efforts gave scientists and historians reason to doubt Boxhall's position. It was time to apply a higher degree of scientific analysis to the sinking if anyone ever wanted to find the great liner.

- By 1984, talk of finding *Titanic* garnered little press. By this time, most people had resigned themselves to the belief that she would never be found. Two scientific groups refused to give up. The Wood's Hole Oceanographic Institution's Deep Submergence Laboratory headed by Dr. Robert Ballard, and IFREMER (officially, the *Institute Français de Recherches pour l'Expolitations des Mers* or the French Institute for Research and Exploitation of the Seas), decided to join together for a joint expedition. The National Geographic Society and French citizens, via taxes, picked up most of the cost. The purpose of the joint venture was to test underwater equipment and technology. And, maybe—just maybe—find *Titanic* in the process.

Once again the Office of Naval Research, citing national security, funded the development of the submersible to be used for the Woods Hole/IFREMER expedition. On July 1, 1985, the French research vessel arrived on site and began searching areas ignored by the previous Grimm expeditions by using side-scanning sonar to search for the wreck.

On July 9, the Woods Hole group arrived with two remote controlled submersibles to help with the search. Between July 1 and August 7, the two ships searched 85% of the 150 square miles of seabed targeted as possible sites for the wreck. Running out of time the French ship departed for another assignment on August 7. Ballard and a group of scientists, using the Woods Hole research vessel *Knorr*, departed from the Azores on August 15 to continue the search in the North Atlantic.

- Since the Navy was paying much of the tab for the search, the *Knorr* first had to detour far south of the Azores to film the wreckage of the nuclear submarine *Scorpion*, which had been lost in 1968 with all hands.

The submersibles photographed the wreckage, the photos of which are still classified. *Knorr* then steamed to find *Titanic*, arriving in the vicinity of her sinking on August 22, 1985. The submersibles searched some of the areas identified by the Grimm expeditions to confirm that the few things found by Grimm were not part of the famous wreck. Thereafter the cameras were turned on in the areas missed by the French expedition. Ballard's idea was to try and find the ship's debris field because it would be larger and easier to find then the hull itself. Day after day *Knorr* steamed a course over the ocean, towing the submersibles behind her. The tedious process numbed the scientists, who quickly grew tired watching grainy black and white images of ocean floor roll by for hours on end. All of that was about to change.

- At 1:00 a.m. on September 1, 1985, the cameras picked up signs of man-made debris. Ballard, who was asleep in his quarters, was awakened and summoned to the control room. By the time he arrived a picture of one of *Titanic's* massive boilers was visible on the television monitor. *Titanic* had been found. Unfortunately, *Knorr* had just one day left before she had to return to port. Wasting no time, Ballard guided the submersible around the site to take as many photos as possible. They revealed that the ship was upright with her bow buried deep in the sandy bottom. The funnels were gone, the port side bridge wing crushed, the forward mast toppled over. The anchors were still in place. Acres of debris surrounded the wrecked hull. Conspicuous by its absence was *Titanic's* entire stern, which was no where to be seen.

Knorr headed home trailed by an airplane trying to get a fix on *Titanic's* location. Wisely, Ballard kept the exact coordinates to himself in an attempt to prevent salvage hunters from disturbing the site. Unfortunately for Ballard, one of his crewmen got access to the coordinates and later offered the information to others, who would not hesitate to use it. The spectacular photos taken on the last day were analyzed on the way home. Only then did Ballard and his crew learn the stern section, in pieces, was resting almost one mile away from the bow, with a huge debris field spread out between the two large pieces of *Titanic*.

The great ship had finally been found. The feeding frenzy was about to begin.

FEEDING FRENZY

Within weeks dozens of proposals were made to raise *Titanic*, salvage her, and allow people to visit her in submersibles (with an opportunity to recover some of the artifacts). Insurance companies quickly jumped into the act, deciding they owned the wreck because they had paid claims many years earlier.

Attempts were also made to protect the site, but because of its location in international waters, the efforts of several governments would be required. That hope quickly proved impossible.

■   Ballard's second trip to the site began in July 1986, this time with a three-man diving submersible named *Alvin*. On July 13, Ballard made his first descent, a 2-1/2 hour dive almost 13,000 feet to the bottom of the Atlantic. A short time after reaching the sea floor *Titanic's* massive bow came into sight—the first time in almost 75 years that anyone had actually seen the famous ship.

Alvin made 11 dives on the site during the next two weeks, thoroughly photographing every foot of the wreck and debris field. More than 50,000 photographs and 100 hours of video footage were captured. Ballard and his crew returned home as heroes a second time.

Two weeks later, Jack Grimm announced he was going to retrieve artifacts from the wreck and sell them, and he was going to do so with the help of IFREMER.

ARTIFACT RECOVERY

The French government sponsored IFREMER, and as such chose to work with a company called Titanic Ventures from Connecticut instead of Jack Grimm. IFREMER provided the ships and submersibles to do so. More than thirty dives to the site recovered 1,800 artifacts and thousands of feet of film of the entire site.

■   The move outraged Ballard, who wanted the site preserved. Others echoed his belief, calling those who recovered artifacts grave robbers. The United States Congress passed a law in late 1986 to protect the site, but it was ineffectual because *Titanic* lies in international waters.

■   A television show in 1986 called *Return to the Titanic . . . Live* justified the preservationists' concerns that the recovered artifacts were not being maintained correctly, and might be sold to the highest bidder. The artifacts were toured around Europe for several years before, fortunately, they were stored by the French government instead of being sold. Meanwhile, the French government required that ownership of the artifacts be defined before they would be returned to Titanic Ventures, as required by the original agreement with IFREMER.

The public was given the opportunity to prove ownership of any of the artifacts, and if ownership could be proved, they would have to pay a portion of the funds expended to recover them. Only one item was claimed, a watch identified by a survivor as having been owned by her father. It was given to the survivor to keep for the rest of her lifetime, and then returned to the collection upon her death.

- Titanic Ventures was eventually absorbed into a new company called RMS Titanic, Inc. (RMST), which acquired the artifacts when the French government released them. In 1991, a series of dives on the wreck launched by the Russian research vessel *Akademik Mstislav Keldysh* resulted in an IMAX movie called *Titanica*, which showed the site and the recovery of the artifacts. It was the *Akademik Keldysh* that James Cameron chartered to film the underwater scenes for his movie *Titanic*.

- In September 1992, Jack Grimm once again entered the picture, this time with a Tennessee group called Marex-Titanic, Inc. to salvage the wreckage. Titanic Ventures, and now RMST, filed suit in a United States District Court to halt the salvage—and won. Grimm decided, finally, to leave *Titanic* to others.

With the French and now the United States District Court giving RMST sole rights to salvage the wreck, it wasn't long before the Canadian and British courts followed suit, each deciding it was best to give one organization the legal rights to salvage the ship as opposed to letting anyone with the technology to do so. This way, the artifacts could be preserved and kept on display or in a museum.

- Over the years RMST has recovered more than 6,000 artifacts from the debris field. The courts have maintained that nothing inside the hull or attached to it can be salvaged. All of the items removed from the seabed have been carefully preserved and maintained. In 1997, RMST began a series of traveling exhibits that have visited several cities in the United States, Canada, and more recently, Europe. Millions of people have visited the exhibits. The plan is that eventually, all of this material will be housed in one permanent museum, although its location has yet to be decided.

Although RMST has the legal right to salvage the wreck, it is becoming clear that other less-scrupulous individuals and organizations are attempting to fund, and find, the wreck for their own agendas. It probably won't be too long before *Titanic* artifacts, some real and some fake, will be circulating for sale.

> *"The ship is its own memorial. Leave it there"* (*Titanic* survivor Eva Hart).

Never again will *Titanic* rest in peace.

CHAPTER 19

A FEW MORE FACTS...

Several people on *Carpathia* and other ships passing through the area photographed the iceberg *Titanic* struck. Someone even shot some movie film, which still exists. Although there were dozens of large of icebergs in the vicinity, this one was identifiable because of the black and red paint smeared along its side.

- All 35 of *Titanic's* engineers remained at their stations in the engine and electrical generating rooms—and died there. King George V later decreed that all British marine engineers wear the insignia of their rank next to a royal purple background to remember their brave colleagues on *Titanic*.

- Hindsight suggests that First Officer William Murdoch's decision to order Quartermaster Hichens to turn the ship "hard-a-starboard," was probably the wrong one. Had *Titanic* rammed the iceberg head-on, the first four compartments probably would have been crushed. Many of the people in the bow, mostly Third Class single men and the black gang crew (firemen, stokers, trimmers, etc.) would have died. However, the ship probably would have remained afloat, at least long enough for rescue ships to come to the aid of the passengers and crew. *Titanic* thus might have survived to sail another day. Murdoch's problem, however, was that he had just seconds within which to make his decision. He knew that ramming an iceberg would kill a lot of people, and his years of training had taught him to save lives and disaster at all cost. Given the circumstances of the event, it is unlikely Murdoch, Captain Smith, or any other officer would have chosen to ram the iceberg instead of trying to go around it.

- Although most people were duly impressed with the mammoth size of *Titanic* and her sister ship *Olympic*, some believed the new ships were too big and carried too many people. The *Olympic*-class ships displaced twice the tonnage of the next largest ship afloat. However, the passenger liners then under construction in Germany, scheduled for launch in

1914, were larger than *Titanic*. Today, the *Queen Mary* and most of the popular cruise ships are much larger than *Titanic*.

- The unidentified child (mentioned in an earlier chapter) recovered and buried in Halifax was later tentatively identified as Gosta Paulson. Gosta had been traveling with his mother and two siblings. As it turns out, it was long believed he was buried in a grave only a few feet from his mother. Neither of Gosta's siblings survived. In 2002, however, DNA testing confirmed the child was actually two-year-old Urho Abraham Panula, who perished with his mother and four siblings. None of the family survived, and as far as is known none of their bodies were recovered.

- Bagpiper Eugene Daly's brother and sister were with him on *Titanic*; both survived. "Erin's Lament," the tune Daly was playing is popularly known as "Lament," and can be found on numerous current CDs and recordings.

- The British Postal Service had assigned the number "7" to *Titanic*. The number was hand stamped on all correspondence handled on the ship. After the disaster the number was officially retired.

- Some of the surviving British crewmen awaiting transportation back to England were invited to work behind the counter of the Woolworth store in New York. They were allowed to keep all the money they collected from sales.

- First Officer Murdoch was engaged to be married, and the wedding was scheduled one week after *Titanic* was supposed to complete her maiden voyage. Murdoch's fiancé lived another 58 years. She never married.

- Fireman Thomas Hart was reported lost on *Titanic*, and his mother was officially notified of his death. On May 8, Hart walked into his mother's house, causing her to pass out from the shock. Hart had lost his identification papers in a bar and was too embarrassed to return home. Whoever took Hart's papers used them to secure a job on *Titanic* and almost certainly went down with the ship. The imposter has never been identified.

- The 1958 movie *A Night to Remember* portrayed Captain Stanley Lord of the *Californian* in a highly negative light—close enough to *Titanic* to help without the desire to do so. In 1959, a still-seething Lord entered the office of the British Mercantile Marine Service Association and announced, "I'm Lord of the *Californian*." Initially, no one knew what he was talking about. Lord spent the remaining three years of his life trying without success to get a new hearing to clear his name. His children are still trying to clear his name.

- Passenger William Stead, who told his dinner companions that a cursed Egyptian mummy that had killed everyone who came into contact with it was on the ship, did not survive the sinking. Ironically, his false story outlived him. There was no mummy on the ship, but the tale continues to make the rounds on the internet.

- What really happened to Captain E. J. Smith? Several accounts by survivors place him on the port side of the bridge shortly before the big wave washed over it. If so, he either drowned quickly or was crushed when the forward funnel fell over, killing several people in the water including John Jacob Astor.

There are dozens of different stories about Smith's last moments, including one in which he supposedly swam up to a lifeboat with a small baby in his arms, handed it to the passengers, and swam away to his death. Since all the babies who were saved were accounted for by those who saved them, this story is untrue.

- Second Officer Lightoller once said of the British hearings,

> "In Washington it was of little consequence, but in London it was very necessary to keep one's hands on the whitewash brush."

- Steward P. Keene reported,

> "One of the engineers got horribly jammed when the doors in the bulkheads were closed. His injuries were terrible, and, as there was no chance of releasing him, he implored that he might be shot to be put out of his misery. This, I have been told, was done."

Steward Keene's story is almost certainly untrue. Other than the guns carried by the ship's officers, no others are known to have been carried on board. No one ever stepped forward to confirm the story.

- The hull number for *Titanic*, assigned by the British government, was 390904. When some of the working-class Catholic employees in Belfast saw this in a mirror image, they read the words "NO POPE." This was enough for them to stop construction. Management had to assure the workers that the number was just a coincidence. However, some believed this "coincidence" spelled doom.

- Did one of the officers shoot himself? Several survivors testified they saw one of the officers put a revolver to his head and shoot himself shortly before the ship sank. No one could agree about who it was, if in fact it happened at all.

If one of the officers did shoot himself, who could it have been? Lightoller, Boxhall, Lowe and Pitman survived, leaving Captain Smith, Chief Officer Wilde, First Officer Murdoch, Sixth Officer Moody, and Purser McElroy.

Smith did not have a pistol, and there are no accounts that Moody was issued one that night. Many accounts have speculated that Murdoch took his own life because he felt responsible for the collision (he was the watch officer at the time the ship struck the iceberg). No one who knew Murdoch well believed he would have shot himself. Purser McElroy was seen in the water by three survivors.

Wilde was the only other person known to have had a pistol that night. Little is known about Wilde. Few of the survivors knew who he was and for the most part, the surviving officers did not remember seeing him after they started launching the lifeboats. If one of the officers did shoot himself, it was either Murdoch or Wilde. It is doubtful at this late date we will ever know for sure.

- The name *Titanic* was sanded off the thirteen surviving lifeboats on Friday, April 19. The following day the boats were hoisted up to the second floor of a warehouse and stored there (where they were later joined by Collapsible A). The total value of the lifeboats was determined to be $4,520, which represented the entire salvage value of *Titanic*. According to U.S. Maritime Law, that sum was the total amount that might have been paid out in claims. This is the reason most damage claims were filed in Great Britain. The lifeboats were eventually moved and disappear from the historical record. In all likelihood they were placed upon another White Star Line ship. But no one knows for sure.

- It seems that Sir Cosmo and Lady Lucy Duff Gordon just couldn't do anything right. The day after they were rescued by *Carpathia*, the couple arranged to have a photograph taken of them and the ten other survivors on Lifeboat 1–all sporting big smiles. Considered tacky at best, the photograph added fuel to subsequent rumors that Sir Cosmo had paid off the crew to not go back and pick up survivors.

- In 1898, 14 years before *Titanic* sank and nine years before the ship's design was even conceived, author Morgan Robertson published a book called *Futility*. It was a short passage about a huge passenger liner that collided with an iceberg on her maiden voyage.

The name of the fictitious ship in *Futility* was *Titan*. The dimensions of *Titan* were spelled out in the book. The similarities between it and the real *Titanic* are striking:

	Titan	*Titanic*
Length	800 feet	882.5 feet
Top Speed	25 knots	25 knots
Number of passengers	2,000	2,200
Registered	British	British
Displacement	70,000 tons	66,000 tons
Propellers	3	3
Lifeboats	24	20
Watertight bulkheads	19	15
Time of voyage	April	April
Side striking the iceberg	starboard	starboard

Robertson died in 1915. He lived long enough to see his fictitious story come true.

■ In August 1912, Madeleine Astor gave birth to a boy; John Jacob Astor V. Madeleine later married William K. Dick, a wealthy businessman. She gave up her claim to the Astor fortune by doing so. Later she divorced Dick and married again, this time to prize-fighter Enzo Fiermonte. She divorced him in 1938. Madeleine Force Astor Dick Fiermonte died in Palm Beach in 1940 at the age of 47. John Jacob Astor V died in 1992 at the age of 79.

■ One of the survivors in Lifeboat 7 was actress Dorothy Gibson. Exactly one month after *Titanic* sank, Gibson co-wrote and starred in a one-reel silent movie called *Saved from the Titanic*. In the movie, she wore the same dress she had worn the night the real *Titanic* sank. Unfortunately, no known copies of the film are in existence.

■ Margaret "Molly" Brown died in 1932. She was never called "Unsinkable Molly Brown" while she lived. It was not until 1960 when Meredith Willson wrote the Broadway musical *The Unsinkable Molly Brown* that Molly Brown earned her unforgettable nickname.

■ In 1848 the seaport town of Cobh, Ireland, changed its name to Queenstown in honor of Queen Victoria. In 1922, Queenstown was once again renamed Cobh.
Queenstown was the last port *Titanic* visited. In 1915, Queenstown was propelled once again into the front page of world events when *Lusitania* was torpedoed and sunk just a handful of miles off the port, and the ship's survivors were taken there.

■ Every choice we make, no matter how insignificant it may seem at the time, can be a matter of life and death. And so it was on *Titanic*.

Titanic carried 197 adult First Class male passengers. Of these, 124 traveled alone (unaccompanied), and 53 traveled with their wives and/or children (accompanied). Their seemingly trivial fork in the road that terrible evening of April 14, 1912, a decision made by either a crew member or themselves, was whether to wait on the starboard or port side of the ship while the lifeboats were being loaded.

Second Officer Lightoller supervised the loading of the even-numbered lifeboats on the port side. His strict orders were that *only* women and children would fill them. The loading of the starboard odd-numbered lifeboats was overseen by First Officer Murdoch. Unlike Lightoller's directive, however, Murdoch ordered crewmen to load women and children *first*. If there was additional room in a boat thereafter, men were allowed to climb aboard. The slight difference in the wording of these orders saved some men—while simultaneously dooming others to extinction.

Only 34 of the original 124 "unaccompanied" First Class males (or 27%) survived. Of that number, 27 secured slots in Murdoch's starboard lifeboats, while only two were allowed aboard lifeboats launched from the port side (in both cases they were ordered into them by Lightholler to help row). The remaining five survivors went into the water and somehow managed to get into one of the two collapsibles.

Only 19 of the original 53 "accompanied" adult males (or 36%) survived. Not a single survivor from this group was allowed into a lifeboat launched by Lightholler. Of those 19 who lived, 15 were allowed by Murdoch to accompany their wives and/or children into the starboard boats, and one was later pulled into a boat from the water. The remaining three men placed their wives into one of Lightholler's lifeboats on the port side and then walked 90 feet across the ship to the starboard side, where they secured a seat in one of Murdoch's boats and joined their families on the *Carpathia* a few hours later.

Every choice we make, no matter how insignificant it may seem at the time, can be a matter of life and death. And so it was on *Titanic* for First Class male passengers.

FREQUENTLY ASKED QUESTIONS

Over the years, visitors to the various *Titanic* Artifact Expositions have asked me a wide range of questions. Below is a partial list of these questions and answers.

Q) Was Captain Smith trying to set a speed record?

A) No. He was steaming at the same speed he had been for most of the trip. He knew he did not have enough coal to set any speed record. (Smith also knew *Titanic* was not fast enough to break the current transatlantic record, which stood until 1926.) He was also four hours behind schedule, so he could not even beat *Olympic's* maiden voyage time.

Q) Why were so many First Class passengers saved and not Third Class passengers?

A) In raw numbers, almost as many Third Class passengers survived (173) as did First Class travelers (201). The difference is in the percentage. Most First Class passengers survived because their rooms were near the Boat Deck, they had servants who took care of them, and they followed the crew's orders when told to get into the lifeboats. Most of the surviving Third Class passengers had English surnames. Unfortunately, most Third Class passengers did not speak English, and could not understand the commands to go up to the Boat Deck. They had to be led to the Boat Deck, and even when they were, most refused to get into a lifeboat. Contrary to popular belief, no Third Class passengers were locked behind gates to prevent them from getting off the ship.

Q) Why did so many crewmen survive when so many passengers did not?

A) The officers made an attempt to make sure each lifeboat had at least five crewmen to row them. Some lifeboats ended up with more, some with less. Of the 212 crew saved, 19 were women and 20 men were pulled out of the water or climbed onto the overturned Lifeboat Collapsible B. Another 90 or so were ordered into the lifeboats to row. The remaining 80 crewmen just happened to be at the right place at the right time and got into a lifeboat. However, hundreds (679) more perished.

Q) Why did the survival rate for men dramatically differ depending upon which side of the Boat Deck men happened to be on?

A) Second Officer Lightoller was in command of loading the lifeboats on the port side. Lightoller held to the rule *women and children only,* and he launched lifeboats with empty seats if there were no more women and children around—even if there were men in the vicinity. On the port side, however, First Officer Murdoch held to the rule *women and children FIRST,* which meant that if he had to launch a lifeboat and there were not any women or children around, he allowed male passengers into the lifeboat and then if there was still room, male crewmembers.

Q) Did Captain Smith really say that it was *"every man for himself?"*

A) Yes. When water was swirling about his feet on the bridge, he gave that command to release the bridge crew and the Marconi operators so they could try to save themselves.

Q) Was the ship built so fast that someone was sealed inside the hull?

A) No. This rumor is essentially an urban legend. The ship was not built that fast and there were not any sealed compartments on *Titanic*.

Q) Is there any truth behind the existence of Jack Dawson, Rose, and the Blue Diamond as depicted in James Cameron's *Titanic*?

A) No. Alas, the story and jewel are nothing more than a Hollywood creation.

Q) Has all the wood on *Titanic* been eaten by micro organisms? If not, what happened to the Grand Staircase, which seems to be missing?

A) This is one of the fascinating mysteries that may now have been solved. When Ballard originally looked inside *Titanic*, no wood was visible—including the First Class Grand Staircase. Bob Ballard believed the wood had been eaten away by microscopic organisms that feed upon organic matter. However, a later investigation probed deeper into the ship and found much of the wood completely intact. So what happened to the massive Grand Staircase? If it had been eaten away, the metal fixtures and fittings would be visible on the deck. They are not. The obvious answer became evident when the movie set of *Titanic* was flooded with 50,000 gallons of water. As the water poured in, the Grand Staircase (rebuilt to the exact specifications of the original), broke free and shot upward. In other words, the whole structure floated. Our best guess today, based upon the evidence that was not left behind (i.e., iron fittings, etc.) is that the massive forces aboard the real *Titanic* shook loose the super-buoyant structure, which shot up through the crystal dome, floated away and eventually dissintigrated somewhere in the Atlantic Ocean.

OF CQD AND SOS

The Marconi Company and many, but not all, telegraph companies used the three letter command CQD to indicate help was needed. Marconi operators, needing something to call it, called CQD Come Quick Danger.

■ In the early 1900s, an international set of commands was developed that all companies were supposed to adopt by 1915. One of the results was the designation of the three-letter combination SOS to signify a call for help. This SOS is still used today.

The SOS call signals the need for immediate assistance. It does not mean Save Our Ship or Save Our Souls. It is, simply, a three-letter combination used to attract help.

- Why was the SOS adopted? Using *Titanic's* plea for help is a perfect example of why it was needed.

When Marconi operator Jack Phillips began his call for help, he sent out the following: CQD MGY CQD MGY. CQD was the call for help, MGY was *Titanic's* unique call sign. The Morse Code indicator for the letters needed to send this message were as follows:

C: dash dot dash dot
Q: dash dash dot dash
D: dash dot dot
M: dash dash
G: dash dash dot
Y: dash dot dash dash

Philips had to tap out the following for each CQD MGY:

Dash dot dash dot dash dash dot dash dash dot dot
dash dash dash dash dot dash dot dash dash.

This was confusing to say the least, and as the situation on *Titanic* worsened, other ships were having trouble understanding Phillip's message. He was clicking as fast has he could, and was making mistakes.

- The letters SOS are very simple, which is why they were picked as a call for help. SOS is a simple:

"dot dot dot dash dash dash dot dot dot."

So Phillips changed over to the SOS later in his transmissions. He now had to send the following "SOS MGY SOS MGY" etc.

Dot dot dot dash dash dash dot dot dot
dash dash dash dash dot dash dot dash dash.

In order to garner attention, he continued sending a series of SOS calls, or SOS SOS SOS SOS MGY SOS SOS SOS SOS MGY

Dash Dash Dash Dot Dot Dot Dash Dash Dash
Dash Dash Dash Dot Dot Dot Dash Dash Dash
Dash Dash Dash Dot Dot Dot Dash Dash Dash
Dash Dash Dash Dot Dot Dot Dash Dash Dash
Dash Dash Dash Dash Dot Dash Dot Dash Dash

- The SOS was now firmly established as a universal call for help. In the phonetic alphabet for Morse Code, the S stands for Sierra and the O is for Oscar. SOS, then, is SIERRA OSCAR SIERRA, and not SAVE OUR SOULS or SAVE OUR SHIP.

OTHER DISASTERS

Halifax, the city that became the final resting place for so many of *Titanic's* dead, suffered a devastating event just a few years later. On December 6, 1917, the French ammunition ship *Mont Blanc*, carrying almost 500,000 pounds of explosives to France, was rammed by another ship in the narrow part of the harbor and caught fire. The crew quickly abandoned ship and tried to spread the word to anyone who would listen. The fire poured black smoke all over the harbor as hundreds of unknowing people lined the banks of the water to watch the spectacular fire. Thousands more watched the event from inside their homes, offices and schools. At 9:05 a.m. the *Mont Blanc* exploded—creating the largest man-made explosion before the atomic bomb in 1945. More than 1,900 people died instantly, some 9,000 more were injured, and more than 350 acres of the northern part of the city was destroyed. The *Mont Blanc* disintegrated. Her anchor landed three miles away. Windows 50 miles away were shattered and the shock wave was felt more than 270 miles away.

- Adding lifeboats to passenger ships contributed to a disaster. On Saturday morning, July 24, 1915, just three years after *Titanic* sank, steamship S.S. *Eastland* rolled over and sank in the Chicago River and drowned more than 800 people, including 22 entire families.

The *Eastland* was a vessel used to transport workers from Chicago to other Lake Michigan cities, and was chartered by private companies on the weekends. *Eastland* had been chartered by the Western Electric Company for their annual picnic in Michigan. Some 2,500 people were crammed on board at the dock under the Clark Street Bridge between LaSalle and Clark streets. Another boatload of Western Electric picnic goers passed by the tied-up *Eastland* and many of those 2,500 passengers moved to the river side of the ship to wave to their friends. The shift in weight capsized *Eastland*, drowning most of the people trapped inside the deck house.

Ironically, *Eastland* was making her second voyage after having been refitted with enough lifeboats to accommodate all her passengers, the result of laws passed after *Titanic* sank. The addition of the required lifeboats to the top deck made the ship top heavy, a condition that almost caused it to sink on her first voyage two days earlier.

- On Friday morning, May 29, 1914, just two years after *Titanic* plunged to the bottom of the Atlantic, the Canadian Pacific Liner *Empress of Ireland* was bound from Quebec, Canada to Liverpool, England with 1,477 people on board. Among the passengers were 171 members of the Salvation Army heading for the Third International Congress in England.

The *Empress of Ireland* was steaming in the middle of the St. Lawrence River on the night of her first day out of Quebec. The Norwegian coal ship *Storstad* was approaching the *Empress* on a correct course to pass on the left. A fog bank suddenly rolled through the area and the captain of the *Empress* ordered his ship to stop because he did not know what course the *Storstad* was taking. The Norwegian coaler steamed out of the fog and crashed into the port side of the *Empress*, opening a hole 14 feet wide and 25 feet high.

The *Empress* filled with water, which flooded the engine rooms and trapped the Third Class passengers in their cabins. She sank in only 14 minutes, dumping hundreds of passengers into the freezing St. Lawrence River. Just as it was with *Titanic*, most of the people in the water died within a handful of minutes because of the freezing water. A total of 1,012 people died that night. There was not enough time to launch even a single lifeboat before the *Empress of Ireland* slipped beneath the surface.

- At 2:10 p.m. on Friday, May 7, 1915, the Cunard Liner *Lusitania* was returning from New York bound for Liverpool on her 201st crossing of the Atlantic. *Lusitania* was one of the fastest ships in the world and was not under the wartime restrictions imposed on most other ships to travel in a convoy to protect them from German U-boats (submarines).

U-boats were waging unrestricted warfare against any ship trying to enter Great Britain, regardless of the type of ship or their country of registry, a fact that angered many in the United States.

On May 7, just 14 miles off the Old Head of Kinsale in Southern Ireland, and just a few miles outside of Queenstown, U-20 spotted the *Lusitania* steaming along on a straight course. *Lusitania* was not following the normal requirement to steam a zig-zag course to make it harder for a U-boat to successfully attack.

The captain of U-20 fired a single torpedo into the starboard side of the forward cargo hold, which detonated and set off another huge secondary explosion. *Lusitania* immediately flooded and started to sink by the bow with a huge list to the starboard. Eighteen minutes after the torpedo struck, she rolled over on her side and sank. Most of the lifeboats on the starboard side were crushed as the ship rolled over, and most of those on the port side, high out of the water and at a dangerous angle, could not be launched. The few lifeboats able to slip their davits were released by cutting their falls, and the drop killed dozens of people in the water under them. In all, 1,201 people died in the disaster.

- No amount of mechanical or technical capability will save a ship if the crew operating her does not follow international rules regarding her safe operation. At 11:10 p.m. on a foggy Wednesday night, July 25, 1956, the luxurious five-year old Italian Liner *Andrea Doria* was rammed by the Swedish-American vessel *Stockholm*, just 60 miles off Nantucket. *Stockholm*'s reinforced steel bow ripped a huge hole in the *Andrea Doria's* starboard side. A missing crucial watertight door and lack of water ballast caused *Andrea Doria* to immediately take on an 18-degree list. Movie cameras on nearby rescue ships and helicopters flying overhead recorded the rescue, allowing thousands of people around the world to watch a live broadcast of the sinking. At 10:00 on July 26 *Andrea Doria* rolled over and sank in 225 feet of water.

Although each ship had detected the other via radar, later inquiry found that the master of *Andrea Doria* turned to the left instead of to the right, as he should have when meeting another ship in the fog. Ultimately, only the fog was blamed for the collision, little compensation for the 52 people who were killed in the initial collision.

- The new and modern RoRo (roll-on, roll-off) passenger and car ferry *Estonia* left her home port of Tallinn, Estonia, for an overnight trip across the Baltic Sea to Stockholm, Sweden, at 5:00 p.m. on September 27, 1994. By all accounts it was a routine voyage. The middle portion of the trip was very rough because of the high waves and 20 mph winds that occur in the region, and many passengers became seasick. The *Estonia* had a slight list to starboard because of the cargo and motor vehicles stowed inside.

Just before 1:00 a.m. a large metallic bang was heard from the area of the bow. Crew members sent to investigate could not find anything wrong. *Estonia* steamed on at 14 knots in waves approaching six feet high. Ten minutes later several more loud noises were heard, which caused many passengers and crew to leave their compartments and investigate. At 1:15 a.m. part of the watertight shield surrounding the bow doors (which open to allow vehicles to drive off) separated and tons of water poured into the vehicle deck. *Estonia* took on a heavy starboard list while hundreds of panicked people poured out of their cabins fearing the ship would capsize. Their fears were realized.

At 1:22 a.m. the first Mayday call went out, and by 1:30 *Estonia* was on her starboard side. Twenty minutes later (35 minutes after taking on water), *Estonia* sank. It took two hours for rescue ships to arrive. *Estonia* sank so rapidly that few life rafts were launched. The freezing water had the same effect on these unfortunates as it had on *Titanic's* passengers. Only 128 survivors were pulled from the water. Another 757 souls were lost, many trapped in their cabins as the ship went down.

GLOSSARY

This glossary is provided to help readers understand some of the terminology used in this book.

Aft: toward the back of the ship.

Amidships: the middle portion of the ship.

Astern: toward the back of the ship.

Barge: a small flat-bottomed, unpowered floating platform that was pushed or towed into position. Used to carry coal, equipment or other bulk items.

Berth: the place where a ship is docked at a wharf *or* a place to sleep (such as bed).

Bilge: the inside of the double bottom of the ship.

Black gang: name for the firemen, stokers, trimmers and everyone else working down in the boiler room. They quickly became covered in coal dust.

Boat Deck: topmost deck on the ship, from which point lifeboats were stored and launched.

Boatswain: a junior officer in command of the anchor and deck crew.

Bow: the front of the ship.

Bridge: The control center, or point where the captain and his officers control the movements of the ship. Usually the highest or close to the highest deck on the ship.

Bulkhead: a wall between two compartments.

Bunker: place to store coal.

Capsize: if a ship becomes unbalanced with too much weight on one side, the ship will tip over toward that side. Generally, this is the most common occurrence when a ship sinks.

Capstan: a revolving cylinder used for hoisting weights by winding in a cable or chain.

Collier: a barge used to transport coal to the side of a ship.

Collapsible (Englehardt boat): a boat made with canvas sides and a wooden bottom. Stored on ship with the sides folded down, it was the crew's responsibility to build up the side supports before launching the boat. There were four collapsibles on *Titanic*.

Corridor: a hallway or passageway.

Compartment: a room.

Crow's Nest: a small platform high on the foreword mast used by the lookouts to stand on.

Davit: a small crane used to lower the lifeboats, two were required for each lifeboat.

Deck: the nautical term for the floor.

Displacement: the volume of water, in tons, displaced by a ship, which is one of the measures of its size. The amount of water a ship displaces must exceed the actual weight of the ship.

Docking bridge: an open platform running the width of the ship on top of the poop deck that contained equipment to communicate with the bridge. Used primarily when in port to help with docking the ship.

Dry Dock: enclosed area where water is pumped out of to allow construction or repair of a ship.

Double Bottom: a series of sealed compartments covering the entire bottom of the ship, designed to prevent flooding if the ship strikes a reef or underwater obstacle. Usually the compartments were filled with water for ballast.

Double Hull: sealed compartments similar to the double bottom but extending along the sides of a ship. It is designed to prevent flooding if something penetrates the outside skin of the ship. *Titanic* did not have a double hull, and might have survived if it had been built with this design feature.

Fall: ropes attached to boats and the davits, used to lower the boats to the water.

Fireman: a person who tended the fires in the boilers.

First Class: the best accommodations on the ship, with various levels of "upgrades" available. First Class passengers paid the highest rate and received access to all of the ship's amenities.

Forecastle (fo'c'sle): a small raised deck at the bow of a ship.

Forepeak: the most forward compartment of the ship.

Forward: toward the front (bow).

Funnel: another name for smokestack. Technically ships don't have smokestacks, they have funnels.

Galley: kitchen where food is prepared.

Gangway: a door in the side of a ship's hull.

Graving Dock: a dry dock ships are placed into, used to fit out a new ship.

Greaser: a crewman whose primary job was to apply grease to all the moving parts of the engines.

Gross Tons: amount of weight a ship can carry.

HMS: initials for His (or Her) Majesty's Ship, for vessels of the Royal Navy.

Hull: the enclosed frame of a ship.

Iceberg: floating mass of freshwater ice that floats with only one-eighth of its mass above the surface.

Joiner: a crewman who worked as a carpenter or cabinetmaker.

Keel: the lowest part of the ship *or* the lowest structural member upon which the rest of the ship is constructed.

Knot: a unit of speed (1.15 miles per hour) *or* distance (2,000 yards).

List: A tilt off the center of the keel. If the weight of a ship becomes unbalanced, the ship will lean to one side or the other.

Lough: (as in Belfast Lough): a bay or an inlet of the sea.

Marconi: the brand name of the wireless telegraph unit carried on *Titanic,* owned and staffed by the Marconi Company.

Masthead light: a bright white light located at the top of the mast.

Nautical mile: speed equivalent to approximately 1.3 miles per hour

Orlop (deck): lowest actual deck of a ship, the deck above the tank top on *Titanic.*

Poop Deck: a raised deck at the very stern (rear) of the ship.

Port: if standing on the deck of a ship looking forward, the port side is the left side of the ship.

Promenade deck: a public place for the passengers to walk. Each class had its own promenade deck.

Quartermaster: a junior officer responsible for the navigation of the ship. On *Titanic,* they were responsible for manning the ship's wheel.

RMS: in the early part of the 20th century, initials for Royal Mail Steamer *or* Royal Mail Steamship.

Reciprocating engine: a high-pressure steam-driven engine with pistons that turn a crankshaft, which then turns a propeller.

Second Class: a class of accommodations better than Third Class but not as good as First Class. Second Class passengers were afforded many amenities that Third Class passengers were not.

Sidelights: a large light located on the side of the bridge, colored red for port and green for starboard. These allow other ships to determine the course, speed, and distance at night.

Starboard: if standing on the deck of a ship looking forward, the starboard side is the right side of the ship.

Steerage: (or Third Class): the part of the ship allocated to the cheapest and largest class of accommodations, placed in the lowest portions of the ship, usually in the stern near the steering apparatus. Accommodations were usually nothing more than a berth in a dormitory-type room.

Stern: the rear of the ship.

Stoker: a crewman who fed coal into the ship's furnace, usually with a shovel-like tool.

Third Class: see Steerage.

Telegraph: a mechanical device used to transmit speed and direction (forward or reverse) information from the bridge to the engine room and steering room.

Tiller: lever used to turn a ship's rudder.

Ton: weight equal to 2,000 pounds or 20 hundredweight (cwt).

Transverse bulkhead: bulkheads going across the width of the ship.

Trimmer: a member of the crew who distributes coal from the coal bunker to the stoker who shovels it into the boiler fires.

Triple-Expansion Engine: a steam engine with at least three cylinders. *Titanic's* engines had four: a high pressure, a medium pressure and two low pressure cylinders.

Upper deck(s): the topmost decks on the ship exposed to the open air.

Well Deck: a part of the upper deck that sits slightly lower than the decks around it. There were two well decks on *Titanic,* one fore and one aft. These comprised the Third Class promenade areas.

Where to find additional information.

BIBLIOGRAPHY

BOOKS

Following is a list of some of my favorite books relating to the Titanic disaster. If you would like to further your education about the *Titanic*, these are the books where you should start. All are generally available at bookstores or via one of the Internet sites. Additionally, the Titanic Historical Society out of Indian Orchard, Massachusetts publishes a bi-annual magazine that contains exceptional articles related to *Titanic*.

Archibold, Rick and Dana McCauley. *Last Dinner on the Titanic:* Toronto: Madison Press, 1997

Ballard, Robert D. *The Discovery of the Titanic.* New York: Warner, 1987.

Beesley, Lawrence. *The Loss of the SS Titanic.* Boston: Houghton Mifflin, 1912.

Brown, Daavid G. The Last Log of the *Titanic.* New York: International Marine, 2001

Bullock, Shane F. *A Titanic Hero: Thomas Andrews, Shipbuilder.* Baltimore: Norman, Remington 1913.

Caplan, Bruce M., editor, *The Sinking of the Titanic: 1912 Survivor Accounts.* Seattle: Seattle Miracle Press, 1997

Davie, Michael. *Titanic: the Death and Life of a Legend.* London: Bodley Head, 1986.

Eaton, John P. and Charles Haas. *Titanic: A Journey Through Time.* W. W. Norton, 1999.

Eaton, John P. and Charles Haas. *Titanic: Destination Disaster.* New York: W. W. Norton, 1987.

Eaton, John P. and Charles Haas. *Titanic: Triumph and Tragedy.* New York: W. W. Norton, 1988.

Geller, Judith B., Titanic: Women and Children First. New York: W. W. Norton, 1998

Gracie, Archibald. *The Truth About the Titanic.* New York: Kennerly, 1913.

Hoffman, William and Jack Grimm. *Beyond Reach: The Search for the Titanic.* New York: Beaufort, 1982.

Kuntz, Tom. ed. *The Titanic Disaster Hearings: The Official Transcripts of the 1912 Senate Investigation.* New York: Pocket Books, 1998

Lightoller, Charles Herbert. *The Titanic and Other Ships.* London: Nicholson and Watson, 1935.

Lord, Walter. *A Night to Remember.* New York: Holt, Rinehart and Winston, 1955.

Lord, Walter. *The Miracle of Dunkirk.* New York: William Morrow, 1976.

Lord, Walter. *The Night Lives On.* New York: William Morrow, 1986.

McCluskie, Tom. *Anatomy of the Titanic.* London: PRC Publishing Ltd, 1998.

Merideth, Lee W. *Titanic Names: A Complete List of the Passengers and Crew.* Sunnyvale, Rocklin Press. 2002

Pellegrino, Charles. *Her Name, Titanic.* New York: Avon Books, 1988.

Simpson, Colin. *The Lusitania.* Boston: Little, Brown and Company, 1972.

Wade, Wynn Craig. *The Titanic: the End of a Dream.* New York: Penquin, 1979.

Winocour, Jack, ed. *The Story of the Titanic as told by its Survivors.* New York: Dover Publications, Inc., 1960.

PERIODICALS

Ballard, Robert D. "How We Found *Titanic*." *National Geographic*, (December 1985).

Carrothers, John C. "Lord of the *Californian*." *United States Naval Institute Proceedings* 94 (March 1968).

Carrothers, John C. "The *Titanic* Disaster," *United States Naval Institute Proceedings* 88 (April 1962).

Lord, Walter: "Maiden Voyage." *American Heritage*, December 1955.

DOCUMENTS

Great Britain, Parliamentary Debates (Commons), 5th series, 37–42, April 15–October 25, 1912.

U.S. Congress, Senate, *Hearings of a Subcommittee of the Senate Commerce Committee pursuant to S. Res. 283, to Investigate the Causes leading to the Wreck of the White Star Liner "Titanic."* 62nd Congress, 2nd session, 1912. S. Doc 726 (#6167).

U.S. Congress, Senate, *Loss of the Steamship 'Titanic': Report of a Formal Investigation...as conducted by the British Government, Presented by Mr. Smith,* 62nd Congress, 2nd session, 20 August 1912, S. Doc. 933 (#6179).

U.S. Congress, Senate, *Report of the Senate Committee on Commerce pursuant to S. Res. 283, Directing the Committee to Investigate the Causes of the Sinking of the 'Titanic' with speeches by William Alden Smith and Isador Rayner,* 62nd Congress, 2nd session, 28 May 1912, S. Rept. 806 (#6127).

INTERNET SITES

Following is a brief list of some of the better Internet sites that contain much useful information. These were all active sites when this edition was published, but I do not guarantee they are still active when you read this.

Encyclopedia Smithsonian:
    http://www.si.edu/resource/faq/nmah/titanic.htm
Encyclopedia Titanica (the ultimate *Titanic* source)
    http://www.encyclopedia-titanica.org
Molly Brown House: http://mollybrown.com
RMS Titanic, Inc. (artifact recovery on list of ongoing exhibitions)
http://www.titanic-online.com
Rocklin Press (publisher of *1912 Facts About Titanic* and *Titanic Names: A Complete List of the Passengers and Crew*):
    http://www.factsabouttitanic.com
Titanic Books: http://www.titanicbooksite.com
Titanic Diagram: http://members.aol.com/lorbus
Titanic Historical Society: http://titanic1.org
Titanic International Society: http://www.titanicinternational.org
Titanic News Channel: http://www.titanicnewschannel.com/
Titanic Website Links:
    http://www.geocities.com/athens/agora/6683/links.html
Wreck of the *Titanic*: http://www.flash.net/~rfm/index/contents.html

INDEX

A Night to Remember, 178, 230
Abbott, Eugene, 68
Abbott, Mrs. Stanton, 68, 178, 187, 192
Abbott, Rossmore, 68
Abelseth, Karen, 69
Abelseth, Olaus, 69
Abrahamsson, August, 70-71
Adriatic, 5, 45, 49, 68
Ahlin, Johanna, 71
Ajax, 43, 83
Akademik Mstislav Keldysh, 227
Aks, Leah, 68, 73, 164-165, 183
Aks, Frank Philip, 68, 73, 165
Aldworth, Charles, 95
Algerine, 203
Allen, Elisabeth, 77
Allison, Hudson J.C. family, 77, 134, 158, 164
Alvin, 226
America, 96, 107
American Inquiry, 214
American Red Cross, 199
Amerika, 123
anchors, 11, 23, 43, 225
Anderson, Dame Judith, 80
Anderson, Father Roger B.T., 194
Andersson, Alfrida, 68
Andersson, Anders, 68
Andersson, August, 70
Andrea Doria, 72, 239
Andreasson, Paul, 70
Andrews, Kornelia, 78
Andrews, Thomas, 11, 51, arrives on the bridge,
    138, feels collision, 136, knows *Titanic* will sink,
    150, last seen, 175, returns from tour, 139, sea
    trials, 41, 65, signed transfer papers, 43, status of
    ship, 141, the fire, 66, tour With Smith, 138, **64**
Antillian, 123
Appleton, Mrs. Edward, 79, 92
Arnold, Josef, 71
Arnold, Josephine, 71
Artagaveytia, Ramon, 96
Asplund, Carl, family, 67
Astor, John Jacob IV, 91, 148, 171-173, body
    recovered, 202, dies, 177, last seen with Smith,
    231, Queenstown, 107, **90**
Astor, John J. V, 233
Astor, Madeleine Force, 91, 107, 148, 164-165,
    172-173, 233, **90**
Athinai, 123
Atlantic, 5-6, 13
Aubert, Madame Leontine, 91, 162
Augustsson, Albert, 70
Ayoub, Banoura, 88

Backstrom, Karl, 68
Backstrom, Maria, 68
Baclini, Mrs. Solomon, 88
Bacon, Robert, 112
Bailey, Joseph, 168
Bailey, Percy A., 71, 75
Ballard, Dr. Robert, 224-226, 235
Baltic, 5, 49, 122-123, 195

Barkworth, Algernon, 176
"Baron von Drachstedt", 89, 150
Barrett, Frederick, 136, 152, 166
Baxter, Mrs. James, 155
Baxter, Queeg, 155
Bazzani, Albina, 158
Beauchamp, George, 136
Beaumont, J.C.H., 57
Becker, Mrs. Allen (Nellie) family, 72, 119, 164-165,
    183, 191, 193, 199
Beckwith, Richard, 153
Beesley, Lawrence, 134, 165, 219, **104**
Beken, Frank, 84-85
Belfast Lough, 31, 40-43
Belfast, Ireland, 4, 6, 29, 35
Belford, Walter, 135
Bell, Joseph, 58, 66, 136-137
Bertram, Tom, 83
Bidois, Rosalie, 91
Bill, Mr. E.W., 112
Bingham, John Charles, Lord Mersey, 215
binoculars, 126, 128
Bird, Ellen, 78, 158-159
Bishop, Dickinson H., 93, 150
Bishop, Helen Walton, 93, 150
Bjornstrom-Steffansson, Mauritz, 79, 133, 174
Blair, David, 47, 50, 126
Blair, Nancy, 50
Blank, Henry, 89, 134
blue ice, 129
Boiler Room 1: 150
Boiler Room 5: 66, 113, 119, 132, 136, 138-139,
    152, 166, 187
Boiler Room 6: 66, 132-133, 136, 139, 152, 166, 187
Bonnell, Caroline, 134
Bowyer, George, 36, 81-82, 85
Boxhall, Joseph, 39, 47, 82, 136, 151, 232,
    biography, 56, dies, 220, fires green rockets, 171,
    186, 189, goes on a tour, 137, Lifeboat 2,
    170-171, 185, 189, reprimands Ismay, 154,
    returns from tour, 139, sees another ship, 152,
    sent on a second tour, 138, shoots stars, 124,
    sights *Carpathia*, 189, *Titanic's* position, 139, 189,
    211, 223-224
Bradley, George, 77, 163
Brayton, George A., 77, 163
Bremen, 210
Brice, Walter T., 57
Bride, Harold, 43, 59, 99, 117, 121, 137, 139,
    Carpathia answers, 142, called by Wm. A. Smith,
    214, "*every man for himself*", 175, goes to bed, 125,
    helps Cottam, 197, ice message from *Californian*,
    124, last survivor off *Carpathia*, 200, Lifeboat B,
    176-177, 184, sea trials, 41, **118**
Bridge Wing, 25, 137
Bright, Arthur, 174
Britannic, 10, 59, 169, 219, 221
British Board of Trade, 36-37, fire, 65, lifeboat
    requirements, 215, regulations for lifeboats, 27,
    67, regulations for rockets, 210, Report of Survey
    of an Immigrant Ship, 64, sea trials, 43, *Titanic's*

departure, 63, *Titanic's* sea trials, 39, 41, villain for not adding enough lifeboats, 218
British Inquiry, 215-216, 231
Brown, Edith, 168, 184
Brown, Margaret Tobin "Molly", 91, 153, 155-156, 188, 233, **90**
Brown, Mildred, 77, 164
Brown, Mrs. John M., 79, 92, 174
Browne, Father Francis M., 75, 85, 96, 107-109
Bucknell, Mrs. William, 158
Buley, Edward J., 57, 161
Burns, Elizabeth, 96, 157
Buss, Kate, 71
Butt, Archibald W., 76, 173, 197
Byles, Father Thomas R.D., 72, 179, **74**

Café Parisian, 23, 102, 104, 115, 179, **100**
Cairns, Alexander, 95
Calderhead, Edward, 153, 155
Caldwell, Mrs. Albert, 119
Californian, 56, 124, 126-127, 139-140, 152, 205, 209, arrives at *Titanic* site, 194, continues to Boston, 210, in whaling area, 210, message about ice, 123, sunk, 222, **208**
Cameron, James, 23, 227, 235
Candee, Mrs. Edward, 79, 120, 155-156, 219
Cape Cod, 140-141
Cape Race, 125, 117, 127, 140, 195, 197
Cardeza, Mrs. James W.M., 92, 157, 216
Cardeza, Thomas D.M., 92, 157
Carlisle, Alexander, 11, 36-37
Caronia, 122
Carpathia, 73, 140, 153-154, 164-165, 173, 189, 192, 194, 209, arrives in New York, 198-200, 210, 214, 218, call sign, 141, crew paid extra month's salary, 198, follows green rockets, 171, 186, Lifeboat 3, 192, Lifeboat C arrives, 193, lights seen, 188, pickup survivors, 191, Rostron orders it turned around, 142, searches for survivors, 193, speeding toward *Titanic*, 144, 181, 189, steaming through the ice field, 142, 194, steams to New York, 196-197, sunk, 222, unloads lifeboats, 199, **182**
Carruthers, Francis, 41, 43
Carter, Rev. Ernest, 71, 120, 124
Carter, Lilian, 71
Carter, Lucile, 93
Carter, Mrs. William E., 53, 93, 170, 172, 193
Case, Charles, 157
Cavendish, Mrs. Tyrell, 155
cavitation effect, 137
Cedric, 5, 197, 199
Chaffee, Carrie, 79
Chaffee, Herbert, 79
Chapman, Elizabeth, 73
Chapman, John, 73
Cherbourg, France, 45, 85, 87-89, 99, 221
Cherry, Gladys, 79, 158-159
USS Chester, 197-198
Churchill, Sir Winston, 219
Clarke, Maurice H., 63-65
Cleaver, Alice, 77, 164
Clench, Fredrick, 167
coal fire, 152

coal strike, 46, 72, 111, 113
coal, capacity, 12
Cobh Harbor, 107
Coffey, John, 107
Collyer, Harvey, family, 73, 187
committee to raise funds, 198
Compton Jr., Alexander family, 168
Cornell, Mrs. Robert C., 79, 92
Cottam, Harold, 140-141, 143-144, 196-197, 213-214, **182**
Cotterill, Harry, 71, 85
counter-flooding, 15
Countess of Rothes, 79, 158-159, **80**
Coutts, Mrs. William, 71
crash stop, 43
Crosby, Catherine, 150
Crosby, Edward, 150, 156
Crow's nest, 47, 58, 128
Cunard Line, 6-7, 9, 198, 222

Daly, Eugene, 109, 120, 165, 230
Danbom, Ernst, 68
Daniel, Robert, 79
Daniels, Sarah, 77, 134, 158, 164
Davidson, Orian, 77, 157-158, 189
Davidson, Thornton, 77, 157
Davies, Alfred, 69
Davies, John, 69
Davies, Joseph, 69
de Villiers, Madame Berthe, 155, 187
Dean, H.V., 141
Dean, Millvina, 188
DeCaprio, Leonardo, 23
Deck Department, 55, 57
Deck A, 7, 14, 26, 102, 113, 146, 148, 159, 161, 163, 166-167, 171, 174, enclosed promenade, 38, tour, 24, **108**
Deck B, 24, 26, 64, 75, 101-103, 107, 115, 170, tour, 23, **100**
Deck C, 21, 23-24, 66, 103, 113, 116, 135, 147-148, 160, 219, tour, 22
Deck D, 14, 67, 101-103, 132, 142, tour, 21
Deck E, 14-15, 21, 25, 61, 67, 83, 103, 106, 116, 136-137, 161, tour, 19-20
Deck F, 46, 67, 101, 105, 141, tour 18
Deck G, 46, 67, 105, 118, 141-142, 148, tour, 17
Deck Boat, 26, 59, 75, 95, 101, 103, 105-106, 116, 120, 133-135, 145-150, 152-155, 161, 164, 170-171, 173, 175, 178-179, 217, 234-235, tour, 24-25
Deck Orlop, 143, tour, 17
Deck Tank Top, 15, 19, 46, 66, 132, 138, tour, 16
Deck, Bridge, 23
Deck, Forecastle, 11, 23
Deck, Poop, 24, 81, 151
Deck, Well, aft, 22, 24, 179
Deck, Well, forward, 22-24, 66, 130, 133, 160-161
Deutschland, 122-123
Dining Saloon, First Class, 21, 103, 114, 116, 122, 132
Dining Saloon, Second Class, 21, 114, 116, 120, 124
Dining Saloon, Third Class, 19, 101, 114
Dobbins, James, 33
Docking Bridge, 24, 56, 81-82, 133, 151

Dodd, George, 171
Dodge Jr., Washington, 153-154
Dodge, Ruth, 81, 153-154, 186, 188
Dodge, Dr. Washington, 81, 165-166, 192
Dorking, Edward, 135
double bottom, 13-14, 16, 218
double hull, 218
Douglas, Mrs. Walter, 171
Dowagiac, Michigan, 93
Dowdell, Elizabeth, 69
Drew, Marshall, 164, 179, 191
Duff Gordon, Lady Lucille, 93, 160, 216, 219,
    94, 232
Duff Gordon, Sir Cosmo, 93, 160, 185, 219, 94, 232
Duke of Argyll, 31
Dunkirk, 219
Dyer-Edwards, Lucy Noel Martha, see Countess
    of Rothes
Dyker, Adolf, 70
Dyker, Elisabeth, 70
Dymond, Frank, 167

Earnshaw, Olive, 95
SS Eastland, 238
electric bath, 105
electrical supply, 13
Elevator, First Class, 20, 106
Elias, Joseph, 89
Ellis Island, 198
Emmanuel, Virginia, 69
Empress of Britain, 121
Empress of Ireland, 238
Endres, Caroline, 91
Engine Room, 11, 82-83
Engineering Department, 55, 58
Englehardt Collapsible, 26-27, see Lifeboats A, B,
    C and D
English Channel, 35, 45, 84-85, 88, 97
Enquiry Office, 22, 58, 116-117
Entrance, First Class, 22-25, 105, 148, 150
Entrance, Second Class, 23
Estonia, 239-240
Etches, H.S., 154
Eustis, Elizabeth, 97, 133
Evans, Alfred F., 58
Evans, Cyril, 127, 140, 205-207, 209-210
Evans, Edith, 79, 92, 174
Evans, Frank O., 57, 161-162
expansion joint, 26

Fanstone, Alan, 55
Farthing, John, 78
fire, 65, 113, 119
Fleet, Frederick, 58, 125, 127-132, 155
Fletcher, P.W., 59, 85, 99, 120
Florida, 7, 37
Forepeak tank, 17
Fortune, Mrs. Mark, 162
Francatelli, Laura, 160
Franklin, P.A.S., 195-196, 213
Frauenthal, Clara, 153-154
Frauenthal, Henry, 153-154
Frauenthal, Isaac, 153-154
Frick, Henry C., 81

Fry, John R., 65
funnel, 12, 25-26, 34, 103, 192, 225, 232
furnaces, 12
Futility, 232
Futrelle, Jacques and Lily May, 79, 163, 80

Galley, Second Class, 21
gates between classes, 67
Gatti, Luigi, 61, 115
General Room, Third Class, 22
George, Shawneene, 88
Germanic, 6, 49
Germantown, Pennsylvania, 92
Gibson, Dorothy, 233
Gibson, James, 209
Gigantic, 10, 45, 49, 59, 219, 221
Giglio, Victor, 91, 166
Gill, Ernest, 206-207
Goodwin, Frederick, 66, 70
Gracie IV, Col. Archibald, 79, 92-93, 120, 133, 146,
    148, 158, 173-174, 176, 219, 116
Graham, Margaret, 146
Grand Promenade Suite, 23
Grand Promenade, 32
Grand Staircase, First Class, 20, 23-26, 39, 75, 101,
    103, 105, 235-236, 102
Grand Staircase, Second Class, 22, 24, 26, 101
Grand Trunk Railway, 77
Greenfield, William, 89
Grimm, Jack, 223-227
Groves, Charles V., 127, 205, 207, 211
Guggenheim, Benjamin, 91, 163, 166, 90
Gustafsson, Anders, 68
Gustafsson, Johan, 68
Gwinn, William L., 60
Gymnasium, 26, 105, 148, 150, 153

Haas, Aloisia, 71
Haines, Albert M., 57, 135, 163
Halifax, Nova Scotia, 7, 68, 73, 121, 138, 196, bodies
    arrive, 202-203, bodies buried, 202, 204, 230,
    Mackay-Bennett, 210, Mount Blanc, 237, Smith's
    decision to steam to, 137, survivors to, 195
Hamburg America Line, 7
Hamilton, Frederick, 202
Harbeck, William H., 73
Harding, J. Horace, 81
Harland & Wolff Guarantee Group, 51, 60, 62, 65-66,
    101
Harland & Wolff, 4-5, 9, 31, 38, 87, construction, 34,
    modern days, 221, modernization program, 6, Queen's
    Island North shipyard, 29, 221, Titanic sea trials, 41,
    65, White Star Line collaboration, 5, 10
Harland, Edward J., 4
Harper, Annie (Nina), 73
Harper, Henry Sleeper, 153, 157-158, 192
Harper, Rev. John, 73, 75, 164, 76
Harper, Myra, 85, 120, 153, 157-158, 217
Harper, Nina, 75, 164, 76
Harris, Henry B., 80, 173
Harris, Mike, 223
Harris, Rene, 80
Harrison, William H., 65
Hart, Benjamin, 73, 118-119

Hart, Esther, 73, 118-119, 136
Hart, Eva, 73, 118-119, 136, 183, 227
Hart, John E., 149, 155, 159, 161, 166-167, 217
Hart, Thomas, 230
Harter Act, 214
Hartley, Wallace, 61, 116, 125, 150, 175, **116**
Hassab, Hammad, 157-158, 192
HMS *Hawke*, 35-36, 49-50, 56, 59, 81, 84, 169
Hays, Charles M., 77, 156-157, 203
Hays, Clara, 77, 157, 199
Hays, Margaret B., 95, 133, 150
Hector, 43, 83
Hedman, Oscar, 70
Heininen, Wendla, 68
Hellstrom, Hilda, 69
Hemming, Samuel, 123
Hendrickson, Charles, 185
Herald, 42
Herculaneum, 42
Hercules, 42-43, 83
Hichens, Robert, 57, 129-130, 155-156, 188, 229, **190**
Hickson and Company, 4
Hippach, Ida, 97, 134, 172
Hippach, Jean, 97, 134, 172
Hirvonen, Helga, 70
Hocking, Elizabeth family, 71, 73, 75, 119
Hoffman, see Navratil
Hogeboom, Anna, 78
Hogg, George K., 58, 150
O.L. Hollenbeck, 33
Holverson, Mrs. Alexander, 158
Hopkins, Robert J., 57
Hornby, 42
Hosono, Masabumi, 72, 185
Hoyt, Frederick, 173
Hoyt, William, 185-186
Hudson River, 29, 199
Humblen, Adolf, 69
Humphreys, Sidney, 163
Hurst, Walter, 58
Huskisson, 42
Hutchinson, John H., 57, 138

ice shelf, 131, 132
ice warnings, 121-122, 124-125, 127
iceberg, 126, 129, 132, 144, 200, 229
IFREMER, 224, 226
Imrie, William, 3
International Mercantile Marine Company, 5-6, 42, 65, 195, 197, 214-215, 218, 220
International Navigation Company, 5
Ireland, 107-108, 110
Iroquois Theatre fire, 97
Ismay, Joseph B., 7, 31, 33, 112, 197, *Baltic's* message, 122, arrives on *Carpathia*, 193, arrives on the bridge, 138, asks if ship is damaged, 139, called by Wm. A. Smith, 214, Charles Hays, 77, concept for *Titanic*, 9, decides to steam to Halifax, 138, did not attend sea trials, 42, feels collision, 136, gets on Lifeboat C, 169-170, Guggenheim, 92, helps load Lifeboat 5, 154, knows *Titanic* will sink, 150, joins White Star Line, 5, message announcing sinking, 213, message to Franklin, 196, not going to be scapegoat, 212, not guilty of disaster, 215, orders design changes,
38, Promenade Suite, 81, request only 16 lifeboats on *Titanic*, 36, requests maiden voyage date, 34, retires, 220, returns to England as a hero, 218, sea trials, 65, sends messages, 197, status of ship, 141, summoned by Wm. A. Smith, 214, Sunday dinner, 123, villain for not adding enough lifeboats, 218, villain for not reporting fire, 218, **82**
Ismay, Imrie and Company, 4
Ismay, Thomas H., 3-5

Jansson, Carl, 70, 135
Jensen, Carla, 69, 133
Jensen, Hans, 69
Jensen, Niels, 69, 133-134
Jensen, Svend, 69
Jessop, Violet, 59, 169, **60**
Jewell, Archibald, 58, 125, 150
Johansson, Karl, 70
Johansson, Nils, 69
Johns, Thomas, 158
Johnson, Elisabeth, 69
Johnson, James, 135
Jones, Thomas W., 57
Jonsson, Carl, 70
Joughlin, Charles, 153, 162, 176, 180, 187
Jussila, Aina, 70
Jussila, Katriina, 70

Kean, Nora, 75
keel, laid down, 29
Keene, P., 231
kennels, 101
Kensington Palace, 79
Kenyon, Mrs. Frederick, 158
Kink, Anton family, 71
Knorr, 224-225
Krekorian, N., 162
Kreuchen, Emilie, 77

La Touraine, 121
Lapland, 199, 214, 216
LaRoche, Joseph, 89
Larsson-Ronsberg, Edvard, 69
Latimer, Andrew, 75
Lee, Reginald, 58, 125, 127, 129-130, 132
Leitch, Jessie, 73, 164
Lester, James, 69
Lesueur, Gustave, 92, 157
Library, First Class, 24, 113, Lifeboat 1: 27, 154, 178, 185, 216, loading and launch, 159-161, **94, 108**
Lifeboat 2: 27, 173, 185, 189, loading and launch, 170-171
Lifeboat 3: 27, 189, 192, loading and launch, 157-158
Lifeboat 4: 27, 142, 148, 168, 173, 184, 191-192, 194, arrives at *Carpathia*, 193, loading and launch, 171-174, lowered to A Deck, 149, picks up survivors, 186
Lifeboat 5: 27, 95, 166, 170, 186, loading and launch, 153-154
Lifeboat 6: 27, 95, 153, 156, 169, 186-188, loading and launch, 155-157, **190**

Lifeboat 7: 27, 150-151, 154, 156, 186, 192, 233, loading and launch, 150-153
Lifeboat 8: 27, 134, 159, 188-189, loading and launch, 158-159
Lifeboat 9: 27, 57, loading and launch, 162-163
Lifeboat 10: 27, 184, 191, loading and launch, 161-162
Lifeboat 11: 27, 64, 164-165, 188, loading and launch, 163-165
Lifeboat 12: 27, 168, 184, 191-192, arrives at Carpathia, 193, loading and launch, 167-168
Lifeboat 13: 27, 154, 164, 166, 183, 186, 192, loading and launch, 165-166
Lifeboat 14: 27, 161, 168, 184, 186, 191-192, 194, arrives at Carpathia, 193, loading and launch, 168
Lifeboat 15: 27, 64, 166, 194, loading and launch, 167
Lifeboat 16: 27, 186, loading and launch, 168-169
Lifeboat Collapsible A: 27, 160, 169, 175, 187, 192, 194, 232, 234, found with bodies, 203, loading and launch, 178, picked up by Lowe, 191
Lifeboat Collapsible B: 27, 69, 177, 184, 187, 192, 194, loading and launch, 175-177
Lifeboat Collapsible C: 27, 160, 170, 172, 181, 193, loading and launch, 169-170
Lifeboat Collapsible D: 27, 170, 174, 186, 191-192, arrives at Carpathia, 193, loading and launch, 173, picks up survivors, 186, 190
Lifeboat drill, 122
Lifeboats, 25, 34, 67, 103, 181, 194, 199, 214, 217, 235, Board Of Trade requirements, 27, 36-37, description, 27, launching, 146, lost to history, 232, Smith gives orders to launch, 147, Smith orders lifeboats uncovered, 142, tested, 39, 64, tour, 26-27
Lightoller, Charles H., 39, 47, 50, 109, 136, 168, 170, 197, 232, allows Arthur Peuchen to enter a Lifeboat, 155-156, awaits orders from Smith, 147, binoculars, 126, biography, 56, checks Moody's skills, 124, comment on British hearings, 231, comments about calm seas, 124, counting cadence, 177, 192, departure, 81, evacuation at Dunkirk, 219, firearms, 167, knows Titanic will sink, 150, last person to board Carpathia, 193, last time he saw Smith, 177, Lifeboat 1, 161, Lifeboat 4, 149, Lifeboat 4, 171, Lifeboat 4, 172, Lifeboat 10, 161, Lifeboat 12, 167, Lifeboat 12, 192, Lifeboat 16, 168, Lifeboat B, 184, lights of another ship, 148, 152, 211, quote about noise from steam, 145, quote orders from Smith to launch lifeboats, 147, quote, "all hands on deck", 146, quote, firing rockets, 151, quote, passengers flocking to the Boat Deck, 147, relieves Wilde, 123, retires, 220, Ryerson and Lifeboat 4, 172, sensation of being in water, 187, shoots stars, 124, starboard side lifeboats, 142, Straus, 159, uncovers lifeboats, 142, washed overboard, 175-176, "women and children only", 235, 110
Lindell, Edvard, 187, 194, 203
Lindell, Mrs. Edvard, 203
Lindqvist, Eino, 70

Liverpool, 33, 39, 45, 122
London, England, 45
longitudinal bulkheads, 14-15
Longley, Gretchen, 78
Lord, Stanley, 56, 124, 205, 212, brings Californian to a halt, 126, condemned by American inquiry, 215, didn't do anything wrong, 205, hears news about Titanic, 209, looks for survivors, 210, retires, 220, scapegoat, 212, sees lights of a steamer, 127, 206, signal rockets, 207, villain, 230-231, 218, was he negligent?, 211, 208
Lord, Walter, 178
Los Angeles, California, 75
The Loss of the S.S. Titanic, 219
Lounge, First Class, 24, 26, 102, 116, 120, 125, 127
Lowe, Harold, 47, 39, 232, biography, 56, departure, 82, dies, 220, fires revolver, 168, hero, 217, hoists sail on Lifeboat 14, 191, Lifeboat 10, 162, Lifeboat 14, 168, Lifeboat 14, 184, Lifeboat 14, 185, Lifeboat 14, 191, Lifeboat 14, 192, Lifeboat 14, 193, Lifeboat A, 203, Lifeboat test, 64
Lundin, Olga, 69-70
Lundstrom, Thure, 70
Lusitania, 6-7, 9, 234, 239, sunk, 221-222
Lyons, William H., 57, 173

Mackay-Bennett, 202-203, 210
Madill, Georgette, 77
Maioni, Roberta, 79, 158
Majestic, 45, 49, 80
March, John S., 60
Marconi antenna, 12
Marconi Company, 117, 236
Marconi Wireless, 25, 37, 59, 61, 117
Marechal, Pierre, 150
Marex-Titanic, Inc., 227
Marshall, Henry, 75
Marshall, Kate, 75
mast, aft, 12
mast, forward, 12, 225
Master-at-Arms, 20
Mauretania, 6-7, 9, 81, 113, 116, 220
Mayne, Berthe, 155
McCarthy, William, 172
McCawley, T.W., 59-60, 104, 120
McElroy, Hugh W., 58, 169-170, 232
McGhee, Dr. Frank, 193, 196
McGough, James B., 132, 150, 155
meal schedules, 112
Merchant Shipping Act of 1894, 36, 216
Mersey Commission, 215-216
Mesaba, 125
Meyer, Mrs. Edward, 155
Millet, Francis D., 76, 173
Minia, 202-203
Mintram, William, 58
Moen, Sigurd, 69
Montmagny, 203
Moody, James, 39, 47, 123, 232, biography, 56, call from fleet, 129, departure, 82-83 Lifeboat test, 64, Lightoller checks skills, 124, phone call from Fleet, 128, washed overboard, 175
Moor, Belia, 68
Moore, Clarence, 173

Moore, George A., 57, 157-158
Morgan, J.P., 5, 31, 33, 81, 214
Morley, Henry, 75
Mount Blanc, 237
Mount Temple, 194, 209
Murdoch, William M., 47, 109, briefs Smith, 136-137, decision to avoid the iceberg, 229, departure, 81, Ismay, 170, Lifeboat 1, 160, Lifeboat 9, 163, Lifeboat 15, 167, Lifeboat C, 169, offers to let First Class men on board Lifeboat 3, 157, on watch, 127, orders engines stopped, 129, orders Pitman into a Lifeboat, 153, orders stop then full astern, 137, port side lifeboats, 142, relieves Lightoller, 125, shoot himself?, 232, waits to strike the iceberg, 130, *"women and children first"*, 235, **110**

Nackid, Said, family, 88
Najib, Adele, 88
National Geographic Magazine, 223
National Geographic Society, 224
Navigation Room, 25
Navratil Family, 73, 174, 203, **74**
Neptune, 43, 83
Nesbit, Evelyn, 93
New York, 84-85, 87
New York Times, 195-196
New York World, 119
Newell, Arthur W. family, 95, 134, 155
Newsom, Helen, 153
Nichols, Alfred, 57
Nicola-Yarred, Elias, 133
Nicola-Yarred, Jamila, 133
Niklasson, Samuel, 70
Nilsson, Berta, 69
"No Pope", 231
Nomadic, 87-88, 221
Noordam, 122
Noronic, 6
North Atlantic Ice Patrol, 219
North German Lloyd Line, 7
Nourney, Alfred "Baron von Drachstedt", 89, 150
Nutbean, William, 58, 82-83
Nye, Mrs. Elizabeth, 72, 165
Nysten, Anna, 68

O'Loughlin, William F.N., 57, 153
Oceana, 5, 57
Oceanic, 5-6, 39, 45, 58, 84, 92, 203-204
Oceanic Steam Navigation Company, 3, 222
Ogden, Louis, 192
Olliver, Alfred, 153
Olsson, Elina, 70
Olsson, Oscar, 70
Olympic-class, 7, 10, 49
Olympic, 16, 23-24, 45, 49, 57-59, 62, 81, 87, 196, 210, Capt. Smith, 46, 49, collision with *Hawke*, 35-36, 49, 56, 81, 84, 115, construction specs, 10, 29, damage after collision with *Hawke*, 36, did not sink in collision with *Hawke*, 35, fitting out trials, 31, forwards *Titanic* messages, 198, Henry T. Wilde, 47, hull painted white, 29, keel laid down, 10, launch, 29, lost propeller blade, 38, maiden voyage, 33, 114, mammoth

size, 229, message from *Titanic*, 144, New York trip, 46, receives distress calls, 195, retro fit, 218, returns to service, 38, scrapped, 221, sea trials, 41, sinks German submarine, 221, sinks *Nantucket Lightship*, 221, trip to Liverpool, 33, used to simulate tests, 216, **28, 54, 100**
orchestra, 60, 115-116, 125, 150
Osman, Frank, 57, 171
Ostby, Englehart, 95
Ostby, Helene, 95, 153

Palm Court Cafe, 24, 102, 104
Panula, John, family, 68, 230
Parisian, 127, 140, 196
"*Park Lane,*" 20
Paulson, Gosta, 230
Payne, Vivian, 77
Pears, Edith, 77, 158
Pears, Thomas, 76
Penasco y Castellana, Maria, 97, 158
Penasco y Castellana, Victor, 97
Penney, V., 58
Perkis, Walter, 172-173, 192
Pernot, Rene, 91
Perreault, Mary Anne, 77
Persson, Ernst, 69
Petterson, Johan, 71
Peuchen, Arthur, 78, 147, 155-156, 188
Philadelphia, 72, 77
Phillips, John (Jack), 43, 59, 99, 117, 121, 137, 177, breaks into Cottam's message, 141, "*every man for himself*", 175, first CQD, 205, message from *Mesaba*, 125, message from Evans, 206, ordered to send CQD, 139, sea trials, 41, sends CQD messages, 140, 207, sends last transmission, 179, shuts Evans off, 127, **118**
Phillips, Kate, 75
Pirrie, Lord William, 4-7, 9, 31, 33-34, 65
Pitman, Herbert, 39, 47, 92, 136, 153, 232, biography, 56, departure, 81, dies, 220, ordered into Lifeboat, 154
Podesta, John, 58, 82-83
Poingdestre, John T., 57, 153, 167
Pontiac, Michigan, 69
Post Office, 17-18, 138, 142
postal clerks, 60, 118, 142
Potter, Lily, 95
Prentiss, Frank M., 180
Priest, John, 169
Promenade Deck, 24-26, 96, 174
Promenade Suites, 10, 38
Promenade, Officers, 25-26
Promenade, Second Class, 22-23, 26, 103
Promenade, Third Class, 22
propellers, 12
Pugh, Alfred, 83
Pugh, Percy, 83
Purser's Office, 22, 116, 147
Pusey, R.W., 160

Queenstown, 45, 75, 85, 97, 99, 221-222, 239, changed name to Cobh, 234, final port call, 76, *Titanic* arrives, 106-107, 109

Rappahannock, 126
Reading and Writing Room, 24
Reception Room, 21, 59, 103
Red Star Line, 199
Religious services, 119, 122
Republic, 5, 7, 37, 49
restaurant, à la carte, 23, 61, 101, 113, 124, 187
Riihivuori, Sanni, 68
River Lagan, 10, 31, 38, 41-42
River Test, 43, 45, 63, 83-84
rivets, 13
RMS Titanic, Inc., 227
Robbins, Victor, 91
Robert, Mrs. Edward, 77
Robertson, Morgan, 232-233
rockets, 151
Roebling II, Washington A., 81, 157
Romain, Harry, 78
Romaine, Charles H., 78
Roosevelt, Theodore, 76
Rostron, Arthur H., 141, collects last of survivors,
    194, dies, 221, hero, 217, 220, ignores USS
    Chester, 197, Leah Aks, 165, lifeboats returned
    to New York, 214, medal from President Taft,
    215, meets Boxhall, 189, orders *Carpathia*
    turned around, 142, orders firing of rockets,
    189, position, 223, praise for crew, 215,
    preparations to receive survivors, 143, searches
    for survivors, 193, silver loving cup, 198,
    speeds toward *Titanic*, 144, 181, 189, **182**
Rothschild, Mrs. Martin, 155
Rowe, Alfred G., 81
Rowe, George T., 57, 133, 151-152, 166
Royal Mail Steamship Co., 222
rudder, 12, 23, 130
Ryerson, Arthur, family, 93 148, 171-173

Sage, William, family, 66, 71
Salkjelsvik, Anna, 69
Sampson, 211-212
San Francisco earthquake, 73
Sanderson, Harold A., 42-43
Sandstrom, Agnes, 69
Sarnoff, David, 196-197
Saved From the Titanic, 233
Scarrott, Joseph, 57, 149, 184, 191
Schwabe, Gustav, 3
USS *Scorpion*, 224
Scotland Road, 19-20, 103, 106, 149
Scott, Samuel, 33
Scripps Institute of Oceanography, 224
Serraplan, Auguste, 95
Seward, Fred, 119
Shepard, Jonathan, 152
Shipbuilder Magazine, called *Titanic* "practically
    unsinkable", 16
Shutes, Elizabeth, 146
Siebert, Sidney, 173
Slade brothers, 58, 83
Sloan, Peter, 58
Slocombe, Maud, 188
Smith, Capt. Edward J., 47-48, 147, 229, 232,
    Baltic's message, 122-123, arrives on bridge,
    136-137, asks for Wilde, 56, at fault per Mersey

Commission, 216, biography, 49-50, calls Andrews to
the bridge, 136, comments about calm seas, 124,
Commodore of the White Star Line, 49, death of, 177,
231, decision to steam toward Halifax, 138, departure,
63, 65, 81-82, didn't hold a Lifeboat drill, 122, dinner,
115, 124, "*every man for himself*", 175, 235, fire, 66, 119,
gives orders to launch lifeboats, 147, goes to bed, 125,
huge following among passengers, 50, ice warnings,
121-125, 127, iceberg, 131, inspects the ship, 118,
knows *Titanic* will sink, 150, near collision with *New
York*, 84-85, not found responsible for collision with
Hawke, 36, not going to be scapegoat, 212, not setting
a speed record, 234, *Olympic* collision with *Hawke*, 46,
49-50, orders engines half ahead, 138, orders engines
stopped for last time, 39, 145, orders lifeboats
uncovered, 142, plan to go around the ice field, 121,
Queenstown, 99, Report of Survey of an Immigrant
Ship, 65, Royal Naval Reserve, 50, sea trials, 42, sees
another ship, 151-152, status of ship, 141, tours with
Andrews, 138-139, turns the corner, 123, updates
charts, 125, villain for not reporting fire, 218, **48, 108**
Smith, James Clinch, 93, 95, 146, **90**
Smith, John R.J., 60, 138
Smith, Lucian, 153,
Smith, Mrs. Lucien P., 79, 153, 155
Smith, William Alden, 214-215
Smoking Lounge, First Class, 24, 26, 59, 91, 102, 113,
    127, 133-134, 166, 173, 175
Smoking Room, Officers, 25
Smoking Room, Second Class, 23
Smoking Room, Third Class, 22
Stockholm, 239
Soholt, Peter, 69
Southampton, 10, 33, 35, 39, 41, 45-46, 57, 63, 83-84,
    216
Spedden, Frederick, family, 96, 107, 157-158, **96**
Spencer, Mrs. William, 155
Squash Racquet Court, 18, 59, 105, 148
Stanley, Amy, 69
Stanton, Samuel Ward, 89
Stanwyck, Barbara, 80
Stead, William Thomas, 79-80, 119, 231
Steerage class, 67
steering engines, 23
Stengel, Annie May, 153-154
Stengel, Charles, 154
Stephenson, Mrs. Walter, 133
Stephenson, Walter, 97
Stewart, G.V., 209
Stone, Herbert, 206-209
Storstad, 238
Straus, Ida, 78, 158, **78**
Straus, Isador, 78, 158-159, **78**
Strom, Elna, 69
Strom, Selma, 69
structure, frame, 12
structure, bottom, 13
structure, plates, description, 13
Stunke, Mrs. Johanna, 210
Suevic, 7
Sultana, 6
Sunderland, Victor, 133
Svensson, Johan, 165
Swane, George, 77, 164

Swimming Bath, 59, 105
Symans, George T.M., 58, 125, 160

Taft, William H., 76, 79, 197, 214
Taussig, Mrs. Emil, 158
Taussig, Ruth, 158
telegraph, ships, 25
Tenglin, Gunnar, 70, 135
Thaw, Harry, 93
Thayer, John B. family, 171-172, 176, 192-193, 199, 220
Theissinger, Alfred, 135
Titan, 233
RMS *Titanic*, 210, American owned, 214, arrives in Cherbourg, 87, arrives in Queenstown, 107, 109, Board Of Trade on trials, 39, 63, cargo, 53, Cherbourg, 87-88, 97, concept, 9, considered excellent insurance risk, 53, construction specs, 10-11, departs Queenstown, 213, departure from Southampton, 63, designed to be safest ship afloat, 14, distance traveled before hitting iceberg, 131, encounter in Southampton, 83-84, engineers, 229, fastest speed attained, 43, finishing work not completed, 50, first maiden voyage date, 34, first to have an elevator for Second Class passengers, 106, fitting out, 34, food for passengers, 53, found, 225, four hours behind schedule, 109, hull painted black, 29, ice shelf, 132, keel laid down, 10, 29, launch, 31, leaves with over 1,200 empty beds, 50, licensed under Board Of Trade regulations, 27, loss of life, 196, maiden voyage, 40, mammoth size, 229, message to *Olympic*, 144, near collision with *New York*, 85, *New York Times*, 195-196, not "unsinkable", 16, not trying to break a record, 113-114, number of crew on the ship, 62, people on the ship, 213, premier crew, 46, safety, 16, salvage attempt, 223, sea trials, 40-42, second ship of the *Olympic*-class, 7, ship close by, 212, slides across an ice shelf, 131, stern sinks, 183, strikes an iceberg, 131-132, survivors arrive in New York, 198-199, three hours late, 107, turns the corner, 123, two hours late, 97, watertight doors tested, 39, wireless, 7, work delayed because of *Olympic* collision, 36, **8, 28, 30, 32, 40, 54, 98**
Titanic movie, 23, 227, 235
Titanic Ventures, 226-227
Titanica, 227
Traffic, 87, 221
Troutt, Edwina "Winnie", 75, 168, 220
The Truth About Titanic, 219
Tucker, Gilbert, 95
Turkish Bath, 18, 34, 58-59, 105, 116
turning directions, 130

United States Hydrographic Office, 123
United States Office of Naval Research, 224
United States Senate, 213
The Unsinkable Molly Brown, 233,
Uruchurtu, Manuel E., 97

Van Der Planke, Jules, family, 68
Van Derhoef, Mr. Wyckoff, 42
Vanderbilt, George W., 112
Verandah Cafe, 24, 102

Victualling and Vendor Department, 55, 58, 99
Virginian, 195, 209
Vulcan, 43, 83-84

Wanamaker's Department Store, 196-197
Ward, Anna, 92, 157
Warren, Anna S., 153-154
Warren, Frank, 154
Waterloo Station, 66, 75, 87
watertight bulkheads, 16-17, 19, 139, 152, 218
watertight compartments, 14, 19
watertight doors, 15, 39
Webber, Susan, 75
Weir, Col. John, 77
Welin Lifeboat davits, 36
Wells, Mrs. Arthur H., 72, 135
Wennerstrom, August, see August Andersson
Wheel House, 25
Wheeler, Frederick, 112
whistle, 12
White, Mrs. J. Stuart, 119, 134, 159, 188-189
White, Stanford, 93
Wick, Natalie, 134, 158
Widener, George D. family, 92-93, 124, 148, 171-172, 199
Widener, P.A.B., 92
Wilde, Henry T., 47, 135, 142, 147, 232, biography, 55, departure, 63, 81, firearms, 167, Ismay, 170, joins *Titanic* the day of its maiden voyage, 56, letter home, 109, shoot himself? 232
Wilding, Edward, 41
Wilkes, Ellen, 73
Wilkinson, Norman, 175
Williams, Walter, 135
Williamson, James B., 60
Willson, Meredith, 233
Wilson, Helen, 96, 157
Winslet, Kate, 23
Wolff, Gustav, 3-4
Wood's Hole Oceanographic Institution, 224
Woody, Oscar S., 60
Woolner, Hugh, 79, 120, 174
Wright, Frederick, 59, 105, 148
Wright, Marion, 71, 135, 163
White Star Line, 9, 220, approval to build, 10, competition with Cunard, 7, decision for *Titanic* to go directly to Southampton, 38, foreign travelers, 67, Harland & Wolff, 4-5, 10, insurance, 216, laundry facility in Southampton, 52, marketing disaster, 113, never called *Titanic* unsinkable, 16, not guilty of disaster, 215, purchased by Ismay, 3, safety record, 7, ships homeport in Britain, 5, sold to Cunard, 222, suspends crew's salary, 198, villain for not adding enough lifeboats, 218

Yrios, Henrietta, 73

ABOUT THE AUTHOR

Lee W. Merideth has been deeply interested in the *Titanic* disaster for more than 40 years. His interest was triggered by Walter Lord's memorable *A Night to Remember*, a 5th grade reading assignment that has not yet reached its end. Over the course of the ensuing decades Lee accumulated 4,000 index cards with facts and figures, which formed the foundation for *1912 Facts About Titanic*. The revised edition follows the highly acclaimed and successful publication of the first edition published in 1999, which sold more than 35,000 copies in seven printings in four years.

In August 2002, Lee published *Titanic Names: A Complete List of the Passengers and Crew* (Rocklin, 2002), which contains detailed and fascinating information about every person known to have sailed on the doomed liner.

Although studying *Titanic* consumes much of Lee's time, his interests extend into several other areas including World War II naval history. His experiences as a docent on the aircraft carrier USS *Hornet* in Alameda, California, led him to write the bestseller *Grey Ghost: The Story of the Aircraft Carrier Hornet* (Rocklin, 2001), a history of the United States Navy's most decorated warship. *Grey Ghost* is also a self-guided tour of the Aircraft Carrier Hornet Museum.

Lee's other books include *Civil War Times and Civil War Times, Illustrated 30-Year Comprehensive Index* (Historical Indexes, 1989) and the mammoth two-volume *Guide to Civil War Periodicals* (Historical Indexes, 1991, 1995). These combined 110,000 entries have played an instrumental role in helping thousands of students of the Civil War better access and utilize their extensive libraries and collections of Civil War-related periodicals.

A graduate of California Polytechnic State University in San Luis Obispo with a degree in Graphic Communications and a minor in history, Lee is also a retired United States Army officer (Armor). He worked in the printing and publishing industry for more than 30 years before retiring in 2002.

To receive a personally inscribed copy of any of Lee's books, or to schedule Lee to speak to your organization, e-mail him at rocklinpress@earthlink.net, or visit his website rocklinpress.com.